Sense and Solidarity

Sense and Solidarity

JHOLAWALA ECONOMICS
FOR EVERYONE

JEAN DRÈZE

"Either we all live in a decent world,
or nobody does"
ORWELL

permanent black

Published by

PERMANENT BLACK

'Himalayana', Mall Road, Ranikhet Cantt,
Ranikhet 263645
perblack@gmail.com

Distributed by

ORIENT BLACKSWAN PRIVATE LTD

Bangalore Bhopal Bhubaneshwar Chandigarh Chennai
Ernakulam Guwahati Hyderabad Jaipur Kolkata
Lucknow Mumbai New Delhi Patna
www.orientblackswan.com

ISBN 978-81-7824-521-8

Typeset by Guru Typograph Technology,
Crossings Republic, Ghaziabad 201009
Printed and bound by Sapra Brothers, New Delhi 110092

CONTENTS

ACKNOWLEDGEMENTS

TEN ESSAYS IN THIS collection are co-authored with people who are not only valued colleagues but also dear friends: Bela Bhatia, Angus Deaton, Reetika Khera, Siddhartha, Vivek S., and the PROBE Team (Anuradha De, Pushpendra, Claire Noronha, Anita Rampal, Meera Samson, Amarjeet Sinha, and A.K. Shiva Kumar). Their good advice and influence, in fact, extend well beyond the co-authored articles. Many essays, as well as the Introduction, have also benefited from comments or suggestions from Sabina Alkire, Diane Coffey, Nikhil Dey, Haris Gazdar, Ramachandra Guha, Aashish Gupta, Mustafa Haji, Aparna John, Sneha Menon, Sudha Narayanan, Christian Oldiges, Isabel Pimenta, Vandana Prasad, Kumar Rana, C. Rammanohar Reddy, Amartya Sen, and Dean Spears, among others. Last but not least, I received very helpful editorial advice from Naman Garg, Nazar Khalid, and Jessica Pudussery.

Most of the essays in this book were initially published in *The Hindu*, one of India's leading dailies. I am grateful to those of its editors and staff members that I worked with over the years, including Shalini Arun, P. Jacob, Mini Kapoor, Murali N. Krishnaswamy, Nirmala Lakshman, Suresh Nambath, N. Ram, Srinivasan Ramani, N. Ravi, Radhika Santhanam, Siddharth Varadarajan, and R. Vijaya Shankar.

This book would not have seen the light of day without the valuable advice and overwhelming generosity of Rukun Advani and Anuradha Roy. Aside from working on the design of this book as if it were their own, they helped me to clarify my thoughts on many issues. The days I spent with them in their lovely cottage in Ranikhet

(Uttarakhand), where Permanent Black's editorial work happens, are among the happiest in recent memory. The warmest acknowledgement is collective. It goes to all the scholars, students, volunteers, respondents, friends and others who enriched the journeys that led to this book, from academic conferences and field surveys to public meetings and street demonstrations. As discussed in the Introduction, research for action is by nature a collective effort.

Finally, the Department of Economics at Ranchi University (Jharkhand) provided a congenial environment for the preparation of this book. Jharkhand may seem like an odd destination for a development economist, but for me it turned out to be a better vantage point than the national or international capitals of development research. Among many other gaps in this book, I would have liked to write about what I have learnt from the Adivasi (tribal) world in Jharkhand. Tribal communities tend to be seen as relics of the past, and no doubt their lifestyle will evolve, but I see some of their norms and values (equality, co-operation, freedom, honesty, gusto) as the wave of the future. The last essay in this book, "Development and Public-Spiritedness", is partly inspired by their example.

INTRODUCTION

Economics among the
Road Scholars

AROUND THE CORNER FROM my office at Ranchi University in eastern India is a wide avenue that leads into the city, called Kanke Road. If you go there at the crack of dawn, you will see something you may never forget: hundreds of young men, many emaciated and dishevelled, pushing bicycles loaded with more than two hundred kilograms of smuggled coal. Under the cover of darkness, they have walked twenty or thirty kilometres with this stupendous load to sell it in Ranchi and earn just enough to feed their families. Some of them, I am told, dig out the coal from below the land they used to cultivate, before they were forcibly displaced.

This sight often reminds me of George Orwell's 1937 essay "Down the Mine", especially its last sentence: "You and I and the editor of the *Times Lit. Supp.*, and the poets and the Archbishop of Canterbury and Comrade X, author of *Marxism for Infants* – all of us *really* owe the comparative decency of our lives to poor drudges underground, blackened to the eyes, with their throats full of coal dust, driving their shovels forward with arms and belly muscles of steel." Replace underground with "on the road" and shovel with "bicycle", and the sentence applies word for word in Ranchi today.

These young men are known as koilawalas (coal guys). I remember seeing the photograph of a koilawala for the first time in P. Sainath's book *Everybody Loves a Good Drought* (1996). The koilawala of today looks the same. Perhaps he has better footwear, and, quite likely, his

1

children are now going to school. But the nature of his predicament has barely changed. It is not very different from slavery, except that he is driven by economic necessity instead of physical coercion.

Another thought often occurs to me when I see the koilawalas. How come they are in their situation, and I in mine? The only answer I can find is: "chance". Perhaps a few of them drank or gambled away their land, but most are in that situation for no fault of their own. They were born in a poor family of the wrong caste, suffered from undernutrition in childhood, did not get a chance to study, and so on. In a different environment, they might have become geologists, engineers, artists, or hockey champions. But they never had a chance.

In India, as elsewhere, the privileged tend to nurture the illusion that they "deserve" what they have. This illusion, however, evaporates with even the most casual introspection. Sure, some rich people work hard – but so do koilawalas, construction workers, and domestic helpers. Other bases of privilege have little to do with personal merit: our aptitudes, health, inheritance, social connections, and other assets derive from contingencies (such as the accident of birth) over which we have no control. Even our education reflects inherited circumstances, and our parents' and teachers' efforts, far more than our own. All this is without going into the fact that wealth and power often build on corruption, exploitation, and crime.

If our situation is more a matter of chance than personal merit, then surely the privileged have a responsibility towards those who are left behind. We cannot prove that the privileged owe something to the rest, any more than we can prove that theft is wrong. But both can be thought of as sensible principles of a good society.

None of this, of course, tells us what should be done to ensure that everyone is able to live with dignity. Some people believe that the best thing to do for the koilawalas is to create a business-friendly environment so that the economy grows faster. Others might advise the koilawalas that armed struggle is the only way to change the system. I hope that this book will convince you – or reinforce your conviction – that there are other options too.

Social Development

For want of a better phrase, the essays in this book can be said to deal with various aspects of India's "social development" in the broadest sense. Social development is often reduced to specific matters on which quantitative indicators happen to be available, such as child health, elementary education, and gender inequality. These matters are undoubtedly important, and figure prominently in the essays. However, there is a great deal more to social development, seen as the endeavour to create a good society.

The abolition of caste, for instance, can be regarded as a critical aspect of social development in this large sense. Quantitative indicators on the abominations of the caste system are scarce (perhaps no accident), yet leaving out this issue from the ambit of social development would be like ignoring "the monster that crosses our path", as Ambedkar described the caste system. Similar remarks apply to patriarchy and other forms of arbitrary power. The expansion of democracy – still very limited in India, as elsewhere – is another natural concern here.

Going beyond these obvious examples, the abolition of violence, or at least of armed conflict, also seems to me an integral part of social development. The same applies to the progress of ethics and social norms. To illustrate: the spread of civic sense and public-spiritedness can be of great help in preventing corruption, crime, exploitation, and environmental vandalism among other anti-social activities. Then there is the destructive power of modern technology (for instance, through nuclear war or climate change), which has reached frightening proportions and keeps growing. Unless ethical development catches up with technological progress, humanity – or even life on earth – may not survive much longer.

The essays that follow do not make more than tentative forays into these big issues, but they are influenced by this concern to enlarge the boundaries of social development. As Noam Chomsky says, it is useful to distinguish between our visions ("the conception of a future society that animates what we actually do") and our goals ("the choices and tasks that are within reach"). This book is largely about goals – and action – in the field of social development, but I hope that it will also contribute to a clearer vision of the sort of society we can aspire to create.

Let me add that efforts to get closer to our goals often present opportunities to further our visions as well. When all the children in a village study together in a good school, the caste system takes a blow. Women who come out of their homes to earn their own wages on local public works are also chipping away at patriarchy. Communities that run their own ration shop to avoid being at the mercy of a corrupt dealer, or resist the corporate plunder of local natural resources, are practising far-reaching principles of self-management and self-governance. The right to information is quietly taking some power away from the state and putting it in people's hands. Taken together, these efforts represent an important counter to forces acting in opposite directions – towards greater inequity, irrationality, and concentration of power.

On Research and Action

The essays reflect an abiding interest in what might be called action-oriented research, or "research for action". This essentially refers to research aimed at contributing to practical change. Research for action is still research – it need not involve compromises with scientific methods or objective enquiry. However, it differs in some important ways from the conventional approach to research in academic circles. I tried to share a few thoughts on this, fifteen years ago, in a short article called "On Research and Action".[1] In particular, I argued for the complementarity of research and action, and against the conventional view that involvement in action detracts from objective enquiry. That article was just a couple of pages long, but it prompted more

---

[1] Drèze 2002.

responses than most of my other writings – some appreciative, others not (one good friend described it as "shitty"). I take this opportunity to clarify some of the basic ideas of research for action, as I understand them.[2]

First, action-oriented research is not a stand-alone activity. Rather, it is part of a larger effort to achieve practical change through democratic action, that is, action based on democratic means and institutions – public debate, the media, the courts, the electoral process, street action, among others. Research can help with arguments and evidence that contribute to more effective action. This perspective would naturally inform the subject and method of our research. To illustrate, one useful form of action-oriented research is to counter some of the propaganda that appears in the mainstream media (various examples are discussed in this book). Academic research rarely concerns itself with this, and in any case, its long-drawn time frame makes it an ineffective response to media propaganda. This is a situation where action-oriented research has an important role, and even becomes a form of democratic action in itself.

Second, if research is to contribute to action, it must be presented in a clear and reader-friendly manner, preferably to a wide audience. This is important, because social scientists have a tendency to talk among themselves and slip into "verbose phraseology", as one of my revered teachers at the Indian Statistical Institute used to put it. In academic circles, complicating matters can be quite rewarding. That applies to economics in particular: another esteemed teacher once told me, "so-and-so is a great economist – very few people can understand him." In action-oriented writing, by contrast, it often helps to remember the KISS principle: keep it simple, sweetie.

Third, action-oriented research resists the common tendency to think of the government as the main agent of change. In

---

[2] The article mentioned elaborates several points being made here in condensed form, particularly the relation between commitment and objectivity as well as the learning value of action.

development economics, it is customary to end a research paper with a few comments on its "policy implications". This typically reflects an attempt to give the research a practical twist, but based on the assumption that government policy is the prime mover. Public policy, of course, is very important, but there are also other means of bringing about practical change. And even public policy, in a democratic country, is the outcome of democratic processes that involve not only the government but also a range of non-government institutions. Research for action addresses itself to the public at large, not just to the government.

Fourth, action-oriented research disputes the conventional view of action and research as antagonistic activities, and even sees complementarities across the two. The basis of the conventional view, influential in academic circles, is that involvement in action detracts from objectivity. However, objectivity requires intellectual honesty, not an abdication of convictions. In any case, academic institutions are not, in the first place, neutral ground – they tend to be well integrated with other institutions of power, such as the government, funding agencies, and the corporate sector. Further, action can be a great eye-opener, and thus contribute to more enlightened research, just as research can lead to more effective action. For instance, engagement with the media, the legal system, and political parties can vastly sharpen our understanding of the institutions of democracy. And there is nothing like a few days in jail to see the state from a new angle.[3]

Fifth, research for action makes special demands on ethical standards. Ethical lapses in academic papers (plagiarism, opportunism, fudging, selective reporting of results, and so on) may or may not have serious consequences. The stakes tend to be much higher when research is linked in one way or another with real-life action. Another

---

[3] The concept of positional objectivity, based on the recognition that "what we can observe depends on our position *vis-à-vis* the objects of observation" (Sen 1993), can help us understand this issue. On related ideas, see also Rapoport 1960.

ethical issue is that action-oriented research, especially on social development, often brings us in direct contact (through field surveys or other activities) with people who are struggling with extreme forms of poverty and exploitation. In such situations it becomes difficult to stay aloof, making this another good reason for seeking ways of linking research with action.

Sixth, a related demand of action-oriented research is to avoid obligations to funding agencies and institutions that may stifle our freedom of expression or action. Indeed, the dependence of academic research on funding agencies is a serious matter, with even some Ph.D. work now being paid for by the World Bank and the corporate sector. Some funding agencies are relatively principled and independent, but many are an integral part of the structures of power. Keeping a distance from them may require a low-cost working style, or efforts to explore ethical sources of funding such as individual donations from people who share or support the spirit of the project.

Last but not least, research for action regards the pursuit of knowledge as a collective endeavour. When we get involved in action, we inevitably develop strong views on the issues at hand. Sometimes we are even under pressure to take simplistic or one-sided positions. That may not be the worst of sins, since there are also professional biases and pressures to conform – of a different kind – in academic circles. However, it calls for some safeguards, mainly through dialogue and arguments with people of different views. Researchers, action-oriented or not, can turn dangerous when they think of themselves as experts who are competent to design public policies on their own. Discussion, dialogue, and debate are essential to avoid this trap.

Research for action is a simple idea and there is no need to make a song and dance about it. Many researchers, even in academia, are eager to see their research contribute to practical change in one way or another. However, the academic environment often dulls this aspiration, partly because of its suspicion of organised action, and partly because of the pressure to use research as a means of career advancement.

Needless to say, research for action is not the only valid form of research. Nor is research for action intrinsically a good thing – much depends on what sort of action it is geared to. The limited claim being made here is that research for action carries possibilities that are commonly underestimated, especially in a country like India where relatively sound democratic institutions coexist with massive social problems.

Hard Work No Pay

This book often makes use of the findings and insights of a series of field surveys conducted over the years with student volunteers, mainly during the summer holidays. Most of these surveys were planned in collaboration with Dr Reetika Khera (Associate Professor at the Indian Institute of Technology, Delhi) and other like-minded scholars. The first time we tried to mobilise student volunteers, we had a small research grant, so we felt that we should give them some token remuneration – the minimum wage applicable to casual labourers. We circulated an appeal called "Hard Work, Low Pay". The response was overwhelming. From the following year on, we dropped the remuneration and modified the appeal to "Hard Work, No Pay". The response was even better, with more and more students applying from all over India each time the appeal was circulated. In most cases, the survey teams also included local volunteers or activists, often from underprivileged backgrounds.

This approach turned out to be very useful in many ways. To start with, it enabled us to complete most of the surveys on a shoe-string budget. The survey costs (a tiny fraction of what the government or NGOs typically spend on comparable surveys, not to speak of international organisations) were met by collecting donations from well-wishers – "voluntary donations in rupees with no strings attached" being the basic principle. This freed us from any obligation to funding agencies, the government, or corporate donors.

Dispensing with financial incentives for field investigators also turned out to enhance the quality of the survey work. The volunteers were driven by passion, not money. Most of them went well beyond the call of duty to reach sample households over hill and high water, polish their questionnaires late into the night, and hold extended group discussions about the survey findings. Their living conditions in the field were spartan: they often slept on the floor in the nearest verandah, ate simple food, latched on to crowded buses, and walked long distances in torrid heat. None of this deterred them.

Further, the whole exercise (not only the survey, but also the training and debriefing workshops, as well as follow-up activities) had lasting value as a means of fostering the spirit of voluntarism among the students. For many, it was an eye-opening experience to spend time in the nooks and crannies of rural India, seeing for themselves the daily struggles of ordinary people against grinding poverty, the brutality of labour contractors, the indifference of the bureaucracy. This is not to say that the experience always changed their lives – many of them returned to the pursuit of career and family life after the surveys. But in many cases, judging by their own accounts, it had a lasting influence on their outlook. And some of the volunteers did later become leading practitioners of action-oriented research.

Not all volunteers, of course, joined in the spirit we had hoped. Some had joined up mainly to pad their CVs. Others seemed to be hoping to sample the local rice beer, or to end up in the same team as their sweethearts (real or imagined). And, as in all team work, there were occasional tensions and irritations. Overall, however, there was remarkable goodwill and energy among the survey teams.

The surveys aimed at high-quality data collection, both quantitative and qualitative, facilitated by careful training and debriefing workshops. However, they were not restricted to data collection. In many cases, the work plan also included some real action – for instance, public hearings, social audits, and even the odd effort to catch some of the crooks who are constantly trying to siphon off development funds in rural India. These activities usually took place after rather than during the survey – research and action have their own methods and should not be mixed casually. But we did learn a great deal from them and considered them an integral part of the exercise.

I take this opportunity to express my appreciation of all the students and local volunteers who participated in these surveys over the years. I have fond memories of the times we spent talking with people, visiting schools, and inspecting ration shops from the hills of Chamba district to the forests of Kalahandi and the dusty plains of Bihar. Aside from being highly rewarding at a personal level, the experience boosted my confidence in the possibility of doing things (not just field surveys) differently – based on principles of freedom, co-operation, and enthusiasm rather than the drudgery of employer–employee relationships. The wage labour system strikes me as a little archaic – better than slavery, but still based on control and subordination. The profit motive, too, is quite crude, and its alleged virtues are much exaggerated in mainstream economics. It will take time to get rid of these norms, but some sections of the economy and society (including academia) have already moved away from them in substantial measure, and hopefully their domain will shrink further over time.

Evidence, Experience, and Enlightenment

There is another reason why involvement in action and participation in field surveys are valuable activities for a researcher: they enrich personal experience of the issues of interest. Research and experience can be thought of as two complementary ways of enhancing our understanding of these issues.[4]

Nowadays there is in development economics a tendency to devalue experience and to insist on "evidence". The buzzword is "evidence-

---

[4] This idea can be regarded as one of the foundations of statistical inference, and therefore, of science. Bayesian statistics, of which classical statistics are a special case, require a "prior" (that is, a probability distribution that captures our initial beliefs), and provide a method for revising the prior in the light of new information. Experience is a natural source of prior beliefs.

based policy", where the word evidence essentially stands for statistical analysis. Sometimes it is even treated as more or less synonymous with randomised-controlled trials (RCTs). I am told that getting funding for development research, or even in some universities doing a Ph.D. in development economics, is increasingly difficult unless something like an RCT is involved. The idea is that this is the only foolproof way, or at least the best way, of demonstrating "causality" between interventions and outcomes.[5]

RCTs can certainly be a useful source of insights. But I submit that if we were to restrict ourselves to RCTs, or even to statistical analysis, as the evidential basis of public policy, we would not get very far. Quite often, in fact, we would miss out on very important knowledge. Let me try to explain.

Statistical analysis, important as it is, is often overrated in economics, while other means of learning, including experience, are undervalued. Studies based on statistical analysis have the reputation of being "rigorous", but in practice they can go wrong in numerous ways – even those published in peer-reviewed journals. The data may not be reliable: even large, renowned datasets like India's National Sample Survey or National Family Health Survey are sometimes misleading. The analysts may lack a sound understanding of the data. Coding errors may creep in. The statistical models being used may not be appropriate. The underlying assumptions may not apply. The authors may lack honesty and nudge the analysis towards particular results (how many have the willpower to resist that, if, say, their Ph.D. or tenure is at stake?). It is no wonder that efforts at the independent replication of results published in peer-reviewed economic journals have often had poor success rates.[6] Further, the same results can be

---

[5] There is a large literature on the validity of this claim; see e.g. Deaton and Cartwright 2016 and earlier studies cited there. The concerns discussed here apply *even* if this claim is accepted.

[6] See e.g. Chang and Li 2015, who "assert that economic research is usually not replicable" based on an attempt to replicate the key results of sixty-seven papers published in "well-regarded economic journals"; see also Young 2016, with specific reference to RCTs. To be fair, the standards of transparency

reported in very different ways (even turned upside down) by different authors, depending on their respective convictions. And then there is, in the economic literature, a huge "publication bias": if one study shows, say, that the deworming of schoolchildren has a statistically significant effect on pupil achievements, while another finds no such relation, the former is far more likely to be published than the latter. Ideally, they should be read together.

This is not hair-splitting. Consider for instance the economic literature on social policy in India. There is quite a jumble of studies here: some are really insightful, others are deeply misleading. If someone were to rely on that literature alone to form a view on India's social policies (as many students of development economics are under pressure to do), she would learn very little. In order to learn from "rigorous studies", it really helps to read them in the light of other information, such as the views of the people concerned, as well as direct experience.

Is experience a form of evidence? It seems to me that it is, though mainly for ourselves. When we move about, observe the way things work and listen to people, some patterns emerge. In principle, that information can be treated with the same rigour as statistical data. Of course, personal experience can be misleading, but so can statistical analysis. The real problem in treating experience as a form of evidence is that it is difficult to share. If I trust someone, I would be able to benefit from her experience, and to that extent experience would become a form of communicable evidence. But when we write for a wide audience, we cannot always expect readers to trust our knowledge. In fact, when academic papers quote "knowledgeable informants", I am often suspicious – who counts as a knowledgeable informant, and how does the author know that an informant is not only knowledgeable but also trustworthy? So-called knowledgeable informants, from government officials to NGO workers and

---

in data analysis are growing, at least in the best economic journals, and replicability may improve over time. As things stand, however, this is a serious and resilient problem.

community leaders, often have professional biases, personal prejudices, or various reasons to mislead the researcher. Thus, the notion of knowledgeable informant does not go very far in helping us to treat experience as a form of evidence. What does help is a forum where people can share their experiences, discuss them, and submit them to scrutiny.

In scientific journals, the author's experience is not generally considered admissible evidence. Every important statement is expected to be substantiated, if not with data, then with reference to an earlier study, also published in a credible journal. This is understandable: we cannot expect the editor of a scientific journal to accept what we say at face value. This convention, however, evacuates a great deal of useful knowledge from the literature. In a book, the author has more latitude to draw on his or her personal experience, and then there are journals like the *Economic and Political Weekly* (EPW) where this is also possible. In fact, the EPW's tremendous success may have something to do with the fact that it provides such space while being committed to sound research.[7]

There is an interesting dilemma here for academic research – if the standards of evidence are too high, then little may be learnt, but if they are too low, what we learn (or think we learn) may not be reliable. The world of policy-making and public action, however, is different from that of academic research. In that universe, we have good reason to make constructive use of experience. Indeed, without it, we would be deprived of rich sources of insight and forced to take decisions based on very limited knowledge.

Public Policy and Democratic Practice

A simple example may help illustrate these issues. During the last few years, India's National Rural Employment Guarantee Act

[7] Methodical "qualitative research" also makes some room, in principle, for integrating evidence with experience, though much depends on how it is done. For instance, participant observation would contribute to experience, but getting a case study done by a research assistant would not.

(NREGA) has been afflicted with a series of problems related to wage payments, including corruption and delays. Consider the simple question – should the payments be made through banks or post offices? In answering this, one could make good use of a number of facts, or rather observations, on which there is likely to be wide agreement among experienced people. For instance, it is relatively well understood that post offices are generally closer to homes, but more vulnerable to corruption, at least when it comes to NREGA payments. The first proposition in the preceding sentence can be backed by statistical evidence (for instance, data on the density of banks and post offices in rural areas), but the second – about corruption – is more a matter of common knowledge. Personally, I am quite confident about it, not only because I have often observed post-office corruption in NREGA wage payments, but also because the vulnerabilities of the post office are easy to understand. On the other hand, if a hard-nosed economist asks me, "what evidence do you have that corruption tends to be higher in post offices than in banks?", I would be at a loss to cite any statistical evidence of it, let alone an RCT. And of course I may be wrong. But if policy-makers were to wait for "rigorous" evidence on this and other relevant aspects of wage payments before taking a decision, nothing would move. The best they can do is use statistical evidence along with other relevant information – that is the way things tend to work in the real world, and rightly so.

Let us pursue the example a little further, because I have simplified the issue. For instance, it is not always true that banks are less corrupt than post offices: some local "co-operative banks" are very corrupt, while post-office corruption may be relatively low in some of India's better-governed states. One can imagine a very interesting consultation on these matters taking place among a group of people who might include, say, bank managers, post-office representatives, government officials, development economists, and some NREGA workers or union leaders. Various questions are likely to arise – whether the post offices can be reformed, whether the reach of the banking system can be expanded, and so on. Hopefully, the discussion will proceed towards a better understanding of the problem and its possible solutions. The economists may well be able to contribute important insights, whether based on statistical evidence or other sources of knowledge (say, theoretical reasoning or qualitative research). If the participants come from adequately diverse backgrounds, and make a genuine effort to learn from each other, there is a good chance that progress will be made.

The last sentence, of course, begins with a big "if". Depending on how and why (and by whom) it is convened, this sort of consultation may be vitiated by conflicts of interest, the absence of key participants, the power of influential consultants, or other biases. Leaving that aside for now, the point being made here is that this process of mutual learning involves much more than "evidence" as it tends to be understood in development economics today. Evidence is certainly an important part of it, but if the discussion were to be confined to formal evidence, it would not go very far. For one thing, the problem at hand has numerous aspects on which hard evidence is lacking, and perhaps difficult to generate. For another, whatever the reach of statistical evidence, other sources of enlightenment (including experience) have much to contribute.

Going beyond this illustration, public policy in India is best seen as an outcome of democratic practice. No doubt some would prefer it to be left to technical experts, insulated from the hustle and bustle of public debate. As it happens, that is the trend today (with more and more decisions being taken behind the ramparts of the prime minister's office or the finance ministry), but it does not strike me as a healthy one. Indeed, the knowledge of accredited experts is often more limited than they think. Also, their values tend to be over-influenced by the privileged circles in which they move. Democratic practice is a more exacting process, but I believe that it is ultimately more effective and appropriate. It is also essential to clarify the goals and priorities of public policy, something no amount of expertise can do on its own.

The case for "evidence-based policy" has to be seen in this light. If the idea is to bring more evidence to bear on public policy, there is much to be said for it. This endeavour, however, is likely to be all the more useful if we bear in mind that evidence is more than RCTs, knowledge more than evidence, policy more than knowledge, and action more than policy.[8]

Experience and Values

Aside from being a valid form of evidence (at least for the person concerned), experience can also be very useful in helping us to clarify our values. This is important, since economic policy and public action necessarily involve value judgements about goals and priorities. Even the most committed advocate of evidence-based policy is likely to agree that evidence, on its own, cannot translate into policy advice unless we are clear about what we are trying to achieve and why.

Here again, an example may help. India has some rudimentary schemes of social security pensions for widows, the elderly, and persons with disabilities. Their coverage, and the pension amounts, are very modest as things stand, and there is a view that these schemes should be expanded and perhaps even universalised. Presented with this proposal, an economist is likely to look into various features of pension schemes – for instance, their impact on poverty, their administrative costs, their vulnerability to fraud, and so on. A number of studies have looked into this and found that India's pension schemes are doing quite well in many ways.

These analyses are very useful, but what is no less useful is to spend some time with widows and the elderly and ask them about their lives. If you have a heart, their pain and helplessness will move you

[8] A useful distinction can also be made between knowledge and understanding. The latter is more demanding than the former. Sound policy-making requires both. It also requires clarity about goals and values – more on that in the next section.

like no statistical evidence is likely to. You will also understand that, despite their meagreness, social security pensions mean a lot to poor widows and the elderly for it gives them some independence and dignity and helps them enjoy small comforts, such as getting their spectacles repaired. Quite likely, the central government's failure to raise old-age pensions above their abysmal level of Rs 200 per month for the last twelve years (even as the pensions of government employees went up by leaps and bounds) will then strike you as deep injustice. In short, lived experience can help us put statistical data in perspective and form a more enlightened view on the priorities of social policy.

Fiction and literature can help, too, despite seeming far removed from "evidence". Bibhutibhushan Bandyopadhyay's classic novel *Pather Panchali* (turned into a film by Satyajit Ray) begins with a very perceptive description of the daily life of Indir Thakrun, an elderly widow. It tells us a great deal not only about how she lives, but also about how she feels. As many avid readers of fiction affirm, the empathy arising from sharing in the lives of fictional characters can be more intense and certainly no less illuminating than real-life encounters. Similarly, reading Dalit autobiographies (e.g. those of Shantabai Kamble, Laxman Gaikwad, Om Prakash Valmiki or Daya Pawar) can tell us things about caste – and its horrors – that would be hard to fathom from academic textbooks or survey data. If we are concerned with social development, we have good reason to take interest in these matters.

All this, of course, is difficult terrain. It is certainly possible to be carried away by personal experience, just as it is possible to miss important aspects of reality when we confine our attention to statistical data.[9] What tends to work best is to make good use of both,

---

[9] In this connection, I often remember a comment received many years ago from the late Ashok Rudra, one of India's finest economists and public intellectuals. He was kind enough to read a paper of mine, where I quoted an old widow who was sharing the pain she had felt when her sons abandoned her: "I suffered so much to bring them up, and what did I get in return?" she said. Ashok Rudra immediately wrote in the margin: "typical blackmail".

and to engage with people who may have a different experience, or different views.

Jholawala Economics

There is no such thing as jholawala economics and I disown in advance anyone who claims to be a jholawala economist enthused by my writings. Jholawala economics is just an expression I have made up for the title of this book. However, I can say a few words about the inspiration behind it.

"Jholawala" has become a term of abuse in India's corporate-sponsored media. Jhola, in Hindi, refers to the sort of cheap sling bag that many Indian activists used to carry (nowadays, a backpack is more likely), and jholawala is a person with a jhola. So jholawala is basically a disparaging reference to activists. The term is part of the business media's propaganda against what they consider subversive ideas, such as the welfare state, minimum wages, and environmental regulation. An important part of this propaganda is to create a convenient vocabulary, for instance by using derogatory terms like "freebies" and "handouts" to refer to valuable and valued social security schemes. Similarly, the term jholawala helps marginalise critics of business-driven public policies.

Economists are generally more respectful, but most of them are also quite sceptical of jholawalas. They often say things like "good intentions are not enough" or "effective policy-making requires sound theory", implying that jholawalas are well meaning but confused. The scepticism is handsomely reciprocated: jholawalas are in no hurry to learn economics, and often dismiss economists as docile servants of the establishment.

This mutual suspicion is unfortunate. Jholawalas can make much better use of economics – a very enlightening discipline, if it is studied

---

Clearly, personal testimonies can be interpreted in very different ways, just like statistical data.

with a critical mind. The insights of game theory, for example, are a dream for the peace activist. They show, among other things, that conflicts can easily get out of hand, no matter how rational the players may be – something we also know from everyday experience. That sounds like a good argument for seeking nuclear disarmament. Game theory's insights on the collectively irrational nature of selfish behaviour (for instance, in "prisoners' dilemma" situations) are also of much interest to critics of the established economic order.

On the other side, jholawalas and their work deserve more appreciation from economists. True, jholawalas are often woolly-headed, intolerant, or prone to herd behaviour. But they tend to have a relatively good view of the dark underbelly of the system, because they are well placed to see it. Many of them are also well informed, at least on the issues that concern them. The reason is that they are passionate about these issues, so they keep track of the details, much like football fans who read the fine print of the sports page. Economists (myself included) often look embarrassingly ignorant by comparison.

To illustrate, few economists – if any – come close to India's best right-to-information activists in terms of their understanding of corruption and how it can be fought. It is mainly activists, not economists, who have developed the principles of a series of anti-corruption legislations concerned inter alia with the right to information, grievance redressal, whistle-blowing, and the right to public service. Interestingly, even recent surveys of the economic literature on corruption rarely refer to the right to information – a simple but powerful idea that has gone a long way in India. Instead, the focus in these surveys tends to be on more conventional measures like fostering competition among government agencies, reducing the scope for discretion, and better use of auctions. These measures, of course, are also important – here as in other fields, there is much scope for mutual learning.

Thus, the reference to jholawala economics in the title is intended to serve a dual purpose. First, it affirms the validity of "research for action" in economics. Second, it is an invitation to mutual learning between economists and so-called jholawalas. It is an odd idea that the proper attire for an economist is a corporate briefcase rather than a jhola. Ideally, economists should be found not only in universities, governments, and the corporate sector, but also among the public at large – working with civic organisations, trade unions, political parties, alternative media, the peace movement, or just freelance. Of course, economists generally like their work to be well paid, so they tend to gravitate towards the centres of privilege and power.[10] But nothing prevents economists from mingling with the jholawalas if they are so inclined – and vice versa.

Scheme of the Book

A few months ago, I read somewhere that publishing a collection of one's op-eds as a book was "the ultimate vanity". That came as a large spoke in the wheel of this book project, halting it for a time, but I revived it for two reasons. One is that the topics of these essays are, sadly, alive and well. India is still grappling with hunger, poverty, inequality, corruption, conflict, and related issues. The arguments in this book have not lost their relevance.

The second reason is that this collection of essays provides some sort of retrospective on the course of social policy in India between 2000 and 2017. Despite India's general inertia in this field, there were some important initiatives over this period, such as the introduction of midday meals in primary schools and the enactment of the National Rural Employment Guarantee Act. As befits a democracy, these initiatives emerged out of lively public debates. Others, notably in

---

[10] In fact, this applies even to those inclined to simple living. A well-known economist tends to be bombarded with invitations to deliver keynote addresses at international conferences, release books authored by influential people, give memorial lectures, advise governments, and join countless boards. Declining these invitations, however unwelcome, is often difficult. That leaves little time for engaging with different circles.

the field of health care, failed to materialise. This book may help to understand some of these advances and setbacks, as well as the debates that accompanied them and continue today.

The essays have been arranged thematically, with a top-up of miscellaneous issues in the last section. Each thematic section begins with a short headnote which puts the essays in perspective. Within each section, the essays appear in chronological order. Since the date of publication often helps to understand the context, it is footnoted at the start of each essay. The chronological arrangement will help, hopefully, to give the reader a sense of how social policy evolved over time.

In a few cases, I have merged two short essays into one longer piece. Some titles have been modified – the original titles and sources are mentioned at the end of the book.

I have not revised the essays, except for some streamlining here and there, e.g. to correct an error, avoid repetition, or revise a careless statement. In order to keep the book as readable as possible I have also refrained from the temptation of adding footnotes to them. However, each section closes with Notes, where I have done my best to retrieve the original statistical and bibliographical sources.[11] The notes also include the odd clarification, and a short update here and there.

---

[11] For further guidance to the literature on social policy in India, see Drèze and Sen 2013, Drèze 2016a, and Drèze and Khera 2017.

1

DROUGHT AND HUNGER

THIS COLLECTION OF ESSAYS begins on a grim note: stories of drought and hunger in the early 2000s. I doubt that many communities on earth face worse living conditions than those we observed among the Sahariyas of western Madhya Pradesh, the Bhuiyans of Palamau, and the Pahari Korwas of Surguja in Chhattisgarh. This experience was harrowing but also valuable, for it informed and inspired much that happened later.

The opening essay, "Starving the Poor", is a critique of the accumulation of excess foodgrain stocks by the Government of India in early 2001. The stockholding was approaching 50 million tonnes – about ten quintals per household below the poverty line. Meanwhile, drought conditions were developing in large swathes of the country, with regular reports of acute hunger and even starvation deaths. The government's gigantic hoarding of foodgrain, far in excess of official norms, seemed to intensify the hardship in the countryside. A case needed to be made for using these foodstocks to organise public works and other relief measures.

Around this time I found myself sitting in Kavita Srivastava's kitchen in Jaipur, with Colin Gonsalvez and Yug Chaudhry. Kavita, an old friend, was active in the People's Union for Civil Liberties (PUCL) and was also convenor of the Akal Sangharsh Samiti, a coalition of citizens' organisations formed to defend the interests of drought-affected people in Rajasthan. Colin, a supreme court lawyer, was Director of the Human Rights Law Network, where Yug also worked (later, Yug became an eminent lawyer in his own right). When I shared my worries over starvation in the shadow of ballooning foodstocks, Colin and Yug immediately suggested a Public Interest Litigation (PIL). A few weeks later, a writ petition on this matter was filed by the PUCL in the supreme court. That was the beginning of the so-called "right to food case" (*PUCL vs Union of India and Others, Writ Petition [Civil] 196 of 2001*), which went on for sixteen years.[1] Over time, the case had a bearing on many of the social programmes discussed in this book, especially midday meals, the Integrated Child Development Services, and the public distribution system (PDS). The case also facilitated the growth of a wider campaign for the right to food.

Meanwhile, however, people continued to go hungry in the shadow of gigantic – and ever-growing – foodgrain stocks. The other essays in this section consist of first-hand accounts of people's living conditions in some of India's poorest states – Chhattisgarh, Jharkhand, Madhya Pradesh, and Odisha (earlier "Orissa"). Everywhere, there was a striking shortage of social support for vulnerable groups. But there were pointers to possible interventions, such as the midday meal programme in tribal areas of Odisha, and drought relief work in western India. In the South, of course, particularly in Kerala and Tamil Nadu, some of these programmes had already been taken much further.

In India, drought is a time of distress that often also brings about social or political change. The events of 2001–3 led to many lessons being learnt, as well as public mobilisation, and paved the way for many of the social policy initiatives discussed later in this book.

---

[1] The petition was eventually dismissed on 10 February 2017 (just before this book came to completion), on the grounds that the National Food Security Act 2013 took care of the concerns it had raised. The National Food Security Act, however, addresses only some of these concerns.

Starving the Poor[*]

There is no greater scam in India at this time than the so-called "food subsidy". Under a fig leaf of "food security", the government is keeping millions of tonnes of food out of the reach of the poor.

Even at the best of times, undernutrition in India is extraordinary. According to the second National Family Health Survey (1998–9), about half of all Indian children are chronically undernourished. The latest Human Development Report places India at the bottom of the international scale in this respect, with only Bangladesh doing worse. This year, with drought affecting large parts of the country for the second or third time in a row, undernourishment and starvation could increase.

Against this background, unsuspecting observers may welcome the Indian government's decision to spend about Rs 10,000 crores on the "food subsidy" – the common assumption being that it will help bring food within the reach of poor families. Far from it. The food subsidy is essentially the deficit of the Food Corporation of India (FCI), whose operations are now chiefly geared to keeping food prices *up* rather than down. This has been achieved, temporarily at least, by accumulating massive amounts of food in FCI godowns. Today, foodgrain stocks are approaching 50 million tonnes.

The Indian public is so used to large numbers that it is easy to lose sight of the staggering scale of this hoard. It may help to think of it as the equivalent of one tonne of food for *each* household under the poverty line. If all the sacks of grain lying in the FCI godowns were lined up in a row, they would stretch for a million kilometres – more

[*]February 2001.

than twice the distance from the earth to the moon. When millions of people are undernourished, if not starving, hoarding food on this scale – at an enormous cost – seems tantamount to mass murder.

There are two major reasons why the food subsidy is so large at this time. One is the FCI's high operating costs, including the costs incurred on storage. According to one estimate, these costs accounted for nearly half the total food subsidy in the mid 1990s. The second reason is that the FCI is currently buying far more food than it is selling. The difference is a net addition to the stocks, which are growing by leaps and bounds.

Ordinary households benefit very little from this "subsidy". In fact, what they gain on the one hand from subsidised food obtained from the PDS pales in comparison with what they lose on the other by paying higher food prices in the market. This is all the more true if we keep in mind the low quality of PDS foodgrains. In some areas, it is reported that even poor households see little point in purchasing food from ration shops rather than from the open market because the lower price in the ration shops is more than offset by the poor quality of their grain. These households, in other words, gain nothing from subsidised PDS sales; on the contrary, they bear the burden of high food prices as a result of the FCI's hoarding operations.

Meanwhile, unintended constituents are feeding at the "food security" trough: rats and worms have a full stomach, even as PDS dealers and other intermediaries siphon off large quantities of grain to sell it on the black market – or rather, the open market. According to the Planning Commission, over the country as a whole 36 per cent of PDS wheat and 31 per cent of PDS rice is appropriated by private parties. All this boosts the "food subsidy" while doing substantially nothing for the hungry.

The obvious question arises: What prevents the government from using this mountain of grain to fund a constructive expansion of the public distribution system, food-for-work schemes, and other anti-poverty programmes? Possible reasons include political inertia, orga-nisational gaps, and reluctance to bear the financial costs (e.g. the non-wage component of food-for-work schemes). Removing these hurdles is an urgent political task at this time of widespread hardship.

It would be a mistake, however, to assume that income-generation programmes will by themselves succeed in absorbing the existing foodstock. Several recent studies show that it is only at very low levels of income that foodgrain consumption rises with additional income; beyond that, income increases lead to a higher consumption of pulses, vegetables, milk, fat, and related items, but foodgrain consumption remains more or less unchanged. This suggests that, beyond a point, income-generation programmes will not help to resolve the fundamental imbalance between foodgrain demand and supply at the prevailing price. Resolving that imbalance ultimately calls for a decline in the relative price of foodgrains. That, however, conflicts with a paramount objective of food policy at this time, namely the continuation of relatively *high* foodgrain prices.

The conviction that food prices have to be "supported" (i.e. kept high) is so strong and so widespread that it has clouded any reasoned analysis of the ensuing social consequences. Many people, especially the poor, would gain from a decline in food prices. For agricultural labourers, migrant workers, slum dwellers – in short, all those among the poor who buy most of their food in the market – cheaper food would be a blessing. People in drought-stricken areas that are ill served by the PDS would also get substantial relief from being able to buy cheap food in the market instead of being at the mercy of the PDS mafia.

What about farmers? As it is, they have not been doing too well in recent years, with the slowdown of agricultural growth in the 1990s followed by widespread drought. Their livelihood is further threatened, in some cases, by the imminent lifting of quantitative restrictions on agricultural imports in compliance with WTO regulations. Against this background, is it not imperative to sustain high foodgrain prices?

There are two answers to this question. One is that the poorer sections of the farming community benefit very little, if at all, from price-support measures. Consider for instance small farmers in, say, Orissa or Jharkhand or Chhattisgarh. These typically sell little grain, if any, in the market; instead, they tend to combine subsistence farming with labour migration and other income-earning activities that allow them to buy non-food commodities. So, higher food prices would not help them. What would help them is an improvement in productivity, via, for instance, technological innovation and crop diversification. There is an enormous potential for productivity improvement in large parts of the eastern region, which has been grossly neglected. Instead, massive resources have been spent on promoting unsustainable farming patterns in Punjab, Haryana, and other privileged areas.

The second answer is that, whatever the pros and cons of lower food prices, it is in any case *not possible* to sustain artificially high prices, short of destroying or exporting the surplus food. Storing surplus food only postpones the problem. Worse, it aggravates it, by giving farmers misleading signals to the effect that they should continue growing more foodgrains instead of diversifying their crops. Sooner or later, this is bound to lead to a glut in the foodgrain market and a collapse of market prices, defeating the price-support policy. In fact, a decline in market prices has already happened this year in some parts of the country. The glut is likely to intensify after the rabi (winter) harvest, especially as private traders are unlikely to risk buying large quantities of food. It is reported that plans are afoot to deal with this impending "crisis" through the official procurement of up to another 20 million tonnes of wheat. But this – to use a paradoxical metaphor for enlarging the size of a mountain – only amounts to digging the hole deeper and deeper.

Temporarily keeping prices up by storing food at massive public expense is not an effective way of helping needy farmers. Insofar as supporting food prices is a sensible objective, the only sustainable and equitable way of going about it is to generate income among the poor. At this time of widespread drought, all parties involved have a strong interest in food stocks being used without delay for massive income-generation programmes.

Fragile Lifelines,
Robust Oppression*

The recent "starvation deaths" in Kashipur prompted me to re-examine some field notes I had written in April 1999 during a long walk through the "KBK" (Kalahandi-Bolangir-Koraput) region of Orissa. As it happens, the walk started in Kashipur. I do not presume to have gained a vast knowledge of the area during this brief journey, but some deep impressions remain.

The breathtaking beauty of western Orissa, and the brighter aspects of tribal life – so beautifully conveyed in Gopinath Mohanty's novel *Paraja* – did not leave any illusion about the harsh conditions of life in the area. I remember how one old man, barely half my height, kindly allowed me to have a go at carrying the load he was taking to the market. I collapsed under the weight. He had another 15 km to go. For this excruciating labour he would earn Rs 12 or so at a time when rice cost Rs 10 per kg in the market.

Beyond this anecdote lies a sea of hardship and deprivation. In village after village, poor people survived on a spartan diet (e.g. rice and salt), drank unsafe water, and had virtually no access to health care. Diarrhoea was a common cause of death. Real wages were incredibly low. Even on public works programmes, labourers earned as little as Rs 25 a day.

There were many signs of a crisis of traditional livelihoods, especially in areas that used to practise shifting cultivation. One elderly man sighed: "In the old days, a single woman's work was enough to feed the family; now, even if the whole family works, we go hungry."

*September 2001.

Massive environmental degradation had contributed to this crisis. In many villages, the surrounding forests had been decimated and forest-based economic activities were virtually over. In some areas, these had been compensated by the expansion of other occupations, such as weaving and cash crops. Elsewhere, labour migration (often described as "going abroad", e.g. to Nagpur or Hyderabad) was the overwhelming survival strategy. Many villages were almost bereft of adult males.

Another prime cause of economic backwardness in KBK is the rampant exploitation and corruption. Local Adivasis and Dalits are sitting ducks for unscrupulous traders, moneylenders, contractors, and bureaucrats. Enormous sums have been poured into "development" programmes of all hues with no tangible results. In Bhawanipatna, a contractor (who turned out to be a fresh graduate from St Stephen's College in Delhi) offered a candid account of the commissions that were due to various officials for any development work at the gram panchayat level: 3 per cent for the block development officer (BDO), 5 per cent for the junior engineer, 5 per cent for the gram panchayat extension officer, 5 per cent for the block chairman, 2 per cent for the block clerk, 2 per cent for the block cashier (*sic*). When I asked him what happened if, say, the BDO were an honest person, he exclaimed, "If the BDO is honest, he will stick to his 3 per cent!"

Everywhere we went, the condition of local public services was abysmal. There were plenty of vacant posts in schools, health centres, and administrative offices – government employees strive to avoid being posted in this difficult area. The schooling system was in shambles. I was startled, for instance, to find fairly large villages without a single primary school, something unthinkable in most other states today. The silver lining was the midday meal programme: school-going children were getting a cooked lunch instead of the usual monthly grain rations.

The PDS had all the familiar flaws. Most people had ration cards, and their official entitlements were far from negligible: 10 kg of rice per month for families in the "below poverty line" (BPL) category, at

Rs 2 per kg. But delivery was inadequate and unpredictable. When food happened to reach the local ration shop, people had to rush there at short notice (a whole day's walk in some cases), and rice was distributed first-come-first-served, with those arriving "late" getting nothing. In two villages where I examined people's ration cards, the average BPL family had received 40 kg of rice over the preceding twelve months instead of the official 120 kg. In Orissa, as elsewhere, officials blame the people for the low offtake of grain under the PDS, but the real problem lies in defective supply arrangements.

Behind all these failures is an overarching problem of political marginalisation. As one woman saw it, "There is no point complaining – nobody is going to listen."

In many villages I heard something I have not often heard elsewhere in India: land productivity is declining. Perhaps this trend can be reversed, but it is clear that the long-term answer to rampant poverty in the KBK region is economic diversification. This was already happening in some places, and there was evident potential for more. Meanwhile, however, the region appears to be going through a phase of extreme vulnerability: traditional livelihoods have collapsed and alternative economic activities have not yet developed.

These general impressions are corroborated by secondary data. Indeed, recent statistics on Orissa's economy make for depressing reading. To illustrate: during the 1990s, the agricultural sector did not grow at all; real agricultural wages stagnated; and foodgrain production declined at about 3 per cent per year. These are all-Orissa figures; the KBK region probably fares worse.

Viewed in the light of this development catastrophe, the recent starvation deaths in Kashipur are no surprise. The 1990s witnessed a protracted crisis of traditional livelihoods in western Orissa. Then came a prolonged drought, when the government stabbed the people in the back by hoarding gigantic amounts of food to placate affluent farmers while the hungry millions bore the brunt of high food prices. Finally, in July 2001, relief programmes were prematurely discontinued, just as impoverished farmers and labourers braced themselves for the hardest season of the year. By a cruel irony, the latest tragedy is excessive rain, which, I am told, has destroyed the maize crop in Kashipur.

There are many lessons to learn from Kashipur's starvation deaths, seen from a broader perspective. In the few lines that remain, let me share one thought. In areas like KBK, there is an urgent need for social security arrangements of a permanent nature involving, for instance, guaranteed slack-season employment combined with direct transfers for those unable to work. The country's massive foodgrain stocks present a unique opportunity to put such arrangements in place. This is how we should think of these stocks, rather than seeing them as a reserve to be rushed to the starving on a temporary and ad hoc basis.

The Right to Food
and Public Accountability*

In the month of October, Surguja district in Chhattisgarh looks like a land of milk and honey. Endless waves of green fields, lush forests, and clear streams give an impression of natural abundance. These delightful surroundings, however, hide a harsh struggle for survival. Yields are low in Surguja, and most farmers are unable to grow enough food to cover their subsistence needs. When food runs out, they have to migrate in search of work. Those unable to migrate try to make ends meet by keeping a little livestock, selling wood, or collecting tendu and other minor forest products. Hunger is widespread, and so are basic diseases like gastroenteritis, which caused hundreds of deaths in Wadrafnagar block last August.

The dismal record of development programmes in the district bears some responsibility for this state of affairs. It would be an exaggeration to say that all these programmes have "failed". Examples of useful interventions include the installation of handpumps in many hamlets, state purchases of tendu at subsidised rates, and a major expansion of school facilities. However, these are islands of relative success in a sea of inefficiency, corruption, and exploitation. Even though large sums have been spent on development schemes, most villages in Surguja are still wanting in basic facilities such as a decent approach road, a health centre, and electricity.

The PDS fits into this broader pattern of dismal basic services, rooted in a breakdown of public accountability. A brief reconnaissance of Wadrafnagar block suggests that the PDS here is virtually non-

*December 2001.

functional. In village after village, ration cards are full of blank entries. The main reason seems to be that the poor are unable to overcome all the hurdles involved in drawing their rations. Consider Jhapar, a tribal village near the U.P. border. It takes about three hours to walk from there to the local ration shop, twelve km away. The shop opens only two or three days each month (in September it was open for only a day). The opening time is arbitrary and unpredictable. When word reaches Jhapar that grain is being distributed, eligible households have to rustle up enough cash to buy their monthly quota of rice – about Rs 130, not a small amount in this subsistence economy. For most people in Jhapar, producing this sum at short notice is very difficult. Among those who are able to raise the cash, and then spend a day walking to the ration shop and back, some find the shop closed, others are told the shop has run out of rice. Few succeed in reaching the end of this obstacle course, most are reconciled to the fact that it is all a futile rigmarole. They know they are being short-changed, and they know even better that little can be done about it. As one resident put it, "*Hamari baat koi naheen manega – hum log lathi chalane wale naheen hai*" (No-one's going to listen to us – we aren't the sort that wield lathis).

Many of these hurdles arise from the fact that the ration-shop dealer has a strong incentive to deprive his customers and sell the grain in the open market. In disadvantaged areas like Wadrafnagar, the public simply does not have enough clout to resist this fraud. Many people have no knowledge whatsoever of their entitlements. In some villages, for instance, they have been told that the monthly quota is only 10 kg, as against the official norm of 20 kg.

In the larger villages on the main road to Ambikapur (the district headquarters), the situation is different. Here people know their entitlements and have the means of keeping the local dealer on his toes, for instance through elected representatives or vigilance committees. As a result, offtake from the ration shops is much higher. In fact, dealers bitterly complain that the public does not "allow" them to sell in the open market, making the entire business unviable. Indeed, the official commissions are insufficient to cover operational costs (including customary bribes at the FCI godowns). Local dealers envy their counterparts in remote areas for being able to fleece the public without much resistance. The whole system looks like it has been designed to fail. Given the inadequacy of official commissions, only those who have enough clout to resist public scrutiny and sell in the open market are likely to bid for ration-shop licences. And once corrupt dealers are in control of the licences, the door is wide open for large-scale diversion of the PDS grain to the market. According to one dealer, who spoke relatively openly, barely 25 per cent of the food lifted from FCI godowns in Surguja reaches the intended households.

Surguja's experience suggests that the PDS is in urgent need of drastic reform, with a special focus on public accountability. Various steps could be taken to improve this. First, better use can be made of both carrot and stick when handling ration-shop dealers. Their commissions should be raised, making it possible for them to work honestly, and, conditional on that, firm action should be taken against corrupt dealers. Second, gram panchayats and gram sabhas should be empowered to appoint and dismiss ration-shop operators. In Madhya Pradesh and Chhattisgarh, the devolution of supervisory powers to panchayati raj institutions has been used with good effect in other contexts, and this approach can be extended to the PDS. Third, in areas such as Surguja, there is a strong case for abolishing the distinction between BPL and non-BPL households. Aside from creating artificial social divisions in the villages, this distinction has undermined public pressure for an improved PDS (since non-BPL households no longer have a stake in it), and led to the exclusion of large numbers of poor households. Finally, the right to food calls for greater attention from popular organisations and social movements. There is little hope of radical change based on government initiatives alone.

It is possible to see the right to food as an ideal focus of popular mobilisation at this time of unprecedented "hunger amidst plenty". In

Wadrafnagar, people were shocked to hear that food mountains lie idle in FCI godowns across the country (and even in Wadrafnagar block itself). Even otherwise, there is a strong undercurrent of resentment about the rampant exploitation of local communities at the hands of babus and sahukars (moneylenders), of which the breakdown of the PDS is one manifestation. Efforts to translate this resentment into constructive action are likely to be rewarding.

A good example of the galvanising effects of public accountability came up in Raghunathnagar, the site of last August's gastroenteritis epidemic. After this incident, which caused a public uproar, the local health centre was promptly revamped. Now there are qualified doctors, plenty of medicines, and feverish activity – the best health outpost I have seen. It took a slew of deaths, however, to bring about the metamorphosis.

Perhaps the most effective means of banishing hunger and starvation from Surguja is an "employment guarantee" programme. Even a limited guarantee (restricted, say, to the lean season) could go a long way. The country's gigantic foodstocks have made such programmes more affordable than ever, and there is no dearth of opportunities for labour-intensive public works here. Most villages in Wadrafnagar, however, had seen no relief works for many years. This year, as usual, no relief work had been organised in any of the villages we visited, except Pandari where some cosmetic work was organised for five days shortly before the chief minister's visit last August. Even there, labourers were yet to be paid, two months after the event. It is a cruel irony for "relief" to translate into work without payment. Here again, the lack of public accountability is the key issue.

Memories of Kusumatand*

(with Bela Bhatia)

On 9 July 2002, the normally sleepy block headquarters in Manatu (Palamau district, Jharkhand) were overwhelmed by thousands of poor people who had assembled there for a public hearing on hunger and the right to food. This public hearing had been called in response to a critical situation: three starvation deaths had been reported in the village of Kusumatand in May.

We visited Kusumatand three times, in late June and early July, initially with a joint fact-finding team of the Gram Swaraj Abhiyan (GSA) and the right to food campaign. The team conducted a survey of twenty-one randomly selected households in the hamlet, cross-examined neighbours and relatives of the victims, and interviewed various officials at the block headquarters. We were shocked by what we saw and heard.

Kusumatand is a hamlet of about seventy-five houses on the outskirts of Manatu gram panchayat. The majority of the villagers are Bhuiyans, others are mainly Muslims and Adivasis. They possess no land, or are virtually landless. Most of them survive by seasonal labour migration, e.g. to Rohtas district in Bihar, where they earn 3 to 4 kg of grain per day for harvesting or transplanting. They also earn a little by cultivation, collecting tendu leaves, and such casual labour as they are able to find. Local employment opportunities being very limited, most households in Kusumatand find it hard to survive during the lean months.

*August 2002.

Our main purpose was to investigate the reported starvation deaths, but we found that the entire hamlet lived in a state of semi-starvation. Most people in Kusumatand survive on small quantities of khudi (broken rice), supplemented with whatever wild food may be available in the season, such as mahua (a tree flower), chakora (a wild spinach), or gethi (a local tuber). The mahua season was now coming to an end and many people were eating lumps of plain chakora. Some had nothing else to eat. Of twenty-one sample households, twenty said they frequently skipped meals for want of anything to eat. Comestibles other than rice and wild food were virtually absent in Kusumatand.

As for expenditure on non-food items, more than half the sample households said it was nil in an ordinary month. They bought clothes once a year, if at all, their meagre earnings going almost exclusively on food. They use sand or ashes to wash with (not a very effective method, judging from the abysmal levels of hygiene in the hamlet), and do without "luxuries" such as tea and bidis. Only two households out of twenty-one said all adult members wore chappals (slippers); only seven owned a blanket or a quilt. Many houses contain nothing other than basic cooking utensils.

Even potable water is missing. Most households drink visibly contaminated water drawn from shallow wells. A sample from one of the wells turned out to be full of worms.

The abject state of life in Kusumatand has other evident symptoms, such as an absence of the usual signs of hospitality. None of the sample households were able to offer the simplest refreshment; they did not even offer water, perhaps knowing how polluted it was. The laughter of children is seldom heard here and very few can be seen playing or running. They tend to stand by listlessly, ill-clad and undernourished.

Health conditions in the village have the character of a humanitarian emergency. During our brief survey, we encountered a plethora of ailments, including tuberculosis, marasmus, polio, epilepsy, paralysis, blindness, conjunctivitis, diarrhoea, chronic backache and headache, toothache, and various mental illnesses. There are no health facilities in the village, and even the Auxiliary Nurse Midwife (ANM) never visits. Private treatment is available in Manatu, but few can afford it. The public health centre has little to offer. This helps to understand why people in Kusumatand often die from the combined burden of malnutrition, weakness, and hunger-related disease. This, it appears, is what happened to Sundar Bhuiyan, Kunti Devi, and Basanti Devi – the three victims who are said to have starved. These deaths, related by surviving relatives, are extreme symptoms of endemic hunger in the area as a whole. In each case, the sequence was similar: chronic hunger and exhaustion, then a prolonged period of precarious survival on wild food, and finally a brief and fatal illness (e.g. an acute stomach ache). The surviving members of these families continue to live in dreadful poverty and are liable to die at any time in a similar way.

Consider for instance the surviving members of Kunti Devi's family. Her husband, Bageshwar Bhuiyan, suffers from TB and is unable to work. His illness goes untreated because he has no money and the staff at the local health centre charge patients for TB drugs that are meant to be given free. The burden of looking after him and his six children falls on his mother, a courageous seventy-year-old widow who walks to Manatu from time to time to glean broken rice from the local mill. The rice is barely fit for human consumption, but there is nothing much else to be had – the family survives almost exclusively on wild food. Their house collapsed a few months ago and the family had to take refuge in a corner of Bageshwar's brother's house. Except for one cooking pot and a few rags, the family owns absolutely nothing – not even a blanket or a pair of chappals.

Kusumatand's predicament reflects the dismal failure of development programmes and welfare schemes in the area. Even the most basic institutional framework necessary for their success is missing. There are no functional gram panchayats in Manatu (panchayat elections are yet to be held in Jharkhand), so village communities are like ships without rudders. All development schemes are run directly from the block office. Government officers have stopped visiting the villages, allegedly because the area is under Naxalite control. The Maoist Communist

Centre (MCC) certainly has a strong presence in Manatu, but "Naxal prabhavit kshetr" (Naxal-affected area) has also become a convenient all-purpose excuse for government employees to abscond. The new block development officer (BDO) is no exception. He comes to Manatu twice a week for brief consultations with the local contractors, who have a strong hold on the area's scanty development schemes. It is common knowledge that there is an understanding between the MCC and the contractors, who are tolerated as long as they pay the mandatory "taxes". After government officers, contractors, and the MCC have taken their share of development funds, little is left for substantive work.

Life in Kusumatand is a vicious circle of poverty, hunger, illiteracy, and powerlessness. Most people there have no notion of their rights and entitlements. The sarkar (government) is an abstract entity with little bearing on their lives. They have never seen the face of the panchayat secretary or BDO. The village has no approach road, no school, no electricity, no health facility, nothing. All this within three km of the block headquarters.

The public hearing on 9 July was partly aimed at breaking this vicious circle of deprivation and disempowerment. The hearing, convened by the GSA, was attended by more than 2000 people (mainly Dalits and Adivasis) from the surrounding villages. Women participated in large numbers.

The hearing began with a presentation of the findings of a survey of 36 villages of Manatu block completed by the GSA in early July. The survey exposed the disastrous state of public services and welfare programmes in the area. To illustrate, only 17 of the 36 survey villages have a primary school, and 9 of the 17 schools have been closed for more than a year. Of the 8 functional schools, 5 have a single teacher. Taken together, the 36 villages have only 12 teachers for more than 2000 children in the 6–11 age group.

Stark irregularities in the functioning of the PDS also came to light. Many people complained that despite their extreme poverty they had no BPL card. Even those who had one, received just a fraction of the subsidised rice they were entitled to buy with it. Their ration cards were often blank, or full of fake entries. Some participants said they were too poor to buy PDS rations (when available) even at the subsidised prices. According to a recent analysis of National Sample Survey data, only 20 per cent of the grain released through the PDS in Jharkhand reaches the intended households – the rest is siphoned off.

Similar irregularities were evident in other food-related programmes. For instance, no drought relief has been organised in the area, even though Manatu was declared drought-affected in November 2001. There are no midday meals in any of the local schools (Jharkhand has not yet implemented the supreme court orders on this). And child care centres for children below the age of six years, also known as anganwadis, are closed most of the time.

While food was the main focus of the hearing, people brought up other pressing problems, such as clean water, schooling, roads, electricity, and health care. The participants listened with remarkable attention for nearly five hours. The public hearing was clearly a new experience for them, greeted with a mixture of puzzlement, interest, and hope. It was also an opportunity to confront government officials who had ignored them for an eternity. The BDO initially took refuge in his office with the son of the erstwhile zamindar (landlord) of Manatu, who was eager to give him "advice". Later he did sit through the hearing and assured the participants that he would address their complaints. His promises did not carry much weight with the audience.

The gathering ended with a resolve to build a larger campaign on these issues. How far this can be done in Manatu's oppressive environment remains to be seen, but the public hearing has at least clarified the challenges to be faced and affirmed the possibility of change.

The Dark Well of Hunger*

The Chambal area of Madhya Pradesh is not exactly a green and pleasant land. Here and there one finds islands of irrigated land, owned mainly by Thakurs, Sikhs, Jats, and other powerful communities. Elsewhere lie vast stretches of rocky land, degraded forest, and desiccated ravines. Marooned in this inhospitable terrain are hundreds of thousands of Sahariyas who eke out a living from survival activities like selling wood, making baskets, and seasonal migration. My stomach churns every time I think about their living conditions in the hamlets surrounding Chharch, a remote settlement of about 500 houses tucked away in a desolate valley of Shivpuri district.

Travelling from Gwalior to Shivpuri, and then on to Pohri and finally Chharch, is like descending deeper and deeper into a dark well of poverty and hunger. Between Shivpuri and Pohri, one goes through a stretch of thirty-five km of parched land, with no sign of economic activity. It is hard to understand how people make a living in this environment. At the block headquarters in Pohri, there are clear signs of the devastating effects of drought: unemployment, dry wells, dead cattle, a crippling recession in the local bazaar.

The situation gets worse as one proceeds from Pohri to Chharch, near the Rajasthan border. According to local Bharatiya Janata Party (BJP) activists, fifty-two "starvation deaths" occurred here in recent months. Their account of the facts is not exactly objective, and the precise nature of these deaths is far from clear. What is not in doubt, however, is that people here suffer from horrendous levels of hunger

*May 2003.

and undernutrition, and that many recent deaths are, in one way or another, hunger-related. Beyond these tragedies, there is a larger issue of appalling living conditions in the area.

Travelling from hamlet to hamlet around Chharch, the scenes of undernutrition and disease are chilling. The plight of children is particularly heart-rending; most are severely malnourished. Some look like textbook cases of starvation, their bodies naked, their bellies distended, their skins blistered. Illnesses have deformed many: swollen chests, hunchbacks, squints, scabies, and other such. Adults, especially the women, fare little better. Yet health facilities are virtually invisible in the area. The nearest health facility worth the name is in Pohri, a long and expensive journey.

This year, chronic poverty and hunger have been fatally aggravated by the worst drought in living memory. Crops have withered and traditional sources of livelihood, such as the collection of mahua and tendu, have been obliterated. There is virtually no employment in the area. Migrating is like a game of Russian roulette, the chances of finding work elsewhere being beset by the possibility of dying while trying to find it.

My journey ended in Jigni, a Sahariya village. Most people here survive from whatever little relief employment happens to come their way. Wild berries are there for the gathering, but an overdose of them gives people stomach aches, and in any case the berries are not expected to last very long. Some residents calmly stated that they had not eaten for days.

Ishwar Dei invited me to see her house. Her husband is ill and she looks after four children. She did not look like the poorest person in the village by any means, yet her tiny hut was bare of possessions and provisions. There was a large storage bin in the corner and when I looked at it she guessed my thoughts and said it was empty. She opened it without hesitation and told me to look. I stretched my arm into the bin and shuddered at encountering thick cobwebs. The hearth was cold and there was nothing to eat in the house except for a bunch of berries tied in a dirty cloth. There was no point checking the food situation in other houses. It was clear that Ishwar Dei's predicament was a kind of village template.

Some children insisted on taking me to Nathu's house, saying he really needed help. I followed them with a heavy heart, wondering if there was any end to this deepening misery. Nathu's dwelling was a chamber of horrors. His wife was one of the victims of the recent "starvation deaths" and he himself is a living corpse. He was lying prostrate on a charpai (string cot), immobilised by some sort of spinal injury. Three young children, listless with hunger and disease, were hanging around with nothing to do. I was at a loss over how these people were alive at all, until someone said Nathu had an Annapurna card. This entitles him to 10 kg of grain per month for free – that's about 300 grams per day to be shared between four.

The preceding paragraphs were written last December, after a brief visit to Shivpuri. I returned there last month and travelled widely, through Shivpuri and in the neighbouring districts of Sheopur, Morena, and Gwalior. I went with the faint hope of finding that things had improved as relief works expanded. Instead, I discovered not only that the situation around Chharch remained much the same, but also that the Sahariya communities throughout the region live in the same condition of permanent semi-starvation as the families I had met earlier.

Back in Jigni, I met Nathu again. I was relieved to find him alive but dismayed to hear that his Annapurna card was now useless as the scheme had been discontinued. With the new BPL survey scheduled for the middle of May, many more households are in danger of being quietly dropped from the public distribution system. Midday meals have also been discontinued with the closure of schools for the summer vacation.

Meanwhile, the summer heat has started descending like a heavy lid on the Sahariyas, threatening to snuff out their remaining survival opportunities. In the Pahargarh area of Morena district, many survive by collecting and selling a sort of medicinal root known as sitavar. This may not last much longer, for the rising temperature makes it more difficult to extract the root from the hardened soil and walk long distances without water – Pahargarh is like a desert, dry as toast and with no shade for miles on end. In many villages, people cling to the hope of finding employment in relief works. But these are few and far between, and wage payments are often delayed for weeks if not months.

Ironically, the struggle for survival is likely to get even harder during the rainy season. Even in normal years, this is the hungry season for the Sahariyas, when earning opportunities come to a standstill and they are forced to eat grass, roots, and other wild foods. This year, they are exhausted and impoverished from the very outset. Growing the kharif (summer) crop will call for further sacrifices as there is no money for seeds and most draught animals have perished of hunger and thirst over the summer. Unless relief works are radically expanded, more starvation deaths seem inevitable.

Notes

Starving the Poor

This is the first part of a two-part article published in *The Hindu* on 26–27 February 2001. Official foodgrain stock figures are readily available from the monthly *Foodgrains Bulletin* of the food ministry. The foodgrain stocks continued to increase in the next ten years or so, reaching a peak of 82 million tonnes in July 2012. On the relation between foodgrain consumption and income, see Oldiges 2012.

Fragile Lifelines, Robust Oppression

This essay is based on a padyatra (walk) through the KBK region of Odisha in April 1999, with Rajkishor Mishra. Secondary data on economic trends in Odisha in the 1990s were taken from the annual economic surveys of the Government of India and Government of Odisha (and also Sarmah 2001, for trends in real wages).

The Right to Food and Public Accountability

This essay is based on a visit to Wadrafnagar block of Surguja district in October 2001, with Gangabhai Paikra, following reports of a gastroenteritis epidemic there. Gangabhai and his associates later did sterling work on the right to food and related issues in the area.

Memories of Kusumatand

A more detailed presentation of the survey findings is available in Drèze and Lall 2002, and Gram Swaraj Abhiyan 2002. A resurvey of public facilities in Manatu Block in 2014, conducted by Ankita Aggarwal and others, found that the public distribution system had vastly improved in the intervening period, though people were still receiving less than their entitlements. By that time, most villages in Manatu had basic facilities such as a school and anganwadi, but the functioning of these facilities still left much to be desired.

Panchayat elections were held up for many years in Jharkhand due to litigation in the supreme court about the validity of the Jharkhand Panchayat Raj Act 2001. They were finally held in 2011.

Jharkhand took several years to implement the 2001 supreme court orders on midday meals, but it is now firmly on board. In fact, it is the only BJP-ruled state (as of now) that serves eggs in midday meals.

For updated NSS-based estimates of PDS leakages in Jharkhand (about 85 per cent in 2004–5 and 44 per cent in 2011–12), see Drèze and Khera 2015a. PDS leakages are further discussed in section 7.

The Dark Well of Hunger

The story of what happened later to the Sahariyas of that area, spanning both sides of the Madhya Pradesh–Rajasthan border, is of some interest. In Rajasthan, a series of agitations (from 2001 onwards) around starvation deaths and acute hunger led to some serious action on the part of the government as well as NGOs. Over time, the Sahariyas managed to achieve a modicum of food security (and also freedom from bonded labour), notably with the help of the National Rural Employment Guarantee Act, the public distribution system, midday meals, and related schemes. In Madhya Pradesh, they received less attention, perpetuating their extreme vulnerability. This contrast is briefly discussed in Drèze and Khera with the PEEP team 2014; see also Khera 2008, and Bhatia 2012.

2

POVERTY

ONE OF THE GREATEST difficulties with many social programmes in India is the selection of eligible households.
In the 1990s and early 2000s, the standard approach was
to restrict them to households "below the poverty line" (BPL). The
identification of BPL households, however, was problematic. Caps
on the number of BPL households were imposed state-wise, based
on poverty estimates supplied by the Planning Commission. These
estimates essentially involved a headcount of households with monthly
per capita expenditure (MPCE) below a pre-specified threshold,
called the poverty line, using National Sample Survey (NSS) data.
The poverty estimates themselves are open to various criticisms, as
discussed in some of the essays in this section. But, more importantly,
there is no obvious way of identifying BPL households subject
to these caps.

In the absence of household-wise data on MPCE, poor households
are typically sought to be identified via proxy indicators such as
occupation or asset ownership. For instance, in the 2002 BPL census, these households were identified using a scoring method based
on thirteen proxy indicators. Due to the imprecise nature of the
proxy indicators, compounded by unreliable survey methods, the
entire approach had a hit-or-miss character. The result is that the
list of eligible households tends to be shot through with exclusion
errors (the omission of eligible households) as well as inclusion errors

(the insertion of ineligible households). The stringent nature of the poverty caps, which are based on a relatively low poverty line, does not help matters.

In the early 2000s, many social programmes targeted BPL households. If the central government had had its way, even programmes such as the Integrated Child Development Services (ICDS) and the National Rural Employment Guarantee Act (NREGA) would have been restricted to BPL households. Meanwhile, however, the idea that many of these social benefits should be regarded as a right of poor households, if not all households, gained ground. BPL targeting is obviously difficult to reconcile with a rights approach, since it tends to leave out many poor households. Gradually, BPL targeting gave way to three alternatives.

First, some entitlements were universalised. School meals, for instance, were extended to all children, at least in government and government-assisted schools. That seems to make sense – it would be very odd to feed some children and not others within a school, especially based on unreliable identification criteria such as BPL status.[1]

Second, some programmes were built on the principle of self-selection – allowing people to decide for themselves whether to participate, with some built-in discouragement of well-off households. NREGA is a prime example: every rural household is eligible for a job card, but the work requirement ensures that most NREGA workers come from deprived sections of the population. There is evidence that this self-targeting process works relatively well, at least in the case of NREGA.

Third, in the context of implementing the National Food Security Act (NFSA), some states adopted what is known as the "exclusion approach". The idea is that instead of trying to target poor households,

---

[1] Strictly speaking, there is also an element of self-selection in this programme, since children attending government schools tend to come from underprivileged families.

it is better to identify well-off households (using simple, transparent, and verifiable criteria), exclude them, and include everyone else by default. To illustrate, all rural households in Jharkhand are now eligible for a ration card under the NFSA unless they have a regular government job, a four-wheel vehicle, five acres of irrigated land (or ten acres of any sort of land), or a pacca (brick) house with at least three rooms. The main advantage of this approach is that the risk of excluding poor households is low.

The recent transition away from BPL targeting, with all its arbitrariness and restrictions, seems like a step forward. However, BPL targeting continues in some centrally sponsored programmes such as the Rashtriya Swasthya Bima Yojana (a health insurance programme). This is difficult to justify, all the more so as the BPL lists are terribly outdated in most states. The Socio-Economic and Caste Census of 2011 was supposed to be used to generate new BPL lists, but this has not happened, at least not yet. Perhaps the time has come to abandon the entire approach.

Three of the four essays in this section are concerned with these matters, and with the limitations of official poverty estimates. The fourth essay, "Beyond Small Mercies", discusses social security pensions for widows, the elderly, and the disabled.

The Poverty Trap*

In the good old days, the poverty line was a relatively simple concept. By and large, it was just a statistical benchmark with which to make "poverty comparisons" – for instance, to track poverty over time, or to compare poverty levels in different parts of the country. Many of these comparisons were not particularly sensitive to the choice of poverty line, within a reasonable range. There is even a situation, with the odd name of "first-order stochastic dominance", which arises when the relevant comparison holds for *any* poverty line. For instance, Bihar is clearly poorer than Punjab, wherever one draws the line.

From Statistical Benchmark to Social Division

The choice of poverty line, therefore, was not particularly controversial. One common benchmark was the level of per capita expenditure required to meet pre-specified calorie norms in the base year. One may or may not like this benchmark (the calorie "norms" themselves are quite shaky), but at least it was fairly transparent. There was no claim that reaching the poverty line was a guarantee of being well nourished (since good nutrition requires much more than calorie adequacy), let alone healthy or well educated.

Then came the whole idea of "BPL targeting", that is, of restricting various social benefits (in particular, the public distribution system) to households below the poverty line. This quietly transformed the poverty line from a statistical benchmark into a real-life social

*September–October 2011.

division. The division was all the more artificial as the identification of BPL households was highly unreliable. Indeed, the Planning
Commission uses one method to count the poor, while the ministry
of rural development uses a different method to identify them. This
cannot work, and is just the beginning of a series of conceptual flaws
and implementation problems that plague the BPL census. It is not
surprising that, according to the National Sample Survey (among
other sources), about half of all poor households in rural India
didn't have a BPL card in 2004–5. The "real-life" poverty line
not only divides people, it divides them in a cruel and destructive manner.

The recent Tendulkar Committee Report further complicated
matters by claiming, for the first time, that the poverty line ensures
"adequacy of actual private expenditure . . . on food, education, and
health". That Rs 32 per person per day (the Tendulkar poverty line
for urban areas at today's prices) is wholly insufficient for this purpose
is self-evident to anyone with common sense. It is even clearer when
one looks at the breakdown of the Rs 32 packet, which includes, for
instance, just about one daily rupee for health expenditure. Yet the
experts managed to rustle up technical arguments to substantiate
their claim.

To be fair to the Planning Commission, it is not quite saying
(at least not explicitly) that the PDS should be restricted to BPL
households. It is just saying that the central government's commitment
ends there. But the writing is on the wall, not just for the PDS but
also for other social programmes that are being quietly earmarked
for BPL targeting, conversion to cash transfers, and self-liquidation
as the official poverty estimates go down.

The way forward is not to "fix the poverty numbers" but to find a
way out of this bankrupt approach of BPL targeting. That is the appeal
of universal entitlement programmes such as school meals, ICDS,
and NREGA. Many states are now moving away from BPL targeting in the PDS too: not only states like Tamil Nadu and Himachal
Pradesh that have a long-standing commitment to universalism in

social policy, but also, increasingly, other states, such as Andhra Pradesh and Chhattisgarh, where the PDS extends well beyond the BPL category. The PDS tends to function much better in those states because everyone – or almost everyone – has a strong stake in it. This approach is expensive, but at least it tends to work.

The BPL Club

Nothing illustrates the absurdity of current food policies more poignantly than the plight of Dablu Singh's family in Latehar district, Jharkhand. About two years ago Dablu, a young Adivasi who survives mainly by casual labour, fell from a roof at work and broke his back. He is paralysed for life and needs intensive care. His wife Sumitra looks after him, their daughter, and a small baby (aside from a few goats and hens), and is unable to work for wages. The family is on the verge of starvation.

BPL families in Jharkhand are entitled to 35 kg of rice per month at one rupee per kg. This comes as a great relief to these families, but Dablu's family doesn't have a BPL card.

Meanwhile, the godowns of the Food Corporation of India (FCI) are bursting at the seams yet again. The FCI is lumbered with about 60 million tonnes of wheat and rice and doesn't know where to put the excess stocks. Some want to export them, others want to brew them, others still want to privatise the FCI and be done. Enhancing storage capacity is routinely offered as a solution – but why not distribute some of the excess grain? There is no dearth of families like Dablu's.

Dablu's only hope is that his plight has been noticed. Soon after his accident, he attracted the attention of local journalists, and later of the district collector, local legislator, and others. Everyone agreed that he should get a BPL card by way of immediate relief.

True to the Jharkhand government's tradition of "administration by gesture", the district collector instructed the BDO to "do the needful" and left it at that. From then on, various officers (BDO, SDO,

BSO, so-and-so) passed the buck to each other for a few months. Dablu's well-wishers pleaded his case all the way to Ranchi and even Delhi. Nothing doing – one year down the line, Dablu still didn't have a BPL card.

When the commissioners of the supreme court took the district collector to task, he finally admitted that the entire district administration was powerless to give a BPL card to Dablu without striking someone else off the BPL list. The district has a strict quota of BPL cards, so no-one can be inducted unless someone is dropped. One observer quietly suggested that since Dablu had become a VIP of sorts, he could perhaps be "adjusted" by randomly removing someone.

There rested the matter a few weeks ago, more than a year after a whole team of well-wishers (stretching from Latehar to Delhi) joined forces for Dablu. One is left to speculate about how many tonnes of grain putrefied in the FCI godowns in the meantime. Anyway, the local Block Supply Officer finally managed to find a way forward: someone on the BPL list in Dablu's village had died, and so had his wife, and their son already had a separate BPL card, so it seemed all right to strike off that name from the list and accommodate Dablu. It took just another 10–15 days to complete the job – Dablu finally has a BPL card.

But there is a catch: Dablu may be *deprived* of his BPL card very soon. This is because the BPL list is supposed to be redone after the ongoing BPL census (alias Socio-Economic and Caste Census) is completed. And the methodology of this census is such that Dablu's family meets only one of the seven "deprivation indicators" that make up the BPL score. With a score of one on a scale of zero to seven, Dablu is almost certain to be excluded again.

And just to make it a little harder for people like Dablu to sneak into the BPL club, the Planning Commission has made it clear (in its recent affidavit to the supreme court) that the BPL list is expected to shrink over time, in line with official poverty estimates based on the government's measly poverty line of Rs 26 per person per day in rural areas. This is what Dablu actually needs, as a bare minimum, for essential medical care alone.

Many states have rebelled against the Planning Commission's poverty straitjacket, and expanded the public distribution system well beyond the BPL list. Had Dablu lived in Tamil Nadu, Andhra Pradesh, or even Chhattisgarh, he might not have gone through this ordeal. In Tamil Nadu the PDS is universal – everyone has a ration card. Andhra Pradesh has rejected the BPL framework in favour of an "exclusion approach", whereby everyone is eligible except those who meet well-defined exclusion criteria such as having a government job. Chhattisgarh, for its part, still uses an inclusion approach, but the inclusion criteria are quite broad (e.g. all SC/ST households are eligible) and the PDS covers nearly 80 per cent of the rural population. Further, the list of ration cards is regularly verified and updated.

In areas like rural Latehar, the case for a universal PDS is over-whelming. Indeed, except for a few exploiters (e.g. contractors and moneylenders), there are no rich people there – most move to urban areas. In the villages, almost everyone is either poor or vulnerable to poverty. The local administration is too inept, corrupt, and exploitative to conduct a credible BPL survey or any sort of identification exercise. In these circumstances, a universal PDS makes a lot of sense.

The proposed National Food Security Act (NFSA) is an opportunity to end the BPL nightmare and ensure that a family like Dablu's is entitled to a ration card as a matter of right. Unfortunately, the official draft of the NFSA perpetuates the entire BPL approach under a new name. Meanwhile, the government has lifted the ban on exports of wheat and rice to "solve" the food crisis.

On the Poverty Line*

India's official poverty line has been a subject of lively debate in recent months. The controversy began with an affidavit submitted to the supreme court by the Planning Commission in September 2011, in response to a query (from the court) concerning the poverty line and the role it played, if any, as an eligibility criterion for food subsidies.

The Planning Commission's affidavit, after clarifying the numbers (whereby official poverty lines stood at around Rs 32 per person per day in urban areas and Rs 26 per person per day in rural areas, at June 2011 prices), proceeded to state that the official poverty lines "ensure the adequacy of actual private expenditure per capita near the poverty lines on food, education and health." This caused an instant uproar, with one commentator after another pointing out that the official poverty line is actually a destitution line, which does not guarantee anything above bare subsistence. The point was not difficult to illustrate. For instance, the reference budget associated with the urban poverty line includes princely sums of ten rupees per month for "footwear" and forty rupees per month for health care. The former would just about make it possible to get a sandal strap repaired once a month, and the latter might buy something like the equivalent of an aspirin a day. Similarly, the monthly allowance of thirty rupees for "rent and conveyance" would not go further than a one-way short-distance bus ticket every few days, with nothing left to travel back, let alone pay any sort of rent.

These measly norms reflect the fact that poverty-line standards were set decades ago, at a time when even bare subsistence was far from assured for a large majority of the population. The poverty

---

* April 2012.

line is, of course, regularly updated for price increases, but not for the enhanced requirements of dignified living. Understandably, the poverty line today looks quite out of line with the bare minimum one would wish everyone to have.

The Planning Commission did not exactly cover itself with glory by defending the original statement, based on the Tendulkar Committee Report, as "factually correct". Perhaps it meant that the affidavit was a factual rendering of factually incorrect statements made in that report. Indeed, the arguments presented in that report to substantiate the adequacy of the official poverty line are difficult to accept. To illustrate, consider the argument invoked to establish "food adequacy" at the poverty line. Briefly, it consists of observing that food expenditure at the poverty line is typically higher than "normative food expenditure". The latter is defined as follows (hold your breath): "When estimated population from NSS [National Sample Survey] is ranked according to ascending size of food expenditure per capita, normative food expenditure per capita is defined by that level of food expenditure per capita that corresponds to cumulative share of population from NSS that equals the index of malnutrition derived from NFHS-III [third National Family Health Survey] for that state." The "index of malnutrition", for its part, is an unweighted sum of the proportions of underweight children, adult men with a low body mass index (BMI), and adult women with a low BMI. The public can be forgiven for finding this argument a little unconvincing.

It is also interesting to consider other arguments that were used to make a dubious position look acceptable. Planning Commission spokespersons repeatedly stressed that the seemingly paltry amount of "Rs 32 per person per day" (for urban areas) should be put on a monthly basis, and also on a household basis, so that (for an average household of size five) it becomes "Rs 4,800 per household per month". They pointed out that Rs 4,800 per household per month did not sound so unreasonable, and even invited some of their critics to ask themselves whether they were paying more than that for domestic help.

This line of defence is quite revealing. Why would "Rs 4,800 per household per month" seem more acceptable than "Rs 32 per person per day", when it is actually the same thing expressed in different units? The reason, I suspect, is that the monthly figure sounds more familiar – it sounds like the salary routinely paid to many workers in the informal sector. Their employers (including many viewers of the TV channels that hosted these lively debates) have become used to the idea that people somehow get by on this. Living on Rs 32 a day is, in fact, a constant struggle, but the necessity of circumstance has silenced millions of people into extreme forms of parsimony.

Some courageous middle-class citizens volunteered to get a taste of this bitter struggle by living on the poverty line themselves, for a little while. Two young professionals, Tushar Vashisht and Mathew Cherian, tried to live on Rs 26 a day (the rural poverty line) after relocating themselves to a small village in Kerala. A supportive columnist, Harsh Mander, described their experience as "harrowing": "They ate parboiled rice, a tuber and banana and drank black tea: a balanced diet was impossible . . . They found themselves thinking of food the whole day. They walked long distances, and saved money even on soap to wash their clothes . . . It would have been a disaster if they fell ill." As it is, they suffered from fatigue, weight loss, and other consequences of undernutrition – all without having to do manual labour.

As the debate unfolded, a series of issues got a little mixed up, and at times the Planning Commission got more flak than it deserved. For instance, an impression was created that the official poverty line was so low because the Planning Commission had just lowered it. In fact, nothing of the sort had happened: the Tendulkar Committee Report led to an upward – not downward – revision of the rural poverty line. Incredible as it may seem, the poverty line was even lower earlier. Much confusion also grew around other issues, such as the purpose of official poverty lines as well as the relation between poverty estimates and food entitlements under the PDS.

Aside from being a little confusing, the debate ended up missing the main point. What is really startling is not so much that the official poverty line is so low, but that, *even with this low benchmark so many people are below it* – a full 30 per cent of the population in 2009–10, or more than 350 million people. How are these people supposed to live? The belated discovery that it is impossible to have anything like a dignified life on the official poverty line draws attention to the appalling living conditions of the Indian poor, which go largely unnoticed (in privileged circles) because poor people have learnt to bear the deprivations and keep a low profile. This basic message about the terrifying yet hidden nature of mass poverty in India has been somewhat lost in the din of the recent debate.

There is another important lesson to learn from this debate. The dismal living conditions of the Indian poor call for immediate intervention – not a passive wait for economic growth to raise their per capita incomes. According to official data (derived from the National Sample Survey), average per capita expenditure in rural India has been rising at just over *1 per cent per year* or so in the last twenty years, with a slightly higher figure for urban areas. This may well be an underestimate, because of growing under-reporting of per capita expenditure among richer households, but there is no obvious reason why this would apply to poorer households. And the growth rate of per capita expenditure among poorer households is lower than the estimated average of 1 per cent per year. Clearly, it would take a very long time, at that rate, for the poor to realise even a modicum of protection from deprivation. On the other hand, there is evidence that various forms of public support and economic redistribution can make a substantial difference to their lives without delay. There is no case for leaving the poor to their own devices.

Beyond Small Mercies*

It was a new experience, last summer, to go from village to village with student volunteers and listen to elderly women and men. Our main purpose was to understand how pension schemes for widows and the elderly worked in different states (Bihar, Chhattisgarh, Himachal Pradesh, Jharkhand, Madhya Pradesh, Maharashtra, Odisha, Rajasthan, Tamil Nadu, and Uttar Pradesh, to be precise). Testimony after testimony opened our eyes to the critical importance of old-age pensions as a tool of social security in rural India.

The first thing that struck me was the immense number of elderly people, and their miserable plight. They escape our notice most of the time, but if we pay attention they spring up everywhere. They live quiet and unobtrusive lives, some passing time on a broken charpai, others collecting twigs, limping from one place to another, or simply lying ill in the darkness of a shabby backroom. They rarely complain, at least in public, but if you enquire about their well-being, the tales of sorrow are endless.

It is not just in poor households that widows and the elderly have a hard time. Even in relatively well-off families, money is always short, and the comfort of the elderly often takes a back seat. We met plenty of women and men who lived a life of deprivation even as their adult sons built spacious houses or rode motorcycles.

Whenever public meetings were called to talk about social security pensions, elderly women and men came out of their houses in swarms to join the discussion. Those who were not receiving a pension pleaded for help to apply. Pensioners, for their part, complained that the

*December 2013.

pension amount was far too low. Even so, they clung to their bank or post-office passbooks as to precious possessions. In their harsh lives the pension was a chance to enjoy small comforts – relieving pain with some medicine, getting sandals repaired, winning the affection of grandchildren with the odd sweet, or simply avoiding hunger.

The main insight from the survey was the basic soundness of pension schemes as a tool of social security and economic redistribution. Most of the recipients are, by any standard, deprived people who need public support – and indeed have a right to it. Aside from contributing to their economic security, pensions give them some dignity and bargaining power. The administrative costs are very low. The survey (which included verifying pension records in 160 sample villages) did not find any evidence of major fraud in pension schemes. There are leakages here and there, for instance when post-office employees take a cut to disburse pensions, but nothing like the scams that plague many other forms of government expenditure. And the leakages, such as they are, can be dealt with quite easily.

Five Hurdles

Having said this, pension schemes for widows and the elderly have five major flaws as things stand: narrow coverage, bureaucratic procedures, low pension amounts, irregular payments, and high collection costs.

To start with, the coverage of pension schemes is too narrow. According to the central guidelines, social security pensions are meant for BPL families; financial support from the central government is restricted to this category. Some states have launched their own schemes, with their own funds, to expand the coverage of pensions beyond BPL families. But the bulk of pensioners are selected from the BPL category. The unreliable and exclusionary nature of this eligibility criterion is now well understood in other contexts. In the context of pensions, it is all the more inappropriate, because widows and the elderly are often extremely deprived even in relatively well-off households. BPL targeting should be abolished in favour of a universal or near-universal approach, whereby any widow or elderly person who does not meet well-defined exclusion criteria is eligible for a social security pension.

Second, application procedures tend to be very cumbersome. Numerous supporting documents have to be produced, and it often takes years for applications to wind their way up and down different layers of administration – gram panchayat, block, district, state, and back. In Latehar district (Jharkhand), we learnt from the sub-divisional magistrate that pension applications were being forwarded to the state at a snail's pace simply because he had to sign each application six times. With about 13,000 applications pending, that meant 78,000 signatures, for this purpose alone. He was blindly signing application forms even as he was talking to us, without making much of a dent in the backlog.

Third, the amounts of social security pensions are ridiculously low. The central contribution to old-age pensions has remained at an abysmal Rs 200 per month since 2006 – an insult to the elderly. Some states top this up with their own resources, but even the topped-up amounts are measly, except in a few states like Tamil Nadu where the standard pension amount is now Rs 1000 per month. Pension amounts should be increased without delay and indexed to the price level.

Fourth, pension payments are highly irregular in most states. Often, pensioners have to wait for their pension for months, without any idea when the next payment will materialise. This defeats the purpose of old-age pensions, which is to bring some security in people's lives. More than ten years have passed since the supreme court ordered state governments to ensure that social security pensions are promptly paid by the 7th of each month, but few of them have acted on this.

Fifth, even when payments are relatively regular, collecting them is often costly and tedious for old people with little mobility, education, and power. Getting to the nearest bank and queuing for hours can be an absolute ordeal. Post offices are closer, but the convenience comes at a price – corrupt post-office employees often expect an inducement. Alternative options such as postal orders, business correspondents, and cash payments pose their own problems. The central government's odd insistence on fast-tracking the transition to "UID enabled" payments of social security pensions (one of the least appropriate applications of this problematic technology) is likely to be very disruptive - "UID disabled" may well turn out to be a more accurate term in this case.

Signs of Change

All these problems are relatively easy to fix. The main reason why they aren't is that the victims count for so little. But this is changing: widows and the elderly have started agitating for their rights, with a little help from associations such as Ekal Nari Shakti Sangathan and Pension Parishad. Under public pressure, or for other reasons, many states have started improving and expanding their pension schemes – Odisha, Tamil Nadu, Rajasthan, among others. Even Bihar and Jharkhand, the incorrigible laggards in such matters, are developing a serious interest in pension schemes.

Odisha, no paragon of good governance in general, presents one interesting case of sustained effort to strengthen pension schemes. Eligibility conditions have been relaxed and the coverage of pensions has been extended well beyond the ambit of central guidelines. Lists of pension recipients are updated regularly and posted on the internet. Pensioners have well-designed and well-maintained passbooks with details of pension payments. Pensions are promptly paid in cash at the gram panchayat office on the 15th of each month – even on 15th August. This arrangement, very convenient for pensioners, is strictly enforced and appears to work very well.

The central government, for its part, seems unable to get its act together on this issue. The need to put social security pensions on a sounder footing is well accepted in principle, and useful recommendations for this purpose have been made by an expert committee. However, little has been done to implement the recommendations – not even raising the central contribution to old-age pensions above the measly Rs 200 per month. The "savage cuts" (as the rural development minister Jairam Ramesh called them) in social expenditure sought to be imposed by the finance ministry are not going to help matters. The axe of fiscal austerity weighs most heavily on the poor and powerless, including destitute women and men who are expected to get by with Rs 200 per month even as prices go through the roof.

Squaring the Poverty Circle*
(with Angus Deaton)

The Rangarajan expert group on poverty measurement has done a great deal of hard and useful work. In its recent report, it probes a wide range of critical issues – how to set poverty lines, the choice of price indexes for poverty comparisons, the discrepancy between National Sample Surveys (NSS) and the National Accounts Statistics, and more. Massive amounts of data were crunched to shed light on these issues. The report also presents a very helpful summary of earlier "expert group" reports on poverty, chaired by Y.K. Alagh, D.T. Lakdawala, and Suresh Tendulkar, respectively. The combined brainpower of four expert groups is brought to bear on the committee's terms of reference, including, most importantly, whether and how "a particular method can be evolved for empirical estimation of poverty in India."

The Calorie Trap

So what has the expert group come up with? Simplifying a good deal, it has reverted to food intake norms, long sanctified by use if not by logic, until they were discarded by the Tendulkar expert group in 2009. These norms are now extended from calories to include both protein and fat. The food component of the poverty line (for rural and urban areas separately) is the level of food expenditure at the point in the 2011–12 NSS per capita expenditure distribution where households just make the norms. These norms, recently set by the Indian Council of Medical Research (ICMR), take into account the age and sex composition of the population as well as activity levels,

*July 2014.

and, for reasons unclear, they are a good deal lower than previous ICMR recommendations, even at fixed age and activity levels. On top of this, there are two different and not obviously compatible schemes for establishing the non-food components of the poverty line: for some non-food items, the poverty-line expenditure is read off the same fractile of the NSS per capita expenditure distribution as the food component, but for other items it is read off the median of the expenditure distribution. All in all, an elaborate construction of wheels within wheels.

If you find it hard to see the justification for this method, don't worry – there is none. Indeed, nowhere in the report do the authors explain clearly why this is an appropriate method for setting poverty lines in India. It is well known, and clearly recognised by the expert group, that average calorie (or protein) intakes in India do not correlate well at all with nutrition outcomes. In particular, the intake norms adopted by the expert group provide absolutely no guarantee of good nutrition. This is in part because good nutrition depends on many factors other than food intake, such as sanitation, water, health care, and the disease environment. But it is also because of the long-appreciated point that different individuals – and populations – have different requirements, even beyond their variation in age, sex, and activity levels.

The expert group understands the first point very well, but presses on with intake norms, arguing that meeting these norms would still have a "favourable impact" on nutrition "taken in conjunction with public policies for full nutrition support for children in the 0–6 age group and public provisioning of a range of public goods and services . . . on a universal basis." Surely the poverty line should be one that works in India, as it is, not in some imagined Nirvana? As for the second point, the expert group seems to take it as a justification for *discounting* calorie norms by 10 per cent – an arbitrary step in the absence of any information on the joint distribution of intakes and requirements. In short, the expert group's method perpetuates the illusion that the poverty line tells us something about nutrition, when in fact it does nothing of the sort.

Implausible Results

Leaving that aside for the moment, what sort of estimates does the method produce? Interestingly, the rural poverty line proposed by the expert group is *almost the same* as the "Tendulkar poverty line". It looks higher, but, as the authors themselves note, that is mainly because their computations are based on the NSS's "modified mixed reference period", instead of the "mixed reference period" used by Tendulkar. When both methods are used with the same reference period, the Rangarajan poverty line for rural areas is only 6 per cent higher than the Tendulkar poverty line. The corresponding poverty rates are also very similar.

It is for urban areas that the Rangarajan method leads to a substantial upward revision of the poverty line. In the Tendulkar method, there was a single poverty line – the national urban poverty line inherited from earlier expert groups. State-wise urban and rural poverty lines were derived from this single national poverty line by applying suitable price indexes. But in the Rangarajan method there are two poverty lines (rural and urban), obtained by applying the method described above to rural and urban data separately. And, as it turns out, this leads to a much larger gap between rural and urban poverty lines (the latter being higher, in money terms) than in the Tendulkar method. At the raised Rangarajan urban poverty line, urban poverty is almost *double* the corresponding Tendulkar estimate, even though rural poverty rates are much the same using both methods. One odd consequence of this is that for half of India's major states, *urban poverty is higher than rural poverty* according to the Rangarajan expert group. This is highly counterintuitive, and the expert group does nothing to defend the reality of this pattern.

Way Forward

In short, the Rangarajan expert group method is both theoretically and empirically implausible. What, then, is the way forward? Appointing another expert group is unlikely to serve the purpose, given the record of previous expert groups. Perhaps the time has come to abandon the elusive search for a technical method of deriving a poverty line that can be interpreted, in some normative sense, as the minimum cost of dignified living. Would it not be simpler, and more useful, to regard the poverty line as a mere statistical benchmark, and set it in a simple and transparent manner that the public can understand?

The Rangarajan expert group recommends, rightly in our view, that entitlement programmes should not be linked to the poverty line (that is, no more "BPL targeting"). This would effectively restore poverty lines to their original statistical purpose of tracking poverty and making poverty comparisons, without creating an artificial social division between the poor and non-poor. In the statistical approach, the poverty line is just a conventional benchmark – or possibly a set of benchmarks, à la Arjun Sengupta and his colleagues (not mentioned in the Rangarajan report). These benchmarks focus on an important component of poverty – purchasing power – and avoid the unsustainable argument that other components are somehow taken care of in the background.

Even a conventional benchmark, of course, can benefit from having some sort of rationale. But if an intuitively appealing poverty line is to be identified, it is best done by keeping things simple and submitting the line to democratic debate. Clarity and transparency are essential for this purpose. It is in that respect, more than any other, that the Rangarajan report disappoints. By clouding poverty estimation in a fog of technicalities, it hampers inclusive and informed public discussion of the entire issue. In fact, like the Tendulkar method, the Rangarajan method is so abstruse and uses so much hard-to-obtain information that it also frustrates independent verification of the results, again hampering democratic debate.

One might argue that, in India at least, the poverty line is not just a statistical benchmark – it also has a policy purpose. The Rangarajan expert group itself suggests that the line might continue to be used for the purpose of allocating central government funds to different states (in the context of centrally sponsored schemes), if not for the purpose of identifying eligible households. But if the poverty line has a policy purpose, in addition to its statistical purpose, that makes it all the more important for it to lend itself to public scrutiny. One way or another, the selection of a poverty line is a social and political question that needs to be subject to democratic debate; it should not be the prerogative of experts, or groups of experts. Indeed, there is no such thing as an "expert" about who is poor and who is not.

Finally, it is very important to supplement expenditure-based poverty estimates with other indicators of living standards, relating for instance to nutrition, health, education, and the quality of the environment. India's social statistics are awfully out of date, with, for instance, no reliable and comprehensive data on child nutrition since 2005–6 (when the third National Family Health Survey was conducted). Noting this in passing, the Rangarajan expert group "recommends a regular programme of NFHS or NFHS-type surveys". On this at least we agree wholeheartedly with the expert group.

Notes

The Poverty Trap

This is a merged and abridged version of two separate articles, written at a time of sustained debate about the Tendulkar Committee Report (Government of India 2009a). The Socio-Economic and Caste Census (SECC) was completed around the same time, in 2011. It was initially intended as a BPL census, merged with a caste census. Both purposes, however, are yet to be realised to this day (meanwhile, many schemes have moved away from BPL targeting). The SECC, however, was used by several states to identify households eligible under the National Food Security Act 2013.

On the Poverty Line

This is an unpublished essay, but some of it was used in Drèze and Sen 2013. Many economists castigated critics of the Planning Commission for arguing that the poverty line was too low. The main criticism, however, was not that the poverty line was low, but that in spite of being so low the government claimed it was adequate for dignified living. The Planning

Commission never retracted the statement it had made to that effect in the supreme court, based on the Tendulkar Committee report. On Tushar Vashisht and Mathew Cherian's effort to live on the poverty-line level of expenditure, see Mander 2012.

Beyond Small Mercies

For a more detailed presentation of the survey findings, see Chopra and Pudussery 2014. As this book goes to press, the central government's contribution to old-age pensions is still Rs 200 per month, as in 2006. Many state governments, however, top this up and some have also expanded the coverage of social security pensions beyond what the central government provides for (i.e. the BPL category). The central government, for its part, seems to be losing interest in the National Social Assistance Programme in favour of a new pension scheme, Atal Pension Yojana (APY), framed in a very different, contributory mode.

On 28 November 2001, the supreme court directed the state governments to ensure that social security pensions are promptly paid by the seventh of each month. Sixteen years later, however, delayed and irregular payments are still the norm in many states.

For the report of the expert committee (strictly speaking, a "task force", chaired by Mihir Shah) mentioned in the last paragraph, see Government of India 2013a.

Squaring the Poverty Circle

For further discussion of the Rangarajan Committee report (Government of India 2014), including a response to this essay, see Rangarajan and Mahendra Dev 2015. On the lack of correlation between average calorie intake and nutrition outcomes, see e.g. Drèze and Deaton 2009. The multiple-benchmark poverty estimates by Arjun Sengupta and his colleagues are presented in Sengupta, Kannan, and Raveendran 2008.

3

SCHOOL MEALS

THE SIGHT OF SCHOOLCHILDREN enjoying their midday meal is one of the brighter moments Indian villages have to offer today. In well-organised schools, especially, it is a pleasure to see children washing their hands, queuing for their food, reciting something in a chorus before they start to eat, relishing the meal, and milling around a hand-pump to clean their plates. The experience tends to get better every year as more and more schools learn to make good use of the midday meal routine.

One of the first supreme court orders in the "right to food case", mentioned earlier, directed state governments to introduce cooked midday meals in all government and government-assisted primary schools. This order, dated 28 November 2001, actually did nothing more than direct governments to do what they were already supposed to under the National Programme of Nutritional Support for Primary Education (NPNSPE), launched by the central government in 1995. The NPNSPE aimed to provide cooked meals in primary schools, but instead, dry rations (monthly quotas of wheat or rice) had been distributed to schoolchildren until then, and even those were conditional on regular attendance. The court order led the government to do what it intended to do – it was a sort of "nudge", as economists call it.

In due course, midday meals came to be seen as one of India's most effective social programmes (a substantial body of research brings out their positive impact on school attendance, child nutrition, and pupil achievements). The early years, however, were arduous. Schools had no kitchen sheds, children had no plates, hygiene was lacking, and the meals were frugal. Media reports on midday meals in those days (and to some extent even today) tended to show a negative slant. Newspaper and television channels took interest mainly when there was an incident of food poisoning or caste discrimination. This is understandable – it is part of the whistle-blowing role of the media. In the process, however, the quiet progress and growing accomplishments of midday meals failed to get due credit. The first three essays in this section are part of a stream of articles (by various authors) that tried to convey a more balanced picture of the achievements and failures of midday meals at that time.

The last essay fast-forwards to 2015. By then, midday meals were doing relatively well in most states, yet much scope remained for quality improvement. In that respect, one recent breakthrough is the provision of eggs in school meals in many states – up to five times a week in Tamil Nadu. However, some states (including most of the states with a BJP government) are resisting the move under the influence of upper-caste vegetarian lobbies. The resistance was taken to a new plane in May 2015, when the chief minister of Madhya Pradesh, Shivraj Singh Chouhan, vetoed the proposed provision of eggs to young children under ICDS, in three tribal districts, on a pilot basis. Soon enough, there was egg on his own face as the Indian media largely rallied on the side of undernourished children. Evidence also emerged, from a right to information (RTI) application, that the same chief minister had hosted a banquet for Japanese industrialists a few months earlier in Tokyo where meat was served with abandon.

Speaking of Japan, I recently watched a bunch of videos about school meals in that country (available on YouTube) and was bowled over by the way in which the midday meal was creatively used as an opportunity to educate children about nutrition, hygiene, mutual co-operation, environmental responsibility, and more. And, of course, the food (sometimes grown on the school grounds by teachers and children, who also eat together) looked really yummy and nutritious. This made me realise that there is still enormous scope for enhancing the nutritional, educational, and social value of school meals in India. There is every reason to look forward to this great enterprise of public service.

Hunger in the Classroom*

(with Vivek S.)

Ten months have passed since the supreme court directed the state governments to introduce cooked midday meals in all primary schools within six months. Some state governments are implementing the order, but many others are trying to buy time, pleading for central government funding, or even trying to get the order reversed. The supreme court seems determined to enforce the order, but public pressure also has an important role to play in overcoming these hesitations.

In states that have started providing midday meals, various implementation problems have arisen. There have been occasional reports of food poisoning, notably in Pondicherry where hundreds of children recently fell ill after consuming the midday milk. Teachers often complain that midday meals encroach on their time or disrupt classroom processes. And in some states, high-caste parents have objected to the idea of an all-caste lunch, or to the midday meal being prepared by a Dalit cook.

It is, however, important to avoid a loss of nerve in the face of these teething problems. Consider for instance the issue of food poisoning. Occasional incidents of indigestion at school carry little weight against the enormous health gains (present and future) that may be expected from higher school attendance and reduced hunger in the classroom. According to recent investigations by the State Council of Educational Research and Training (SCERT) in Delhi, even in the national capital

*October 2002.

a large proportion of children from poor families go to school with an empty stomach. Better-fed and better-educated children are the key to the future health of the nation.

Similarly, the much-cited problem of encroachment on teacher time is far from insurmountable. The more enterprising states have already appointed helpers to serve the midday meal. In some circumstances, the provision of pre-cooked food can help avoid the disruption of classroom processes. Further, it is important to remember that one of the biggest disruptions of classroom processes in Indian schools arises from the *absence* of a midday meal: children go home for lunch and many do not return.

As far as caste conflicts are concerned, they have a positive counterpart: midday meals challenge traditional caste prejudice and teach children to eat together irrespective of caste. In Karnataka, most cooks are Dalit women, and there appears to be wide acceptance of this arrangement. In Rajasthan, perhaps a more conservative society as far as caste is concerned, significant incidents have occurred, for instance in the form of Rajput parents objecting to the midday meal being cooked by a Dalit woman. But even in Rajasthan, the midday meal programme is on track and there is a good chance that high-caste resistance will melt over time.

This is not to dismiss the problems that have arisen. But these problems are best seen as a useful reminder of the urgency of higher quality standards in midday meal schemes (including adequate infrastructure and hygiene) rather than as an indictment of the entire project. Further, it is important to note that many positive achievements have already emerged from the new midday meal programmes, even though these achievements tend to be less widely publicised than gory tales of food poisoning or caste conflict. In particular, there is growing evidence that school meals have boosted school attendance in many areas. To illustrate, a recent survey of twenty-six villages in Sikar district (Rajasthan) found that school enrolment was much higher than last year in all the schools, and had risen by more than 25 per cent on average. In some "alternative schools" located in deprived hamlets, enrolment nearly doubled after the introduction of midday meals.

One of us recently participated in informal investigations of midday meals in Karnataka, where the programme has been introduced in seven districts on a pilot basis. The overall picture was very encouraging. In most of the eight schools sampled, adequate logistical arrangements (including provision for water) had been made and midday meals were served regularly. No incidents of food poisoning had occurred. Most of the cooks were Dalit women and no objections had been raised, except in one village where high-caste children abstained from the midday meal. By all accounts, school enrolment had increased, and daily attendance was more regular.

There is, in short, little reason for delaying the extension of midday meal programmes to other states. The main stumbling block, here as in many other contexts, is the reluctance of state governments to bear the overhead costs. While grain for the midday meal programme is provided free of cost by the central government, the states are expected to pay for the other ingredients, and also for transport and cooking arrangements. These overhead costs vary, depending on the arrangements being made, but, taking Karnataka's relatively successful model as a benchmark, it appears that a sound midday meal programme calls for a financial allocation of about one rupee per child per day.

Most state governments are reluctant to bear this financial burden, arguing that their coffers are empty. But if the public capitulates to such arguments, the social sectors will never get their due. Ultimately, it is a question of priorities. Indeed, the same state governments that complain of financial bankruptcy often manage to find hundreds of crores of rupees overnight when powerful interests are involved.

To illustrate: a high-level official from the education department in Uttar Pradesh recently mentioned at a workshop in Lucknow that a midday meal programme would cost Rs 680 crores per year, and that the state government was at a loss to find such resources. Yet a few days later, the MLAs of Uttar Pradesh passed a motion raising their own salaries and perks at a potential cost of Rs 425 crores per year for the state exchequer. Commenting on this, a ruling-party MLA complained that existing allowances were "not even sufficient to foot our monthly tea bills" (*Times of India*, 4 September). The full significance of this comment probably escaped most readers, unless they noticed another news item published the same day in the *Hindustan Times*, according to which the ministers of the Mayawati government had consumed Rs 6.71 lakhs worth of "tea and snacks" since May. Such is the state of democracy in Uttar Pradesh that political leaders are allowed to gorge themselves at public expense while children go to school on empty stomachs.

On 28 November 2001, when some state governments argued in the supreme court that midday meals were unaffordable, the bench sternly told them to "cut the flab somewhere else". The advice has not lost its relevance. Besides, there is always the possibility of raising taxes to generate additional revenue. Indeed, taxation rates in India are quite low by international standards. And as pointed out by Dr John Kurian of the Planning Commission, in many states even a moderate surcharge on liquor taxes would be quite enough to fund a midday meal programme. There is no excuse for allowing the continuation of hunger in the classroom.

Food for Equality*

As millions of children flock back to school after the summer vacation, it is worth examining what midday meals have achieved so far and how they can be improved. Tamil Nadu's experience suggests that well-devised school meals have much to contribute to the advancement of elementary education, child nutrition, and social equity. However, these achievements depend a great deal on the quality aspects of midday meals. Ramshackle midday meal programmes can do more harm than good.

Beyond Ghoogri

To illustrate, consider the primary school in Bamhu (Bilaspur district, Chhattisgarh). The midday meal there is prepared in a sooty classroom using a makeshift stove, next to the swarming pupils. The cook struggles with inadequate utensils and takes the help of young children to cut vegetables and clean the rice. After lunch, the classroom turns filthy. The teacher wishes midday meals were discontinued.

Bamhu is a good example of the sort of horror stories that often catch the attention of the media. However, it is important to go beyond these selective anecdotes and form a clearer view of the larger picture. Early hints of it are available from a recent survey initiated by the Centre for Equity Studies (CES), New Delhi. The survey took place in three regions where the scheme is supposed to be in place: Rajasthan, Chhattisgarh, and north Karnataka. In each region, the survey covered twenty-seven randomly selected schools spread over

*July–August 2003.

three districts. The findings suggest that, on the whole, midday meals have made a promising start. The scheme is certainly popular: 91 per cent of the parents sampled wanted it to continue (rising to 96 per cent among scheduled caste and scheduled tribe parents). However, the survey also shows that quality issues need urgent attention if the programme is to realise its full potential.

On the positive side, midday meals were being served regularly in seventy-six of the eighty-one sample schools. Their most impressive achievement so far is to enhance school enrolment and attendance, especially among girls. In the schools sampled, the enrolment of girls in Class 1 rose by 19 per cent after the introduction of midday meals. In Rajasthan, where baseline levels of female school participation were lowest, the corresponding figure is 29 per cent. There is also much informal evidence that daily pupil attendance has improved after the introduction of midday meals. For instance, many parents report that it has become much easier to send their children to school in the morning, as they look forward to eating with other children at noon. Similarly, teachers report that afternoon attendance has improved. Earlier, children went home for lunch, with many not returning.

Another achievement of midday meals is the elimination of classroom hunger. A large proportion of Indian children start the school day on an empty stomach. Without a midday meal, they grow hungry after a while and lose interest in studying, or go home. Where midday meals are in place, this problem has been largely resolved. In areas of endemic hunger, such as in the tribal areas of southern Rajasthan, the school meal also makes an important contribution to food security in general by ensuring that children get at least one square meal a day.

Having said this, the quality of midday meals leaves much to be desired because of the low budget allocations, especially in Rajasthan, where the government spends as little as 50 paise per child per day on recurring costs (compared with one rupee per day or so in Chhattisgarh and Karnataka). Because of inadequate resources, basic facilities are sorely lacking. For instance, very few schools in Rajasthan have a cooking shed. As a result, the cooking process often disrupts teaching activities and hygiene levels are inadequate. Lack of money is also the main reason why most schools in Rajasthan continue to serve ghoogri (sweetened boiled wheat) day after day, instead of varying the menu. An important opportunity has been missed here to enhance children's health by ensuring that they get nutritious food at school.

Caste, Class, and Gender

Recent media reports of upper-caste opposition to school meals in some areas highlight the "socialisation" role of midday meals. Restrictions on the sharing of food play an important role in the perpetuation of caste inequalities. Teaching children to sit and eat together at school, irrespective of caste, is a good way of defying traditional prejudices.

Of course, it is also possible for midday meals to be a tool of the reinforcement rather than the erosion of prevailing social inequalities. In Rajasthan, for example, we came across one village (Joz in Rajsamand district) where Dalit children were asked to drink from separate pitchers. This is a despicable instance of caste discrimination in the classroom which defeats the socialisation role of midday meals.

How common is caste discrimination in the context of midday meals? The CES survey sheds some useful light on this issue. The findings suggest that open discrimination is rare. For instance, we did not find any case of segregated sitting arrangements in the eighty-one schools sampled, or of preferential treatment being given to upper-caste children. Pupils of all social backgrounds seem to be quite happy to sit together and eat the same food. Parents and teachers both claim to welcome the arrangement in most cases, and very few parents among disadvantaged castes felt that their children had ever experienced caste discrimination in the context of the midday meal.

These responses, however, do not rule out subtle forms of caste prejudice and social discrimination. While open objections to the midday meal on caste grounds were rare, upper-caste parents were often sceptical of the scheme, and in a few cases actively opposed it. Some upper-caste parents send their children to school with packed food, or ask them to come home for lunch. Whether this is a manifestation of caste prejudice (as opposed to class privilege) is not always clear, but caste is likely to play a part in many cases.

Further, there does seem to be much upper-caste resistance to the appointment of Dalit cooks. In north Karnataka, half of the cooks in the sample were Dalits, and this arrangement seems to have gained fairly wide acceptance. In Chhattisgarh and Rajasthan, however, Dalit cooks were largely confined to schools with no upper-caste children. We also noted instances of active parental resistance to the appointment of Dalit cooks. In Kolu Pabuji, a village of Jodhpur district, a Rajput parent had thrown sand in the midday meal after discovering the cook was a Meghwal woman. She was promptly replaced by a woman from another caste.

These findings do not detract from the general socialisation value of midday meals. In a sense, they even enhance it: if upper-caste parents initially resist midday meals, there is much value in overcoming that reluctance. There are strong indications that the caste barriers are far from immutable.

The contribution of midday meals to social equality is not confined to the erosion of caste prejudices. They also promote gender equity in several ways. To start with, midday meals dramatically reduce the gender gap in school participation. The reason is that they boost female enrolment much more than male enrolment. One recent study estimates that the provision of a midday meal in the local school is associated with a 50 per cent reduction in the proportion of girls who are out of school. The CES survey also finds clear evidence of a surge in female school participation after midday meals were introduced, particularly in Chhattisgarh and Rajasthan.

Midday meals also create employment opportunities for poor women, especially when, as in Karnataka, the programme guidelines specify that all cooks should be women. In Tamil Nadu, each primary school has three paid staff: a cook, a helper, and an "organiser". Most of them are women, and this has become an important source of female employment in rural areas.

Further, midday meals contribute to the liberation of working women by freeing them from the burden of having to feed their school-going children at noon. As Sudan Mati, a 35-year-old tribal woman from Bilaspur district (Chhattisgarh), puts it: "Since our child has started getting food at school, we don't need to worry about him going hungry, and I don't need to come back after half a day's work to prepare his lunch." This feature is especially helpful to widowed mothers, who often work outside their homes without the benefit of domestic support.

Midday meals also help to reduce class inequalities. Indeed, children enrolled in government schools today come mainly from disadvantaged families. Thus, midday meals can be seen as a form of economic support to the poor. More importantly, perhaps, midday meals facilitate school-going among underprivileged children. This is likely to reduce future class inequalities, since the lack of an education is a major source of economic disadvantage and social marginalisation.

In their innocent garb, midday meals deal a healthy blow to the prevailing inequalities of caste, class, and gender. This is one reason, among others, why midday meals deserve more attention from individuals and organisations committed to social equity.

Midday Meals and the Joy
of Learning*

Feeding is everywhere perceived as an expression of love. The giving and sharing of food can do more to foster friendship and affection than the most eloquent religious sermons. This is well conveyed in the film *Babette's Feast*, where members of a village community who despise each other in spite of going to church every Sunday become friends as they eat and drink together at a wild banquet.

One argument for the provision of cooked midday meals in primary schools is that they make the school environment less hostile for the child. For Indian children, the school is often stifling and unfriendly. Verbal humiliation and physical brutality are common, and children rarely enjoy gestures of appreciation or encouragement from their teachers. In this situation, midday meals can help make children feel at ease in school.

We have already noted the many ways in which midday meals can serve useful purposes, such as boosting school attendance, reducing the gender gap in education, protecting children from classroom hunger, fostering a sense of social equality, generating employment for poor women, and imparting nutrition education to schoolchildren. All these, of course, depend on ensuring that midday meal schemes meet adequate quality standards.

There has been a wave of interesting studies on midday meals during the last few years. Field surveys have been conducted in Bihar, Chhattisgarh, Delhi, Jharkhand, Karnataka, Madhya Pradesh, Orissa,

*July 2006.

Rajasthan, and West Bengal, among other states. A number of useful insights have emerged.

First, midday meals are in place in most primary schools. Some states took several years to implement the supreme court order of 28 November 2001, which, we may recall, directed them to provide cooked midday meals in all primary schools within six months. But ultimately they all fell in line, and the coverage of midday meal schemes is now close to universal. Field studies indicate that the provision of midday meals is fairly regular in most states.

Second, midday meals are popular. Parents and teachers generally want the scheme to continue. There are, as noted, substantial pockets of opposition among upper-caste parents to their children being made to eat with Dalit children, or eating food cooked by a Dalit. And some teachers complain that midday meals disrupt classroom activities. This opposition typically wears out if the scheme is well implemented: over time, midday meals get smoothly integrated in the school routine, and upper-caste parents resign themselves to the fact that "times have changed". In some states, however, haphazard implementation has strengthened the opposition lobby and a backlash against midday meals cannot be ruled out.

Third, children are generally happy to get a midday meal at school. This is not so much because they are hungry, or because the food is better than what they get at home, but because they enjoy sharing a meal with their friends. Many states have started enhancing the variety and nutritional value of midday meals, and this tends to make them even more popular among children. According to a recent study of midday meals in Delhi: "Many [children] were observed enjoying every last grain on their plates, licking their fingers in delight. Rare was the child who did not take the food, and rarer still the school where the meal was not the highlight of the day."

Fourth, midday meals seem to be quite effective in promoting regular school attendance. This is one of the most common findings of recent studies on midday meals. Sometimes the reported effects on school attendance are really impressive. A recent study co-ordinated by the Samaj Pragati Sahyog in Madhya Pradesh found that school enrolment in Class 1 had shot up by 36 per cent within a year after cooked midday meals were introduced. A similar jump in school enrolment among scheduled caste and scheduled tribe children is reported for Jharkhand in a recent report prepared by the Gram Swaraj Abhiyan. These particular figures may be on the high side, due to small samples or reporting biases, but what is not in doubt is that midday meals have major effects on school attendance, especially among girls and disadvantaged families. In this respect, quantitative data corroborate wide-ranging testimonies from teachers, parents, and other observers.

Fifth, midday meals help to break caste barriers and foster a sense of social equality among school-children. This is very important, because the early years of primary school correspond to a vital period in children's lives, when their perceptions of social identity take shape. It is around this age, for instance, that children develop a consciousness of their caste and its place in the social hierarchy. The experience of unsegregated dining can help impart a sense of social equality at this crucial stage. The fact that upper-caste parents often resist this experiment confirms that it does challenge prevailing social norms in an important way.

Sixth, the socialisation value of midday meals is defeated when midday meals themselves become a site of social discrimination. A recent incident in Bhokludih village of Mahasamund district (Chhattisgarh) illustrates the problem, as well as how it can be turned into an opportunity to challenge caste discrimination. In Bhokludih, some Dalit children complained that they were given less food than others, made to sit separately, and prevented from entering the kitchen on the grounds that they were "Chamras". When a local teacher (Kamala Chauhan) took up their cause, she was transferred. On a more positive note, the incident received wide publicity and helped raise public awareness of the need to deal sternly with such incidents of caste discrimination.

Seventh, there is some interesting evidence on the value of midday meals as nutrition supplement. While midday meals certainly help to protect children from classroom hunger, they may or may not lead to a sustained improvement in their nutritional status. In fact, a poor midday meal (say rice and salt) can even be counterproductive, if it kills the appetite and reduces the child's intake of more nutritious home food. In this connection, it is interesting to note that, according to a recent study by Farzana Afridi, the improved midday meal scheme in Madhya Pradesh "reduces the daily calorie deficiency of the average primary schoolgoing child in the survey region by almost 35%, the daily iron deficiency by 25% and meets almost their entire daily protein deficiency." Having said this, there is a long way to go in making full use of midday meals as an opportunity to improve child nutrition. Some states have started enhancing the nutritional value of midday meals (e.g. by providing eggs and fruit), or combining them with micronutrient supplements (e.g. iron and Vitamin A), but the typical school meal is still quite frugal in most cases.

Finally, almost all recent studies of midday meals point to serious quality problems. Basic facilities such as cooking sheds and drinking water are often lacking, with the result that midday meals often interfere with classroom activities. Poor hygiene makes children vulnerable to stomach aches, if not food poisoning. Monotonous menus undermine the nutritional value of midday meals. And social discrimination persists. These problems need to be urgently addressed if midday meals are to realise their full potential.

Supreme court orders on midday meals can be seen as an instructive example of the possibility of constructive judicial intervention to protect children's right to food. However, court orders are little more than a temporary solution. Ultimately, nutritious midday meals need to be recognised as an integral part of a healthy school environment, just like a blackboard or textbook. And this recognition needs to be reflected in permanent legal entitlements as well as in political priorities and financial allocations.

Caste, Class, and Eggs*

Many Indian states have started providing eggs with midday meals, either in schools or in anganwadis or both. This is the best thing that has happened for a long time in the field of social policy.

Indian children are among the most undernourished in the world. They are starved of protein, vitamins, iron, and other essential nutrients. Eating eggs regularly could help them grow, thrive, and think. Indeed, eggs are a kind of super-food for growing children. They contain all the essential nutrients (except Vitamin C).

There are other arguments for including eggs in midday meals. First, most children (especially those from poor families) love eggs. Serving eggs with the midday meal helps boost school attendance and create a child-friendly environment. Second, eggs could give a new lease of life to the Integrated Child Development Services, still a fledgling programme in many states. Third, poultry is a useful source of local employment for rural households and women's self-help groups.

Eggs first appeared in school meals in states like Tamil Nadu and Andhra Pradesh. Today, Tamil Nadu provides eggs five times a week in schools and three times a week in anganwadis. But other states are catching up fast. Odisha, for instance, serves eggs three times a week in anganwadis and twice a week in schools. Among other major states, Bihar, Jharkhand, and West Bengal have recently joined the egg club. Even the poorest states, evidently, can afford it. (The accompanying map shows the state-wise number of eggs being served every week in schools and anganwadis, as this book goes to print.)

*July 2015.

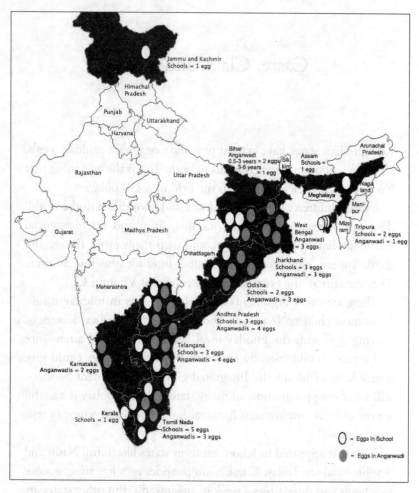

MAP: Number of Eggs Served Each Week to Children in Schools and Anganwadis. *Credit*: Swati Narayan.

The experience so far is overwhelmingly positive. Eggs are extremely popular among children, and quite safe – I am not aware of any incident of food poisoning. Nor is there much by way of complaint from upper-caste parents: wherever eggs are part of the midday meal menu, there is also a vegetarian option (e.g. a banana). In the light of this experience, there is every reason to go for eggs across the country.

Why, then, are egg proposals being repeatedly shot down in a few states, notably Madhya Pradesh, Chhattisgarh, Karnataka, and Rajasthan? In each case, the story is the same: the state government was held hostage to a tiny vegetarian (more precisely, semi-vegan) lobby. As a vegetarian myself, I am dismayed by the attitude of my fellow vegetarians. Surely, vegetarianism is about abstaining from certain food products, not about enforcing the abstention on others.

The egg resisters have been at a loss to come up with a rational argument to defend their position. Leaving aside the more eccentric claims (e.g. elephants prove that there is strength in vegetarianism), their main contention is that there are alternatives, such as milk or bananas. But bananas do not come close to eggs in nutritional value, and milk raises serious safety issues. Being a perishable food, it is also difficult to distribute efficiently. Further, as Mahatma Gandhi pointed out, milk is no more vegetarian than eggs in any rational sense. In any case, why look for alternatives when the humble egg is an effective, safe, well-tested, affordable, and popular option?

Ultimately, the resistance to eggs has to do with caste and class. Restrictions on the choice and sharing of food play a crucial role in the caste system. The self-appointed guardians of these restrictions typically come from the privileged castes, who have a stake in that system. Often they also come from the privileged classes, who can afford nutritious food for their children without having to rely on school meals. Their dogged insistence on having their way is essentially an upper-caste affirmation that "what we say goes".

Chief Minister Shivraj Singh Chouhan's recent veto against eggs in Madhya Pradesh contrasts with the quiet manner in which eggs were introduced in Bihar about a year ago. When Jiten Ram Manjhi, then chief minister of Bihar, heard of the idea of serving eggs in anganwadis, he supported it immediately. Coming from a poor Musahar family, and having known hunger in his childhood, he understood what it would mean for poor children to get an egg at school. He himself explained how he knew many Musahar children who had never eaten an egg. Within a few weeks, the Government of Bihar started implementing the proposal.

Interestingly, there have been no reports of vocal opposition from upper-caste parents in Bihar, or in any other states where eggs were introduced recently. At countless public functions, there are vegetarian and non-vegetarian queues for food, and I have never seen vegetarians run away in disgust – why would the same arrangement be a problem in schools? Contrary to their claims, the anti-egg militants are not voicing the sentiment of a large constituency but acting as an authoritarian minority.

Finally, I sympathise with animal rights activists who are batting for brutalised farm animals. I have seen how pigs are treated in industrial farms, and that is why I gave up meat and fish (not eggs!). But scuttling poor children's right to nutritious food is not the best way to champion the cause of farm animals.

Notes

There is, by now, a large body of research on India's midday meal scheme. Some of the early studies are cited in this section, but there are many more, consolidating the initial evidence of the scheme's positive impact on school attendance and child nutrition; see e.g. Khera 2006, 2013, Drèze and Khera 2009, 2017, Drèze and Sen 2013, and the studies cited there.

Hunger in the Classroom

The reference to an investigation of hunger among schoolchildren in Delhi is based on a personal communication from Dr Janaki Rajan, then director of the State Council for Educational Research and Training (SCERT). The Sikar survey was conducted by local NGOs and presented at a meeting of the Akal Sangharsh Samiti in September 2002.

The essay mentions that most cooks in Karnataka were Dalit women at that time. On 20 April 2004, the supreme court issued an order stating that "in appointments of cooks and helpers, preference shall be given to Dalits, Scheduled Castes and Scheduled Tribes." To this day, however, there are occasional media reports of parents resenting or resisting the appointment of Dalit cooks.

Food for Equality

The findings of the Centre for Equity Studies (CES) survey, only partially available when this essay was written, are presented in Drèze and Goyal 2003. The text refers to an early analysis of the impact of midday meals on female school participation (Drèze and Kingdon 2001), now supplemented with many other studies.

Midday Meals and the Joy of Learning

This essay draws on the literature cited in Drèze and Khera 2009. The findings of the Samaj Pragati Sahyog and Farzana Afridi studies of midday meals in Madhya Pradesh are presented in Jain and Shah 2005, and Afridi 2010, respectively. The Delhi study quoted in the text is a draft version of De, Noronha, and Samson 2008.

Caste, Class, and Eggs

On the nutritional value of eggs, see e.g. Applegate 2000. Credit for the right to information query that drew attention to the non-vegetarian banquet hosted by the chief minister of Madhya Pradesh in Tokyo (as mentioned in the headnote to this section) is due to Ajay Dubey.

4

HEALTH CARE

THE FLAWS OF SOCIAL POLICY in India are nowhere more glaring than in the field of health care. Public expenditure on health has stagnated at around 1 per cent of GDP for the last twenty-five years – a lower ratio than almost anywhere else in the world. The bulk of health expenditure consists of out-of-pocket (OOP) private expenditure, and the provision of health services is also largely private, as well as profit-oriented. In the absence of any effective regulation of the private sector, patients are highly vulnerable to exploitation. The shortcomings of market competition in the field of health care, in terms of efficiency as well as equity, are well understood in mainstream economics. As Kenneth Arrow, one of the greatest economists of the twentieth century, pointed out more than fifty years ago in a seminal article on the subject, "It is the general social consensus, clearly, that the laissez-faire solution for medicine is intolerable."[1]

India's record is particularly dismal in the specific field of public health, which refers to activities such as epidemiological surveillance, immunisation, waste management, water supply, and sanitation. In this respect, India fares poorly not only in comparison with China (as is well known), or almost any East Asian country, but also in comparison with its neighbours in South Asia, with the partial exception

[1] Arrow 1963, p. 967.

of Pakistan. When it comes to sanitation, even Pakistan is ahead of India, as are almost all other countries in the world.

Looking at change over time, rather than at the comparative international picture, there is little to celebrate, except for a few signs of hope. The basic character of India's health care system (highly privatised and very ineffective) has not changed in the last twenty-five years. In 2005, the National Common Minimum Programme of the United Progressive Alliance government promised to raise public expenditure on health to "2 to 3 per cent of GDP", but this never happened. In 2011, the High Level Expert Group on Universal Health Coverage for India (appointed by the Planning Commission) submitted its report to the government – little has been heard of it since. During the last three years, under the National Democratic Alliance government, health policy has been further sidelined. The government did make some grand initial statements about universal health care, and even about health becoming a "fundamental right", but it turned out to be all gong and no dinner.

Coming to the signs of hope, two are worth mentioning. First, there have been sporadic departures from this general apathy in the form of specific health-related initiatives on the part of the central government. For instance, the National Rural Health Mission (launched in 2005–6) initiated a process of sustained improvement in rural health care facilities, later extended to urban areas as well. Similarly, the Janani Suraksha Yojana (JSY) led to an impressive surge in institutional deliveries and possibly contributed to the relatively rapid decline of maternal mortality in recent years.

Second, there has been some action at the state level, not just among the traditional pioneers of social policy in India (such as Kerala and Tamil Nadu), but also in other states, for instance Chhattisgarh, Odisha, and even Bihar. In 2002, Chhattisgarh launched the Mitanin programme of female community health workers, which later became the model for the national deployment of Accredited Social Health Activists (ASHAs). In Odisha, there have been sustained efforts to improve the reach and functioning of health centres as well as anganwadis (child care centres). There are growing indications that these national and state-level initiatives have had significant results.[2]

The essays in this section discuss these deep flaws of India's health care system as well as the signs of hope. They also include a short article on Bangladesh – an early discussion of the fact that Bangladesh is doing much better than India in terms of health indicators, despite being much poorer. That pattern became even clearer later on, for instance from the findings of the Demographic and Health Surveys (known in India as the National Family Health Survey). Today, even Nepal is doing better than India in terms of many health indicators, despite having barely a third of India's per capita GDP. Notwithstanding some recent progress in India, there is still a lot to do to overcome the legacy of decades of inertia in this field.

The last essay presents tentative rankings of Indian states in terms of child development indicators in 2005–6 and 2013–14. Consistent with earlier research, the toppers in both years are Kerala, Tamil Nadu, and Himachal Pradesh.[3] Also in line with earlier findings, Gujarat is a "middle" more than a "model". Bihar is at rock bottom, but it did improve significantly between the two reference years – there is another sign of hope there, not only for Bihar but for all Indian states.

[2] See e.g. Goel and Khera 2015, Khera 2015, Narayan 2016, Sinha 2016, and the last two essays in this section.

[3] For further discussion of these comparative experiences, see Drèze and Sen 2013, and Drèze and Khera 2012.

Health Checkup*

Sometimes the most important things in life are the least talked about. For instance, it is hard to think of anything more important than health for human well-being and the quality of life. And yet, health is virtually absent from public debates and democratic politics in India.

To illustrate, consider the coverage of health issues in the mainstream media. In an earlier analysis of 300 opinion articles published over a period of six months (January to June 2000) in *The Hindu*, it emerged that not *one* of these articles dealt with health-related matters. Just in case, I repeated the exercise this year for the period January–June 2003. This time, I did find an article dealing with health issues – it was about the SARS crisis in China!

This silence would perhaps be tolerable if the Indian population enjoyed good health and adequate health services, but nothing could be further from the truth. Indeed, India's health indicators are among the worst in the world. For instance, according to the latest National Family Health Survey (1998–9), half of all Indian children are undernourished and half of all adult women suffer from anaemia. At the time of the survey, 30 per cent of all children under the age of three years had fever, another 20 per cent had diarrhoea, and another 20 per cent had symptoms of acute respiratory infection. Even after allowing for some overlap between these different groups, this suggests that at least half of all Indian children in that age group suffer from one of these conditions at any given point of time.

*March 2004.

The condition of health services is no less dismal. As a ratio of GDP, public expenditure on health in India is among the lowest in the world – about 1 per cent. The health system is highly privatised. Indeed, only 15 per cent of total health expenditure in India is public expenditure; the rest is private expenditure, such as over-the-counter drug purchases from chemist shops. By contrast, the ratio of public expenditure to total health expenditure is 40 per cent in East Asia, 50 per cent in Latin America, 75 per cent in Europe, and as high as 85 per cent in Britain. In large parts of India, there are no public health facilities worth the name, except for female sterilisation and polio immunisation.

Recent health facility surveys conducted by the International Institute for Population Sciences (Mumbai) give a chilling picture of the state of health centres around the country. To illustrate, only 69 per cent of primary health centres (PHCs) have at least one bed, 20 per cent have a telephone, and 12 per cent enjoy "regular mainte-nance". These are national averages, and the corresponding figures for the poorer states are much worse. In Bihar, for instance, a large majority of PHCs make do without luxuries such as electricity, a weighing machine or even a toilet. It is worth remembering that a PHC is supposed to be a facility of major importance, serving a population of 30,000 or so.

Even when health facilities are available, their utilisation leaves much to be desired. According to a forthcoming Harvard study, absence rates among health workers range between 35 and 58 per cent in different Indian states. A similar picture emerges from an ongoing study of health services in Udaipur district, Rajasthan. More than half the health sub-centres were found to be closed during regular opening hours, and even in the primary health centres and community health centres (larger than PHCs), 36 per cent of the personnel were absent on average. Meanwhile, local residents suffer from horrendous levels of morbidity: one-third of all adults had a cold during the 30 days preceding the survey, 42 per cent had body ache, 33 per cent had fever, 23 per cent suffered from fatigue, 11 per cent had chest pains, and more than half suffered from anaemia. Close to a third found it difficult to draw water from a well and one in five had difficulty standing up from a sitting position.

It is worth noting that even the well-off families in India often do not have access to decent health services. The technology and the expertise exist, but public facilities are highly inefficient and private services are virtually unregulated, leaving patients at the mercy of unscrupulous practitioners. Fraud, over-medication, and unnecessary surgery are the bread and butter of the private health sector. According to a recent study of health services in Mumbai, for instance, about 65 per cent of deliveries performed in the private sector end up with a Caesarean, compared with 9 per cent in the public sector (the latter is close to WHO norms).

If anything, the neglect of health services in public policy has intensified in the liberalisation period. Public expenditure on health declined steadily in the early 1990s, as a share of GDP. The ratio picked up again towards the end of the decade, but mainly because of salary increases (in the wake of the Fifth Pay Commission), without any improvement in real inputs. As the recent budget indicates, the spotlight today is on expensive, high-tech facilities such as modern hospitals, and on vertical programmes sponsored by foreign agencies, such as the pulse-polio programme. Basic health services, for their part, have been grossly neglected, to the extent that the coverage of routine immunisation has shrunk in recent years, according to the Reproductive and Child Health surveys. The decline of infant mortality has also slowed, after a spell of rapid decline in the 1980s.

On the positive side, some states (Kerala, Tamil Nadu, Himachal Pradesh, among others) have recognised the importance of good public health facilities, and planned accordingly. In an illuminating study, Leela Visaria has drawn attention to the comparatively good functioning of health services in states like Tamil Nadu. Last year, I had an opportunity to observe this myself when I visited health centres in three districts of Tamil Nadu (more on this in "The Welfare State in Tamil Nadu"). Used as I am to North India's dilapidated and unfriendly health centres, I was impressed to find tidy and well-equipped premises, abundant stocks of essential medicines, active nurses and doctors, and a general sense of responsibility towards the patients. I also found myself agreeing with an important observation made by Leela Visaria: the social distance between doctors and patients seems to be smaller in Tamil Nadu than in North India, which may help explain the relatively good functioning of health services there. In Tamil Nadu, according to the latest National Family Health Survey, 99 per cent of births are preceded by antenatal checkups and 89 per cent of children are fully vaccinated. The corresponding figures in, say, Uttar Pradesh are 35 and 21 per cent – most women and children there being left to their own devices.

One reason for this contrast is that, in Tamil Nadu, health care has been brought within the ambit of democratic politics. Health and related issues, such as midday meals, are a subject of lively public debate and play an important role in election campaigns. In North India, however, health does not figure on the political agenda, and nor do other basic needs such as elementary education and child nutrition.

The supreme court gave a useful wake-up call to the government on 28 November 2001, with an order calling for the provision of a functional anganwadi in "every settlement". Active implementation of this order could go a long way in protecting Indian children from hunger and disease. Unfortunately, the government has taken little notice of it. In fact, according to the Department of Women and Child Development, a recent proposal to expand the Integrated Child Development Services (ICDS) was "categorically rejected" by the cabinet on the grounds that there was "no money". Meanwhile, lavish public resources are spent on the more influential sections of society – private corporations, the military establishment, public employees, and the so-called "middle classes", among others. Much like the state of health care, however, these anomalies seem to escape the radar of the mainstream media.

India Leapfrogged*

In the context of the recent panic about the growth rate of the Muslim population in India, international data on human development in India and Bangladesh make interesting reading. Surely, India must be far ahead of Bangladesh in this respect? Indeed, Bangladesh is not only poorer (much poorer) than India, but also has a large Muslim population. India, for its part, is now a budding superpower. One would, therefore, expect its citizens to be much healthier, better fed, and better educated than their Bangladeshi neighbours.

Let us examine the evidence. A good starting point is the infant mortality rate: 51 per 1000 live births in Bangladesh compared with 67 per 1000 in India, according to the latest Human Development Report. In other words, infant mortality is much lower in Bangladesh. This is all the more interesting as the positions were reversed not so long ago: in 1990, the infant mortality rate was estimated at 91 per 1000 in Bangladesh, and 80 per 1000 in India. India has been neatly leapfrogged, that too during a period when economic growth was much faster in India than in Bangladesh.

Other indicators relating to child health point in the same direction. According to the same report, 95 per cent of infants in Bangladesh are vaccinated against tuberculosis, and 77 per cent are vaccinated against measles. The corresponding figures in India are only 81 per cent and 67 per cent, respectively. Similarly, 97 per cent of the population in Bangladesh has access to an "improved water source", compared with 84 per cent in India; and 48 per cent of Bangladeshis have access to "improved sanitation", compared with 28 per cent

*September 2004.

of Indians. For good measure, the maternal mortality rate is much lower in Bangladesh than in India: 380 and 540 per 100,000 live births, respectively. Contraceptive prevalence, for its part, is higher in Bangladesh than in India – the "wrong" ranking again!

Perhaps all this has something to do with the fact that public expenditure on health as a proportion of GDP is almost twice as high in Bangladesh (1.6 per cent) as in India (0.9 per cent). The reverse applies to military expenditure, also known as "defence": 2.3 per cent of GDP in India compared with 1.1 per cent in Bangladesh.

So much for health. But in education at least, India must be way ahead? Can Bangladesh boast a fraction of India's Nobel prizes, famous writers, nuclear scientists, eminent scholars? Perhaps not, but Bangladesh appears to be closer to universal primary education than India: it has achieved a "net primary enrolment ratio" of 87 per cent, higher than India's 83 per cent. What is more, Bangladesh has eliminated the gender bias in primary education, in sharp contrast with India where school participation rates continue to be much higher for boys than for girls. Other gender-related indicators also put Bangladesh in a relatively favourable light, compared with India: Bangladesh, for instance, has a higher female–male ratio and much higher rates of female labour force participation.

However, there is a consolation of sorts: the nutrition situation is no better in Bangladesh than in India. In both countries, about half of all children are undernourished. No country in the world fares worse in this respect, but at least India is not alone in the back seat.

Some of these estimates may not be very accurate. Perhaps the ranking would be reversed, in some cases, if precise figures were available. But the general pattern, whereby Bangladesh is now doing better than India in terms of many aspects of social development, is unlikely to reflect measurement errors. This pattern is all the more striking as India used to fare better than Bangladesh in all these respects not so long ago – as recently as the early 1990s in many cases.

Bangladesh is no paradise of human development. Like India, it is still one of the most deprived countries in the world. However, social indicators in Bangladesh are improving quite rapidly. Whether one looks at infant mortality, immunisation rates, school participation, child nutrition, or fertility rates, the message is similar: living conditions are improving steadily, not just for a privileged elite but also for the population at large. In India, social progress is slower and less broad-based, despite much faster economic growth. This is one indication, among many others, that India's development strategy is fundamentally distorted and lopsided.

Health at Sixty-six*

India is now sixty-six years old, and, as it happens, life expectancy in India today is also sixty-six years. That's almost exactly twice as high as life expectancy at the time of Independence – thirty-two years or so. Expanding life expectancy by more than thirty years in a few decades is no small feat. This has never happened in India before, and may never happen again. It is part of what Angus Deaton aptly calls the "great escape" from poverty and deprivation that happened around the world during the last few decades.

However, if we evaluate India's life expectancy achievement of 66 years by contemporary standards, rather than by historical standards, the picture is less rosy. It is not just that life expectancy is much higher in countries like China (73 years), Sri Lanka (75 years), and South Korea (81 years) – countries where living conditions were not much better than in India 66 years ago. Even within South Asia, India has a lower life expectancy than any other country except Pakistan, which is more or less on par with India in this respect. A similar pattern applies to child mortality rates: 61 per thousand live births in India compared with 48 per thousand in Nepal, 46 in Bangladesh, and only 12 in Sri Lanka. The figures are all the more striking in light of the fact that Bangladesh has about half of India's per capita GDP (adjusted for purchasing-power parity), and Nepal one-third.

There is another thing worth bearing in mind when we compare these country averages: health inequality is probably higher in India than in most other countries. The evidence on this is a little patchy,

*August 2013.

but it is a very plausible hypothesis. An illustration from a related field may help. The proportion of stunted children is similar, on average, in India and sub-Saharan Africa. But differences in child stunting rates between different socio-economic groups are much higher in India. And even within households, inequalities are larger in India, where stunting rates rise sharply with birth order. Thus, if we were to compare disadvantaged groups across countries, instead of national averages, India's health indicators would look even less inspiring.

The country's birthday is a good opportunity to reflect on what has gone wrong and why India's health achievements remain so limited even in comparison with its poorer neighbours. In answering this question, it helps to look at Indian states that have done relatively well. The trail-blazer in this field is Kerala, where, interestingly, life expectancy and child mortality today are almost exactly the same as in Sri Lanka. Tamil Nadu, one of India's poorest states at the time of Independence, soon followed Kerala's footsteps and its health indicators are now catching up rapidly with those of Kerala. Himachal Pradesh made a late start, after it became an independent state in 1971, but the speed of progress in health and related fields has been very rapid ever since.

One common feature of these three states is an early drive towards universal elementary education. Kerala began that journey before Independence, and many of its later social achievements build on this foundation. In Tamil Nadu, there were also some important initiatives in the first half of the twentieth century, but the real breakthrough came just after Independence, with a massive expansion of the schooling system. In Himachal Pradesh, elementary education was the overwhelming priority of the state government as soon as the state was formed in 1971. Given the wide-ranging personal and social roles of elementary education, evident from a wealth of studies, this early investment in mass education clearly played a crucial role in the subsequent achievements of these three states, including rapid progress in matters of health and nutrition. India as a whole missed that boat, and is paying a heavy price for it.

Another well-documented determinant of good health, and parti-cularly of child health, is the informed agency of women. A woman who is confined to the house, has never been to school, is not allowed to visit a health centre on her own and receives no special attention during pregnancy is not well placed to look after her children's health, or her own for that matter. These and other shackles continue to restrict the freedoms of Indian women, despite some improvement in specific aspects of gender relations. Gender-related indicators look better in Bangladesh, whether we look at women's work-force participation, or sex differentials in mortality rates, or patterns of school participation, or even women's representation in parliament. For instance, there has been a major expansion of women's workforce participation in Bangladesh in recent years, enabling women to earn some income of their own and also giving them an entry into public life. In India, by contrast, women's workforce participation remains abysmally low – lower than anywhere else in the world except for a few countries of West Asia and North Africa.

A third enabling factor is public action, including well-functioning health services. This is perhaps where there is most to learn from leading states like Kerala, Tamil Nadu, and Himachal Pradesh. There is a tendency to presume that what has been achieved in these states cannot be replicated elsewhere, but this assumption has no basis. Indeed, some other states have already started replicating aspects of these relatively effective health care systems. For instance, Tamil Nadu's exemplary system of free distribution of generic drugs is being emulated in Rajasthan, with promising initial results. And in many states, one can now find at least some anganwadis that begin to resemble Kerala's lively child care centres, aptly described by one observer as having the atmosphere of "a birthday party".

Bangladesh is unlikely to be a model for health services in general, but it has made good progress with simple public health measures that can make a big difference. To illustrate, the proportion of child-ren who are fully immunised, get Vitamin A supplements, are treated with oral rehydration therapy when they have diarrhoea, and were breastfed within an hour of birth was above 80 per cent in each case in Bangladesh in 2007. The corresponding figures for Indian children were uniformly below 50 per cent in the same year. Similarly, the proportion of households defecating in the open (a major health hazard) is around half in India, but less than 10 per cent in Bangladesh. The entire field of public health has been comprehensively neglected in India, with dire consequences.

Elementary education, women's empowerment, and public action have powerful effects on their own, but they also reinforce each other. Public services are more likely to work where people are educated and know their rights, just as the spread of education requires an effective schooling system. Similarly, elementary education contributes to women's empowerment, just as education is more likely to spread in a society where women are active and informed mothers, teachers, voters, and leaders. This complementarity magnifies the scope for rapid progress in the field of health, even at an early stage of development.

Perhaps the biggest puzzle of health policy in India is why it has been such a low priority for so long. Aside from ruining the lives of millions, poor health has huge economic costs for the nation. Yet public expenditure on health has been stagnating for decades at around 1 per cent of GDP, compared with an average of 3 per cent for low- and middle-income countries. While we are still learning how to ensure that health centres have adequate supplies of basic drugs, countries such as Brazil, China, Mexico, Thailand, Vietnam, and others have made decisive progress towards universal health care. Unless health matters receive more attention in democratic politics, it may take another sixty-six years for India to achieve this essential goal.

Small Leap Forward in
Child Health*

The recent release of summary findings from the Rapid Survey on Children (RSOC) has generated remarkably little interest in the mainstream media. The main focus of attention so far has been the indifferent performance of Gujarat in matters of health and nutrition – nothing new there. Related to this, there has also been some speculation about the reasons for the central government's apparent reluctance to release the findings. The substance of the findings, however, has passed largely unnoticed.

This is unfortunate, because there is much to learn from the survey. In fact, the RSOC can be regarded as some sort of substitute for a fourth National Family Health Survey (NFHS). It may be recalled that the third NFHS was conducted almost ten years ago, in 2005–6. Prolonged delays in the completion of the fourth NFHS have created a huge gap in India's social statistics, even as all other South Asian countries conducted regular national health and nutrition surveys. Fortunately, the RSOC survey (conducted in 2013–14) seems to be modelled on the NFHS, generating a wealth of health and nutrition statistics that can be usefully compared with the corresponding findings from the third NFHS.

Overall, the RSOC findings look like relatively good news. They suggest a marked improvement in many aspects of maternal and child nutrition between 2005–6 and 2013–14. But the progress is uneven – fairly rapid in some fields, slow in others.

*September 2015.

At first glance, the biggest change relates to safe delivery. The proportion of institutional deliveries among recent births shot up from 39 per cent in 2005–6 to 79 per cent in 2013–14, and the proportion attended by a skilled health provider rose from 47 per cent to 81 per cent. At least part of this trend is likely to reflect the impact of the Janani Suraksha Yojana, including cash incentives for institutional delivery. This leap forward, however, has not been accompanied by a general breakthrough in maternal care. For instance, the proportion of pregnant women who had at least three antenatal checkups was not much higher in 2013–14 (63 per cent) than in 2005–6 (52 per cent). Similarly, the proportion who consumed "iron and folic acid tablets" for at least ninety days was very low in both years: 23 per cent and 24 per cent respectively. Even the sharp increase in institutional deliveries needs to be taken with a pinch of salt: in some states, many women deliver in health centres for the sake of cash incentives, with very limited real benefits in terms of natal or postnatal care.

Another area of substantial progress is vaccination. The proportion of children with a vaccination card rose from 38 per cent in 2005–6 to 84 per cent in 2013–14, and vaccination coverage rose from 59 to 79 per cent for measles, 55 to 75 per cent for DPT3, and 44 to 65 per cent for "full immunisation". Even with these improved figures, India has some of the lowest child vaccination rates in the world, and lags far behind Bangladesh and even Nepal. But at least there is a hint of accelerated progress, after an alarming phase of near stagnation in routine immunisation. As with institutional deliveries, this pattern can be plausibly attributed to recent health policy initiatives, such as the appointment of Accredited Social Health Activists (ASHAs), who are now actively involved in immunisation programmes along with anganwadi workers and Auxiliary Nurse Midwives (ANMs). Quite likely, these initiatives can also take credit for a substantial improvement in breastfeeding practices: the proportion of children breastfed within an hour of birth rose from just 25 per cent in 2005–6 to 45 per cent in 2013–14.

Turning to other health and nutrition indicators available from these surveys, most of them point to moderate progress between 2005–6 and 2013–14 – more rapid than between NFHS-2 and NFHS-3 (conducted in 1998–9 and 2005–6 respectively), but nowhere as fast as one would hope to see in a booming economy. To illustrate, the proportion of undernourished children declined from 48 to 39 per cent based on height-for-age criteria and from 43 to 29 per cent based on weight-for-age criteria. This is an improvement over the preceding period, when child undernutrition was declining at a glacial pace. Yet much faster progress is required if India is to overcome this colossal problem in a reasonable period of time.

Finally, there are worrying signs of stagnation in some important fields. One of them is access to safe drinking water: 88 per cent in 2005–6 and 91 per cent in 2013–14. The shortfall from universal coverage may not look large, but considering the vital importance of safe water, it is alarming that close to 10 per cent of households are still deprived of it (the corresponding figure in Bangladesh was just 3 per cent in 2007). No less alarming is the slow progress of sanitation: the proportion of sample households defecating in the open declined from 55 per cent in 2005–6 to 46 per cent in 2013–14, or barely one percentage point per year. At that rate, it will take at least another forty years for India to eliminate this problem.

It is useful to read these figures in comparison with similar data (e.g. from the periodic Demographic and Health Surveys) from other South Asian countries, especially Bangladesh and Nepal. These comparisons tend to place India in a poor light. For instance, despite being about twice as rich as Bangladesh in terms of per capita GDP, India lags far behind Bangladesh in terms of child vaccination rates, breastfeeding practices, the incidence of open defecation, access to safe water, and related indicators. The same point applies if we compare India with Nepal, which is even poorer than Bangladesh. This gap reflects India's resilient neglect of health and nutrition matters over a long period of time. The RSOC findings suggest that, in some respects at least, India is finally catching up with its poorer neighbours. They also suggest that the areas of rapid progress (e.g. safe delivery and vaccination) are those where serious action was initiated during the last ten years or so. The need of the hour is to consolidate these initiatives and extend them to other domains where there is still no sign of rapid progress.

Alas, the central government is going in the opposite direction. Financial allocations for the Integrated Child Development Services were slashed by 50 per cent or so in the last union budget, sending a disastrous signal about policy priorities (no matter what compensation state governments may be receiving in the form of higher tax revenue). Health policy is a morass of confusion and inertia, with the health ministry and NITI Aayog talking at cross purposes. The central government is brazenly ignoring its legal obligation to provide for maternity entitlements under the National Food Security Act. Even the sanitation budget has been quietly reduced, soon after the prime minister's announcement that India would be free of defecation in the open within five years. The central government is effectively palming off social policy to the states, with little regard for the consequences of undermining centrally sponsored initiatives that have come to play a critical role in the field of maternal and child health. This does not augur well for another leap forward in the near future.

Kerala Tops, Gujarat Flops,
Bihar Hops*

(with Reetika Khera)

Even as we track the Sensex day after day, humble child statistics that tell us big stories about the country's development strategy get little attention. The early findings of the Rapid Survey on Children 2013–14 (introduced in the preceding essay) present an opportunity to take a fresh look at inter-state contrasts in child development and reflect on what lies behind them.

Helpfully, RSOC figures are comparable with similar data from the third National Family Health Survey (NFHS-3) for 2005–6. In earlier work, published in the *Economic and Political Weekly*, we used NFHS-3 data to construct a simple child development index, analogous to the Human Development Index but based on child-related indicators. This can be done again, with minor modifications, using NFHS-3 as well as RSOC data. This time, the four component indicators are: proportion of children fully immunised; female literacy in the age group of 10–14 years; proportion of births preceded by an antenatal checkup; and proportion of children who are not underweight. In the absence of survey data on age-specific female literacy rates, we use the 2001 and 2011 censuses, respectively, for the literacy indicator. The indicators are normalised using the standard HDI method, and given equal weight.

The results are presented in Table 1. Note that the absolute value of the index is not strictly comparable across years – what can be

*November 2015.

Table 1: Child Development Index, 2005–6 and 2013–14*

2005–6		2013–14	
Kerala	0.955	Kerala	0.958
Tamil Nadu	0.921	Himachal Pradesh	0.866
Himachal Pradesh	0.810	Tamil Nadu	0.863
Punjab	0.800	Punjab	0.789
Maharashtra	0.749	Maharashtra	0.769
Haryana	0.706	Andhra Pradesh	0.762
Jammu &Kashmir	0.694	Karnataka	0.759
West Bengal	0.693	West Bengal	0.722
Karnataka	0.670	Uttarakhand	0.646
Andhra Pradesh	0.669	Haryana	0.627
Uttarakhand	0.635	Chhattisgarh	0.616
Odisha	0.577	Assam	0.553
Chhattisgarh	0.573	**INDIA**	**0.530**
Gujarat	0.561	Odisha	0.525
INDIA	**0.502**	Jammu &Kashmir	0.507
Assam	0.454	Gujarat	0.484
Rajasthan	0.424	Rajasthan	0.394
Madhya Pradesh	0.386	Jharkhand	0.354
Uttar Pradesh	0.333	Madhya Pradesh	0.333
Jharkhand	0.216	Bihar	0.296
Bihar	0.070	Uttar Pradesh	0.144

*In each year, states are ranked in decreasing order of Child Development Index. As explained in the text, absolute values of the index are not strictly comparable between the two reference years, but the rankings can be compared.

Note: The child development index presented here is an unweighted average of the normalised values of four basic indicators: proportion of children aged 12–23 months who are fully immunised; female literacy rate in the age group of 10–14 years; proportion of births preceded by a health checkup; and proportion of children below the age of five years who are *not* underweight. Data on these indicators for 2005–6 and 2013–14 are available from NFHS-3 and the RSOC, respectively (in the absence of age-specific literacy data from these surveys, figures from the Census of India 2001 and 2011 were used for female literacy).

compared is the ranking of states in 2005–6 and 2013–14. As it happens, the ranking is quite similar in both years and its basic features are familiar. At the top of the list come Kerala, Himachal Pradesh, and Tamil Nadu – states that might be called "supermodels" if Gujarat were a model, which it is not. Indeed, Gujarat ranked 14th in the list of twenty major states in 2005–6, and slipped to 15th in 2013–14, with a child development index well below the all-India average.

Predictably enough, the other lagging states belong to the region formerly known by the unflattering acronym of BIMARU – undivided Bihar, Madhya Pradesh, Rajasthan, and Uttar Pradesh. However, some important contrasts have emerged within this region.

Chhattisgarh, for instance, has detached itself from the rest as far as child development is concerned. Indeed, the child development index for Chhattisgarh is above the all-India average, and of course above Gujarat. Uttarakhand is doing even better. Uttar Pradesh, on the other hand, has replaced Bihar at rock bottom.

Bihar is still close to the bottom, but in absolute terms it has progressed a great deal (from an abysmally low base) between 2005–6 and 2013–14. For instance, the proportion of births preceded by an antenatal checkup in Bihar shot up from 34 per cent in 2005–6 to 85 per cent in 2013–14 – the largest improvement among all major states, by a long margin. Similarly, the proportion of children fully immunised jumped from 33 per cent to 60 per cent. For a state that was thought incapable of running basic health services until very recently, this is a real breakthrough.

We explored variants of this index, e.g. using stunting instead of low weight as the nutrition indicator, or looking at breastfeeding instead of antenatal care. While some of these variants lead to a somewhat different ranking, the basic patterns are fairly robust: Kerala, Tamil Nadu, and Himachal Pradesh are at the top, the former BIMARU states (minus Chhattisgarh and Uttarakhand) languish at the bottom, and Gujarat is near the all-India average.

The essay "Health at Sixty-six" (above) discussed the enabling factors that Kerala, Tamil Nadu, and Himachal Pradesh seem to have in common, including the fact that mass schooling was the prime mover in each case. The constructive role of the state also extended, later on, to the provision of a wide range of essential services and facilities – from health care and clean water to social security and basic infrastructure. It is worth noting that active social policies did not prevent these states from doing well in terms of economic growth – on the contrary. Despite regular warnings that this approach is "unsustainable", Kerala, Tamil Nadu, and Himachal Pradesh keep expanding the reach and quality of public services. Tamil Nadu, for instance, has recently introduced pioneering schemes of maternity entitlements, community kitchens, and even nursing rooms at bus stands.

Can other states take a leaf from these successful experiences? Kerala used to be thought of as some sort of anomaly among Indian states, but now Tamil Nadu and Himachal Pradesh are in the same league. And other states, including some that looked like basket cases not so long ago, are catching up too. Here is some food for thought: in terms of each of the four indicators considered here, Bihar today is more or less on par with Tamil Nadu in the early 1990s. This can be read to mean that Bihar is more than twenty years behind Tamil Nadu in this field. But if the gap between Bihar and Tamil Nadu continues to narrow, as it did in the last ten years, this also suggests that Bihar may take less than twenty years to look like Tamil Nadu today as far as child development is concerned. That is certainly a cheerful thought. And if Bihar can catch up, why not every state?

Notes

Health Checkup

For further discussion of the coverage of social issues in the Indian media, see Drèze and Sen 2002. Data from the second National Family Health Survey (NFHS-2) are presented in International Institute for Population Sciences 2000. Figures for public expenditure on health were taken from the latest *World Development Indicators*, published by the World Bank. Health-facility statistics are available from International Institute for Population Sciences 2005. For findings of the "forthcoming Harvard study" and the "ongoing study of health services in Udaipur district", see Chaudhury, *et al.* 2006, and Banerjee, *et al.* 2004, respectively. On Leela Visaria's comparative work on health services in Rajasthan and Tamil Nadu, see e.g. Visaria 2000a, 2000b. For child immunisation data from the Reproductive and Child Health Surveys, see e.g. International Institute for Population Sciences 2006.

India Leapfrogged

This essay is based on data from the *Human Development Report* (latest edition available at that time). The Bangladesh–India contrast in health-related matters (including Bangladesh's huge lead in terms of sanitation, immunisation, breastfeeding practices, and more) became much clearer a few years later, as the availability and reliability of health indicators improved in both countries. For further discussion, see Drèze and Sen 2013.

Health at Sixty-six

Life-expectancy, mortality and GDP figures are from *World Development Indicators* (latest available edition at the time of writing). On stunting in India and sub-Saharan Africa, see Jayachandran and Pande 2013, and earlier work cited there. On the comparative development experiences of Himachal Pradesh, Kerala and Tamil Nadu, see Drèze and Sen 2013, where the contrast between India and Bangladesh is also discussed. The comparative public-health indicators for India and Bangladesh are based on the National Family Health Survey 2005–6 and the Demographic and Health Survey 2007, respectively.

Small Leap Forward in Child Health

This essay is based on summary findings of the Rapid Survey on Children 2013–14 (RSOC), released in August 2015 in the form of state-wise fact-sheets; the final fact-sheets are available on the website of the ministry of women and child development (http://wcd.nic.in/acts/rapid-survey-children-rsoc-2013–14). For further discussion of the 2015–16 budget cuts, see Drèze 2017a.

Kerala Tops, Gujarat Flops, Bihar Hops

This essay was originally posted on the NDTV website. It is also available, along with details of the data and calculations, at www.ideasforindia.in. The child development index mentioned in the text was initially developed in Drèze and Khera 2012.

5

CHILD DEVELOPMENT AND ELEMENTARY EDUCATION

I F THERE IS ONE THING we have learnt from development economics in the last twenty years, it is the importance of elementary education for development. To state the obvious, education is of great help in many of the activities that make life worthwhile, and the process of learning has intrinsic value. Education also contributes to a variety of social goals, including economic progress, demographic change, social equity, and democratic practice. Seen in this light, the low priority attached to universal elementary education in twentieth-century India was a monumental blunder.

The victims were often blamed for their predicament. As recently as 1997, privileged Indians often claimed that "illiterate and semi-literate parents see no reason to send their children to school" (*Times of India*, 15 August 1997) or that literacy is not seen as a basic need among "the vast majority of adult illiterates belonging to the poor economic stratum" (*Indian Express*, same day). This view is one of the myths that were questioned in the Public Report on Basic Education in India, also known as the PROBE report (The PROBE Team, 1999), and firmly disproved soon after that as Indian children flocked to school at accelerating rates. The first essay in this section is a brief overview of the PROBE survey findings. It is included here as a reminder of how grim the schooling situation was in India just twenty years ago.

114

The PROBE report is based on a 1996 survey of primary schools in about 200 villages spread over the large Hindi-speaking states of North India (undivided Bihar, Madhya Pradesh, Rajasthan, and Uttar Pradesh). Ten years later, some members of the PROBE team conducted a re-survey in the same areas. Impressive progress was found in some aspects of the schooling system, including the schooling infrastructure, school participation rates, and the inclusion of disadvantaged groups. However, there was no improvement in classroom activity levels: in 2006, as in 1996, there was no teaching activity at all in half the schools sampled when the investigators arrived. As mentioned below in "Struggling to Learn", simple tests of children's learning achievements gave alarming results: barely half the pupils in Classes 4 and 5, for instance, could do single-digit multiplication in 2006.

It is important, of course, to remember that the PROBE survey (and the follow-up survey in 2006) happened in states that lag behind the rest of India in matters of social development, including elementary education. Companion surveys in Himachal Pradesh found that the schooling situation there was enormously better than in the PROBE states, and the same would also apply, say, in Kerala and Tamil Nadu. In fact, according to the first India Human Development Survey, pupil achievements in government schools in these states are higher than the corresponding all-India averages for children enrolled in *private* schools (who tend to have a relatively privileged background and good home support).[1] Other states tend to be somewhere between these topper states and the lagging states of North India. But there is certainly a massive problem of inadequate quality of school education across the country.

What is truly extraordinary is that this state of affairs is not a political issue in India. Yet the situation is unlikely to improve in the absence of a high-profile national initiative to enhance the quality of

---

[1] See Drèze and Sen 2013, Table 5.3, based on IHDS data for 2004–5. The statement applies to children in the age group of eight to eleven years.

schooling, especially in government schools. The schooling system has already shown its ability to bring about positive change in many fields, including school participation, infrastructural development, and the effective provision of school incentives (from midday meals to free bicycles). Similar energy needs to be brought to bear on the quality of education – India's schooling system will stand or fall on this challenge.

Other essays in this section are concerned mainly with children below the age of six years ("children under six" for short). The PROBE report inspired a similar study of anganwadis (child care centres), known as the Focus on Children Under Six (FOCUS) report. The anganwadi survey happened in 2004, when the Integrated Child Development Services (ICDS) were only beginning to receive serious attention in public policy. As it happens, just before the FOCUS report went to press in 13 December 2006, the supreme court issued a far-reaching order on the ICDS, declaring inter alia that all children under six were entitled to all ICDS services. Along with other efforts to rouse the government from slumber, led, inter alia, by India's right to food campaign, this gave a new lease of life to the programme. "Universalisation with quality", one of the main themes of the FOCUS report, became a widely accepted goal of the ICDS. Progress towards this goal was examined ten years later in a follow-up report called Progress of Children Under Six. Two essays in this section discuss child development in the light of these reports.

Class Struggle[*]

(with the PROBE Team)

The directive principles of the Indian constitution urge the state to provide "free and compulsory education for all children until they complete the age of fourteen years" within a period of ten years. Fifty years after this bold resolution, however, educational deprivation remains endemic, even in the younger age groups. According to the 1991 census, for instance, nearly half of all girls in the age group of 15–19 years are illiterate. The spread of elementary education is so slow that the absolute number of illiterate persons in India is still rising decade after decade. In 1991, it had reached nearly half a billion – more than the total population of the country thirty years earlier.

The Public Report on Basic Education (PROBE) attempts to shed light on the roots of this failure. This report is based on a detailed survey of the schooling system in North India. The survey was conducted in late 1996 in 188 randomly selected villages of Bihar, Madhya Pradesh, Rajasthan, and Uttar Pradesh. These four states account for over half of India's out-of-school children. Aside from making unannounced visits to all the primary schools (more precisely, all schools with a primary section) in the villages sampled, the survey teams interviewed 1221 randomly selected households.

Two Myths

The PROBE survey debunks two myths that have clouded clear thinking about the causes of educational deprivation in rural India.

[*]January 2000.

One resilient myth is that Indian parents have little interest in education. Contrary to this belief, the PROBE survey suggests that an overwhelming majority of parents, even among deprived sections of the population, attach great importance to the education of their children. For instance, a resounding 98 per cent of respondents felt that it was important for boys to go to school. For girls, the corresponding proportion was lower, but still very high: 89 per cent. Similarly, 98 per cent of all parents wanted their sons to receive at least eight years of education, and even for girls a large majority (63 per cent) had the same aspiration. Further, 80 per cent of parents felt that primary education should be made compulsory for all children. This is not to deny that pockets of indifference remain, especially when it comes to female education. Some parents bluntly said it was pointless for a girl to study since she would later be doing domestic work. It would be quite misleading, however, to regard the lack of parental motivation as the main obstacle to the universalisation of elementary education.

Another myth is that economic dependence on child labour is the main reason why poor families are unable to send their children to school. Contrary to this assumption, PROBE data on the time utilisation of children show that out-of-school children perform just two hours of extra work per day on average, compared with schoolgoing children. Further, the direction of causation does not necessarily run from child labour to non-attendance. In many cases, it is the other way around: dropouts take up productive work (of their own choice or through parental pressure) as a "default occupation". Eight-year-old Manoj in Karanjia village of Bihar, for instance, dropped out of school after being bullied by other children, and now spends his time grazing cattle. Even among children whose income-earning activities are essential for the family, the time spent in these activities often leaves much room for other occupations. Bearing in mind that school hours are short (at most six hours a day for 150–200 days in the year), the proportion of children whose work priorities are incompatible with schooling is likely to be small.

The Discouragement Effect

If parents are interested in education, and if child labour is not a major obstacle in most cases, why are so many children out of school? To understand this, the first point to note is that regular school attendance requires a great deal of effort on the part of parents as well as children. To begin with, schooling is expensive, in spite of free education being a constitutional right. The PROBE survey suggests that North Indian parents spend more than Rs 300 per year (on books, slates, clothes, etc.) to send a child to a government primary school. This may sound like a small amount, but it is a major financial burden for poor families, especially those with several children of schoolgoing age. To illustrate, an agricultural labourer in Bihar with two children would have to work for about forty days in the year just to send them to primary school.

In addition to the financial burden, much parental effort is required on a day-to-day basis to motivate children to go to school, ensure they make good progress, and free them from domestic chores. Effort is also needed from the children themselves, especially when the school environment is hostile or boring. The willingness of parents and children to make this effort depends a great deal on what they can expect in return, in terms of the quality of schooling. This basic problem is often *compounded* by other factors, such as the seasonal dependence on child labour and the gender bias in educational aspirations. These aggravating factors, however, should not divert attention from the fundamental mismatch between the quality of school education and the effort required to acquire it.

Dilapidated and Idle Classrooms

There are many aspects to the poor quality of schooling in rural India. First, the physical infrastructure is inadequate. In some villages, there is no infrastructure worth the name. In Vidya (Mandla district, Madhya Pradesh), for example, there is no school building.

Children are huddled in a dark, tiny storeroom and an adjacent open space where the owner keeps domestic animals. In some villages, the building is used by teachers for residential purposes. Elsewhere, the school premises are used as a store (Sawarna in Ujjain district, Madhya Pradesh), police camp (Baruhi in Bhojpur, Bihar), cattle shed (Belri Salehpur in Hardwar, Uttar Pradesh), public latrine (Vangaon in Saharsa, Bihar), or to dry cowdung cakes in (Mujahipur in Muzaffarnagar, Uttar Pradesh). These are extreme cases but even an average school boasts little more than two classrooms, a leaky roof, and some dilapidated furniture. The PROBE survey found that 82 per cent of the schools sampled needed major repair. Two-thirds had leaking roofs, making it difficult to hold classes when it rains.

Second, schools are short of teachers. The primary schools in the PROBE sample had about fifty children enrolled for each teacher, on average. Further, the distribution of teachers between schools is highly uneven, so that the pupil–teacher ratio is much higher than fifty in many schools, and even shoots up to three-digit figures in some cases.

Another aspect of teacher shortage is the continued existence of single-teacher schools (officially abolished under Operation Blackboard). In the sampled villages, 12 per cent of all primary schools had a single teacher. Another 21 per cent had a single teacher present on the day of the survey because the other teachers were absent. Thus, one-third of all schools had, effectively, only a single teacher.

Third, classroom activity is very low. Even among relatively conscientious teachers, coming late and leaving early is accepted practice. Others are worse, as Tejulal of Tigariya Sancha in Madhya Pradesh explained: *"Padhate nahi, turant chutti kar dete hain"* (They don't teach, they send us off at the earliest). In some villages, schools had been closed for a week at a time as the teachers had taken French leave.

Even when the teachers are present, there is little activity in the classroom. Controlling children is the priority. In half the schools sampled, there was no teaching activity at all when the investigators arrived.

Fourth, teaching methods are stultifying. The preferred method is copying – from the board or from textbooks. Even that is hardly monitored. In Golwa village (Ujjain, Madhya Pradesh), the PROBE team found that children's notebooks were filled with meaningless scribbles, page after page.

Teaching aids are seldom available, let alone used. Some schools have received new teaching aids (such as globes) under Operation Blackboard, but these are usually locked up and kept away from the children. In the classroom, the stick remains the most common teaching aid. *"Padhate kam, marte zyada"* (instead of teaching, they beat us) said one boy as he explained why he had dropped out.

Teachers, for their part, feel their work conditions are not conducive to better teaching methods. Three out of four were compelled to do multi-grade teaching. Some teachers deal with this by concentrating their efforts on the higher grades, leaving the younger children to their own devices.

In these circumstances, it is no wonder that pupil achievements are abysmal. The PROBE survey even found numbers of children who were unable to read or write after several years at school. Mohabai of Diwara village in Sawai Madhopur (Rajasthan) is one example. She is one of the few girls in Diwara who managed to reach Class 5. Alas, she is still unable to read or write.

Outlook

While the PROBE survey paints a grim picture of the schooling situation in North India, there is a sense in which these findings are good news. Had child labour or parental motivation been the main obstacles to universal elementary education, the government might have good reason to feel somewhat powerless. On the other hand, much can be done without delay to reduce the costs of schooling (e.g. by providing school meals), and to improve its quality (e.g. by raising teacher–pupil ratios). The main challenge seems to be to build the political commitment required for a radical improvement of the schooling system.

This has already happened in other states, and not just faraway Kerala. In Himachal Pradesh, for instance, elementary education became a top priority of public policy as soon as the state became independent in 1971. In a survey of forty-eight randomly selected villages in Himachal, conducted on the sidelines of the PROBE survey in late 1996, we found that 97 per cent of children in the age group of 6 to 12 years were going to school. Further, primary schools were doing much better in Himachal than in the PROBE states in terms of a range of quality indicators such as teacher–pupil ratios, levels of classroom activity, and parent–teacher co-operation. Universal elementary education had become a widely accepted norm, with 97 per cent of parents sampled wanting at least ten years of education for their daughters. This is all the more telling as Himachal had some of India's lowest literacy rates in the early 1950s. The speed of change was so impressive that we decided to include a chapter on "the schooling revolution in Himachal Pradesh" in the PROBE report. Let us hope similar revolutions happen in other states too.

The Welfare State in
Tamil Nadu*

Sometimes a little bit of fieldwork is worth years of academic study. So I felt last month after returning from a brief reconnaissance of rural Tamil Nadu with a former student. It was a revelation.

Our main object was to visit schools, health centres, and related facilities. I have done this off and on for some years in North India, and it is almost always a depressing experience. Millions of children waste their time and abilities in dysfunctional schools. Health centres, where they exist at all, provide virtually no services other than female sterilisation. Ration shops are closed most of the time. And other public amenities, from roads and electricity to drinking water, also tend to be in a pathetic state.

The situation seems radically different in Tamil Nadu. Though we visited only three districts (Kancheepuram, Nagapattinam, and Dharmapuri), the basic patterns were much the same everywhere and are likely to reflect the general situation in the state. For instance, each of the nine schools we visited enjoyed facilities that would be quite unusual in North India: a tidy building, basic furniture, teaching aids, drinking water, a midday meal, free textbooks, and regular health checkups. More importantly, the teachers were teaching, and most of them were even using the blackboard, a rare sight in North Indian schools. There was, of course, much scope for improvement, but at least children were learning in a fairly decent and stimulating environment.

*May 2003.

It was a joy to observe the midday meal programme in government schools. Everywhere, the meals were served on time according to a well-rehearsed routine. The children obviously enjoyed the experience, and the teachers felt very positive about it. Nowhere did we find any sign of the alleged drawbacks of midday meals, such as stomach upsets or disruptions of classroom activity. Seeing this first-hand, one wakes up to the fact that midday meals should really be seen as an essential feature of any decent primary school, like a blackboard.

We were also impressed with the health centres. They were clean, lively, and well-staffed. Plenty of medicines were available for free, and there were regular inspections. The walls were plastered with charts and posters giving details of the daily routine, facilities available, progress of various programmes, and related information. Patients streamed in and out, evidently at ease with the system. What a contrast with the bare, deserted, gloomy, hostile premises that pass for health centres in North India!

Another pleasant surprise was to find functional anganwadis (child care centres) in most villages. In North India, anganwadis are few and far between, and those that exist have little to offer, when they are open at all. Sometimes the local residents are not even aware of the fact that their village has an anganwadi. In Tamil Nadu, however, a functional anganwadi seems to be regarded as a normal feature of the village environment. Anganwadis have separate buildings, two or three helpers, cooked lunches, teaching aids, health checkups, and regular inspections. The helpers we met were well trained and gave us credible accounts of their daily routine.

The public distribution system (PDS) provides yet another example of the striking contrast between Tamil Nadu and North India as far as social services are concerned. In North India, collecting wheat or rice from the local ration shop is like extracting a tooth. The cardholders are sitting ducks for corrupt dealers, especially in remote areas where the latter have overwhelming power over their customers. Quite often, people have no idea of their entitlements and are unable to take action when cheated. But in Tamil Nadu we found that even uneducated

Dalit women were quite clear about their entitlements and knew how to enforce them. This pattern is consistent with secondary data: the National Sample Survey indicates that households in Tamil Nadu get the bulk of their PDS entitlements, in contrast with North India, where massive quantities of PDS grain end up in the open market.

I am not suggesting that social services in Tamil Nadu are flawless or even adequate. Even there, civic amenities fall short of the norms prescribed, say, by the directive principles of the constitution. Also, there are significant social inequalities in the provision of public services. But at least the rudiments of a credible welfare state are in place, and Tamil Nadu's experience (like Kerala's) points to far-reaching possibilities in this domain.

An obvious question arises as to why social services function so much better in Tamil Nadu or Kerala than in the bulk of North India. The question is beyond the scope of this brief article, but I venture to suggest that the contrast relates in part to the role of women in society. For one thing, women's votes in Tamil Nadu matter a great deal, because women are relatively well informed and vote with their own mind. This forces political leaders to pay attention to women's aspirations, including those relating to health and education. For another, women are the prime movers of social services in Tamil Nadu. All the facilities I have mentioned (with the exception of ration shops) are staffed mainly by women. And everywhere we went, there were signs of their special competence in these matters. It may not be an accident that the only North Indian state whose achievements in the field of social development are comparable to those of Tamil Nadu, namely Himachal Pradesh, also happens to have much in common with Tamil Nadu in terms of the role of women of society.

Children Under Six:
Out of Focus*

The draft Approach Paper to the 11th Plan, prepared by the Planning Commission, has been discussed and criticised from various perspectives. However, little attention has been paid to its worst blind spot: the state of Indian children, particularly those below the age of six.

The facts are well known. About half of all Indian children are undernourished, more than half suffer from anaemia, and a similar proportion escapes full immunisation. This humanitarian catastrophe is not just a loss for the children concerned and their families, and a violation of their fundamental rights, but also a tragedy for the nation as a whole. A decent society cannot be built on the ruins of hunger, malnutrition, and ill health.

Yet one is at a loss to find any serious discussion of these issues in the Approach Paper. Patient search uncovers a little "box", tucked away in the section on Sarva Shiksha Abhiyan, where children under six are finally mentioned. The box (two paragraphs) begins with the grand statement that "development of children is at the center of the 11th Plan", but does not give any inkling of what this actually implies. Instead, it essentially confines itself to the startling suggestion that anganwadis should "concentrate on inculcating good health and hygienic practices among the children".

The anganwadi scheme, officially known as the Integrated Child Development Services (ICDS), is the only major national scheme that addresses the needs of children under six. As things stand, less

*October 2006.

than half these children are registered under the ICDS. The Common Minimum Programme (CMP) clearly states that the UPA government will "universalize ICDS to provide a functional anganwadi in every settlement and ensure full coverage for all children". This step is also required for compliance with recent supreme court orders (*PUCL vs Union of India and Others, Civil Writ Petition 196 of 2001*). It would be natural, therefore, to expect the universalisation of ICDS to be one of the top priorities of the 11th Plan. None of this, however, finds mention in the Approach Paper.

The main argument for universalising the ICDS is that it is an essential means of safeguarding the rights of children under six – including their right to nutrition, health, and pre-school education. These rights are expressed in Article 39(f) of the Indian constitution, which directs the state to ensure that "children are given opportunities and facilities to develop in a healthy manner and in conditions of freedom and dignity". If we take children's rights seriously, an institutional medium is required to provide these "opportunities and facilities". That is the main role of the ICDS centre or anganwadi.

Apathy towards the ICDS in official circles appears to be linked with a perception that this programme is ineffective, if not useless. It is easy to provide superficial support to this claim by citing horror stories of idle anganwadis or food poisoning. These horror stories, however, are not a fair reflection of the general condition of the ICDS. Indeed, recent evidence suggests that the ICDS is actually performing crucial functions in many states, and that there is much scope for consolidating these achievements.

A recent survey of the ICDS, initiated by the Centre for Equity Studies, sheds some light on these issues. The survey, called Focus on Children Under Six (FOCUS), was conducted in May–June 2004 in six states: Chhattisgarh, Himachal Pradesh, Maharashtra, Rajasthan, Tamil Nadu, and Uttar Pradesh. It involved unannounced visits in a random sample of about 200 anganwadis, detailed interviews with local anganwadi workers and helpers, and further interviews with about 500 women (randomly selected among those who had at least one child below the age of six years, enrolled at the local anganwadi).

Among mothers with a child enrolled at the local anganwadi, more than 90 per cent said that the anganwadi opened "regularly". This is consistent with direct observation: nearly 80 per cent of the sample anganwadis were open at the time of the investigators' unannounced visit. Similarly, 94 per cent of the sample mothers stated that supplementary nutrition was being provided at the anganwadi. Even pre-school education, the weakest component of the ICDS, was happening in about half the anganwadis sampled. More than 70 per cent of mothers felt that the ICDS was "important" for their child's welfare.

This is not to deny that the quality of ICDS services needs urgent improvement in many states. But recognising the need for quality improvements is not the same as dismissing the ICDS as a nonfunctional programme. The FOCUS survey does not provide any justification for this defeatist outlook.

In fact, the survey findings highlight the enormous potential of the ICDS. This potential is well demonstrated in Tamil Nadu, where child nutrition has been a political priority for many years. Every anganwadi sampled in Tamil Nadu had an effective feeding programme, and almost all the mothers sampled were satisfied with the quality as well as the quantity of the food. Other basic ICDS services were also in good shape. For instance, 97 per cent of the mothers sampled in Tamil Nadu reported that children were being "weighed regularly", and 86 per cent said that useful educational activities were taking place at the anganwadi. Every single child in the Tamil Nadu sample had been immunised, fully so in a large majority of cases. Perhaps the best sign of real achievement in Tamil Nadu is the fact that 96 per cent of the mothers sampled considered the ICDS to be "important" for their child's well-being, and half of them considered it to be "very important".

While Tamil Nadu is an exemplary case of effective action in this field, success stories are not confined to this particular state.

Maharashtra, for instance, seems to be rapidly catching up with Tamil Nadu. To illustrate, the proportion of sampled mothers who stated that the local anganwadi opened regularly, or that their child was regularly weighed, or that immunisation services were available at the anganwadi, was above 90 per cent in each case. Much as in Tamil Nadu, 93 per cent of the mothers sampled in Maharashtra considered the ICDS to be important for their child's well-being. A large majority (60 per cent) also viewed the anganwadi worker as "a person who can help them in the event of health or nutrition problems in the family". While there were also areas of concern, notably the pre-school education programme, Maharashtra's experience clearly shows that Tamil Nadu's achievements can be emulated elsewhere.

In the northern states, the condition of the ICDS varied a great deal, from fairly encouraging in Himachal Pradesh to very poor in Uttar Pradesh (the usual "basket case" as far as public services are concerned). Even in the lagging states, however, the strong potential of the ICDS clearly emerged in villages with an active anganwadi. It is also important to note that these states have largely reaped as they sowed. Consider for instance the "supplementary nutrition programme" under the ICDS. There is much evidence that the best approach here is to combine nutritious, cooked food for children aged 3–6 years with well-designed "take-home rations" (together with nutrition counselling) for younger children. Yet many states are not even trying to take these simple steps to improve the nutrition component of the ICDS. For instance, in Rajasthan and Uttar Pradesh, children aged 3–6 years get the same bland "ready-to-eat" food (panjiri or murmura) day after day, and younger children get nothing at all. It is no wonder that the mothers sampled in these states were often dissatisfied with the programme.

Similar remarks apply to other hurdles that have plagued the ICDS in the northern states – lack of funds, understaffing, poor infrastructure, erratic supervision, inadequate training, and centralised management, among others. These shortcomings are curable, and their persistence essentially reflects a lack of political interest in the well-being and rights of children. In sharp contrast to Tamil Nadu, where child health and nutrition are lively political issues, the ICDS is at the rock bottom of policy concerns in the northern states.

It is against this background of political indifference to children under six that the CMP commitment "to provide a functional anganwadi in every settlement" was so important. In pursuit of this commitment, the National Advisory Council formulated detailed recommendations on the ICDS in November 2004, along with cost estimates and a proposed time frame for universalisation. These recommendations have been amplified and improved in a number of recent documents, such as the reports of the commissioners of the supreme court and the concluding statement of a convention on "children's right to food" held in Hyderabad in April 2006. Unfortunately, this wave of creative advice appears to be falling on deaf ears. It is certainly not reflected in the draft Approach Paper to the 11th Plan. An opportunity is being missed to rectify the catastrophic neglect of children under six in public policy and economic planning.

Struggling to Learn[*]
(with Anuradha De, Meera Samson, and A.K. Shiva Kumar)

How would you feel if half of the buses and trains that are supposed to be running on a particular day were cancelled at random every day of the year? Quite upset, surely (unless you can afford to fly). Yet, a similar disruption in the daily lives of children has been quietly happening for years on end, without any fuss: in rural North India, on an average day, there is no teaching activity in about half the primary schools.

Positive Changes

In late 1996, the PROBE team surveyed primary schools in about 200 villages of undivided Bihar, Madhya Pradesh, Rajasthan, and Uttar Pradesh – also known as the BIMARU states at that time. In 2006, we revisited the same areas to find out whether and how the schooling situation had changed over ten years. There were many signs of positive change.

First, school enrolment rates have risen sharply, e.g. from 80 to 95 per cent in the age group of 6–12 years. For the first time, the goal of universal school participation is within reach.

Second, social disparities in school enrolment have considerably narrowed. For instance, the gap between boys and girls has virtually disappeared (at the primary level). Enrolment rates among Scheduled

*February 2009.

Caste and Muslim children are very close to the sample average – about 95 per cent in each case. Enrolment among Scheduled Tribe children, however, is lower at 89 per cent.

Third, the schooling infrastructure has improved. For instance, the proportion of schools with at least two pacca (brick) rooms went up from 26 to 84 per cent between 1996 and 2006. Nearly three-fourths of all primary schools now have drinking water facilities. Toilets have been constructed in over 60 per cent of all schools.

Fourth, school incentives are reaching many more. To illustrate, free uniforms were provided in barely 10 per cent of primary schools in 1996, but this went up to more than half in 2006. Similarly, the proportion of schools where free textbooks were distributed was less than half in 1996, but close to 100 per cent in 2006.

Fifth, cooked midday meals have been introduced in primary schools – they were in place in 84 per cent of the sample schools in 2006. The bulk of the gap was in Bihar, where midday meals were still in the process of being initiated at the time of the survey.

Economic growth, rising parental literacy, and the rapid expansion of rural infrastructure and connectivity have certainly facilitated these achievements. But public initiatives such as Sarva Shiksha Abhiyan, supreme court orders on midday meals, and active campaigns for the right to education have also made a major contribution to this new momentum for the universalisation of elementary education.

Inside the Classroom

Having said this, the quality of education remains abysmal for a vast majority of Indian children. To start with, school enrolment does not mean regular attendance. Almost everywhere, children's attendance as noted in the school register was far below enrolment. And actual attendance, as observed by field investigators, was even lower.

Classroom activity levels, too, are very low. One reason for this is the shortage of teachers. Despite a major increase in the number of teachers appointed, the pupil–teacher ratio in the survey areas has shown little improvement over the years. The proportion of schools with only one teacher appointed has remained much the same – about 12 per cent. In 2006, an additional 21 per cent of schools were functioning as single-teacher schools on the day of the survey, on account of teacher absenteeism. Aggravating the situation is the fact that teachers often come late and leave early. Even when they are present, they are not necessarily teaching. In half the sample schools, there was no teaching activity at all when the investigators arrived – in 1996 as well as in 2006.

Even in the active classrooms, pupil achievements were very poor. Teaching methods are dominated by mindless copying and rote learning, e.g. chanting endless mathematical tables or reciting without comprehension. It is, thus, not surprising that children learn little in most schools. For instance, we found that barely half of the children in Classes 4 and 5 could do single-digit multiplication, or a simple division by five.

No Quick Fix

Some quick fixes have been tried, but with limited results. One of them is the appointment of "contract teachers", often seen by state governments as a means of expanding teacher cadres at relatively low cost. In the government primary schools surveyed, contract teachers account for nearly 40 per cent of all teachers. Due to the contractual nature of their appointment, and the fact that they are local residents selected by the gram panchayat, these contract teachers were expected to be more accountable than permanent teachers. This has not happened. The inadequate training and low salaries of contract teachers affect the quality of their work. In some schools, they were certainly more active than the permanent staff; in others, however, their connections with influential people in the village enabled them to take it easy.

Another way of improving school performance, related to the first, is to promote community involvement and decentralised school management. Most of the schools in our sample had a Village Education Committee (VEC) or some other committee of this sort. In many cases, these committees have helped to improve the school infrastructure, select contract teachers, and supervise midday meals. However, they have been much less effective in improving the levels of teaching activity. Power in most committees rests with the president (generally the sarpanch) and the secretary (generally the head-teacher), who need to be held accountable in the first place. With the exception of Parent – Teacher Associations (PTAs), the representation of parents in these committees tends to be nominal, and their active involvement is rare. The survey found numerous instances where committee members did not even know that their name had been included in the committee.

This does not detract from the importance of community participation in reviving classroom activity. But active and informed community participation requires much more than token committees, especially in India's divided and unequal social context.

A third quick fix is greater reliance on private schools. The proliferation of private schools in both urban and rural areas often creates an impression that this is the solution. A closer look at the evidence, however, does not support these expectations. The quality of private schools varies a great deal, and the cheaper ones (those that are accessible to poor families) are not very different from government schools. Their success in attracting children is not always a reflection of better teaching standards; some of them also take advantage of the ignorance of parents, e.g. with misleading claims of being "English medium". Further, a privatised schooling system, where education opportunities depend on one's ability to pay, is inherently inequitable. It also puts girls at a disadvantage: boys accounted for 74 per cent of all children enrolled in private schools in the 2006 survey (compared with 51 per cent of children enrolled in government schools). Private schooling therefore defeats one of the main purposes of universal elementary education – breaking the old barriers of class, caste, and gender in Indian society.

Despite the recent mushrooming of private schools, about 80 per cent of schoolgoing children in the households sampled were enrolled in government schools in 2006 – the same as in 1996. This situation makes it imperative to do something about classroom activity levels in government schools, instead of "giving up" on them.

Like the 1996 baseline, the follow-up study in 2006 included a separate survey in Himachal Pradesh, where we found that the schooling situation was much better. For instance, 99 per cent of all children in the age group of 6–12 years were enrolled, and 92 per cent of those enrolled were at school on the day of the survey, compared with just 66 per cent in the other states. Schools in Himachal also had higher levels of teaching activity. Further, VECs and PTAs were generally functional. Interestingly, this success is not based on any quick fix, but on responsible management of a traditional schooling system, based on government schools and regular teachers, with a little help from a relatively egalitarian social context.

The Future

The title of the last chapter of the PROBE Report, published in 1999, was "Change is Possible". In many ways, this assertion has come true. Much has indeed changed – for the better – in the schooling system during the last ten years or so. The need of the hour is to consolidate the momentum of positive change and extend it to new areas – particularly those of classroom activity and quality education. The forthcoming Right to Education Act may help. But the first step is to stop tolerating the gross injustice that is being done to Indian children by wasting their time day after day in idle classrooms.

Progress of
Children Under Six*

No social programme in India is more exciting, more critical, or more promising than the Integrated Child Development Services (ICDS). A colourful and lively anganwadi, where young children get a taste not only of nutritious food but also of the joy of learning, is a ray of hope for the entire village. The future of Indian children, and indeed of the country, is being shaped in these modest premises managed by local women.

Having said this, the ICDS is also one of India's most neglected schemes. That was one of the key messages of Focus on Children Under Six (FOCUS) report, discussed earlier. A few days before the FOCUS report was released, on 13 December 2006, the supreme court issued far-reaching orders on the ICDS. All children below the age of six years were declared to be entitled to all ICDS services. The Government of India was directed to increase the number of anganwadis from about 7 lakh to 14 lakh (roughly, one per habitation). Settlements with at least forty children below six years but no anganwadi were entitled to being provided with an anganwadi on demand.

These orders were of great help in creating a new momentum for the ICDS. Anganwadis, like schools, came to be regarded as an essential facility for every village. Public expenditure on the ICDS shot up, and the programme also started receiving greater attention in public debates and democratic politics. Repeated attempts by

*September 2016.

commercial interests to invade the programme met with spirited resistance. There were also lively discussions about the "restructuring of ICDS", eventually leading to major improvements in the guidelines.

Against this background, the findings of the recent Progress of Children Under Six (POCUS) report are relatively encouraging. This report is based on a resurvey of the FOCUS districts ten years on (in 2014), and suggests significant quality improvements. Two of the formerly dormant states (Chhattisgarh and Rajasthan) had a much more active ICDS programme by 2014 – Uttar Pradesh, alas, was still far behind. Taking the six FOCUS states together, significant improvements are evident in the quantity and quality of food supplements, the regularity of child attendance, the maintenance of growth charts, and related matters. Consider for instance the proportion of mothers sampled who stated that their child attends the anganwadi regularly, or that immunisation services are provided there, or that pre-school activities under the ICDS benefit their child. In each case, the proportion was 80 per cent or more in 2014, compared with 40 to 50 per cent in 2004. Similarly, the proportion of mothers sampled who felt that the ICDS is "important for their child's welfare" increased from 48 per cent in 2004 to 84 per cent in 2014. The fact that quality improvements took place during a phase of rapid quantitative expansion is good news. As quantitative expansion becomes less urgent, there will hopefully be greater scope for qualitative improvements in the near future.

Further evidence of slow but steady progress in the performance of the ICDS has recently emerged from the Rapid Survey on Children 2013–14 (RSOC). Good practices such as the provision of nutritious food, the maintenance of growth charts, and pre-school education activities at the anganwadi are becoming the norm in large parts of the country. To illustrate, one way of spotting a well-managed anganwadi is to check whether children's growth charts are being maintained. According to the RSOC, this was the case in a large majority of anganwadis in twelve out of twenty major states, including Chhattisgarh, Odisha, and West Bengal aside from the usual suspects.

Of course, the shortfalls remain huge, especially in states like Bihar and Uttar Pradesh. Even in the lagging states, however, there are signs of improvement in ICDS-related indicators. As mentioned earlier, for instance, Bihar achieved the largest improvements in child immunisation and coverage of antenatal care between 2005–6 and 2013–14, starting of course from a very low base.

Another experience of much interest is that of Odisha, one of India's poorest states, not known for exemplary governance. In a recent survey of about 50 randomly selected anganwadis in four districts of Odisha, we found that anganwadis opened regularly and provided most of the prescribed services. Supplementary nutrition is part of the daily routine, with an improved menu, including eggs twice or thrice a week. Pre-school education is taking root: at more than three-quarters of anganwadis, children were able to recite a poem when asked. Health services such as growth monitoring, immunisation, and ante-natal care were also provided regularly, in collaboration with the local Auxiliary Nurse Midwife (ANM) and Accredited Social Health Activist (ASHA). Further, Odisha has developed an effective model of decentralised production of take-home rations for children below the age of three years, involving women's self-help groups. Take-home rations in Odisha include eggs, not only for young children but also for pregnant and lactating women. This is an important innovation: children below three are the most critical age group, yet ICDS has tended to be more focused, so far, on children in the age group of three to six years.

It is also worth noting that significant evidence has emerged, in recent years, of the impact (or potential impact) of the ICDS on the well-being of Indian children. For instance, there is some econometric evidence of positive effects of the ICDS on child nutrition, child education, and related outcomes from recent studies by Gautam Hazarika, Monica Jain, Eeshani Kandpal, Nitya Mittal, Arindam Nandi, and their respective colleagues. Recent findings from the second Indian Human Development Survey (2011–12) and the RSOC also point to a marked acceleration in the progress of child development indicators after 2005–6 (the reference year for the third National Family Health Survey). It is quite plausible that the ICDS has contributed to this, along with related initiatives such as the National Rural Health Mission.

Alas, the Government of India seems to be returning to the days of vacillation on the ICDS that preceded the supreme court orders of December 2006. In the union budget 2015–16, ICDS funds were slashed by a staggering 50 per cent or so, though the cuts were partly reversed later in the year due to public criticism (including dissent from the government's very own minister of women and child development, Maneka Gandhi). The cuts were sought to be justified on the grounds that the share of state governments in the divisible pool of taxes had been raised from 32 to 42 per cent, in line with the recommendations of the Fourteenth Finance Commission. But this does not explain why the axe should have fallen most heavily on children's programmes (not only the ICDS but also school meals). This move sent a disastrous signal about the social priorities of the central government – a signal that could cause much damage down the line. Some state governments, notably the Government of Odisha, have already complained in strong terms about the devastating consequences of the central budget cuts.

These setbacks make it more important than ever before to stand up for children's rights, including their right to the full spectrum of ICDS services – nutrition, health care, and pre-school education. The silver lining is that, despite this slackening of central support, progress appears to continue at the state level. For instance, many states are now serving eggs in anganwadis: Andhra Pradesh, Odisha, Tamil Nadu, Telangana, West Bengal, and even Bihar. Growing attention is being given to pre-school education as a core activity of the ICDS. Uttar Pradesh has finally moved away from panjiri to cooked meals for children in the age group of three to six years. All these are small steps forward, and the overarching pattern of gross neglect of children under six (the most important age group for lifelong health and well-being) continues. But the last ten years or so have at least demonstrated the possibility of accelerated progress in this field. Even the central government's indifference towards the ICDS is not irreversible.

Notes

Class Struggle

This essay is based on the PROBE report (The PROBE Team, 1999). An earlier, longer version with the same title was published in *India Today* as an illustrated cover story, on 13 October 1997. The literacy figures are from India's decennial census.

The Welfare State in Tamil Nadu

For further discussion of the welfare state in Tamil Nadu, see Drèze and Sen 2013, Vivek S. 2015, and earlier studies cited there.

Children Under Six: Out of Focus

This essay is based on early tabulations of the FOCUS survey data. For a more detailed discussion of the ICDS and the FOCUS survey, see Citizens' Initiative for the Rights of Children Under Six 2006, and Drèze 2006.

Struggling to Learn

This essay is based on De, *et al.* 2011, a follow-up to the PROBE report. A longer version was published in *Frontline* on 14 March 2009, under the title "Education: Report Card". More detailed information on pupil achievements in India is available from the India Human Development Surveys, PRATHAM's Annual Status of Education Reports, and the NCERT's National Achievement Surveys.

Progress of Children Under Six

This essay is based on the Progress of Children Under Six report (Centre for Equity Studies 2016) and the RSOC 2013–14 fact-sheets. The Odisha survey is discussed in Khera 2015. Maneka Gandhi's criticisms of the ICDS budget cuts (including her statement that the cuts had made it "a month-to-month suspense on whether we can meet wages") were reported by Reuters, and widely discussed in the Indian media. For further details of recent econometric studies of the ICDS, see Drèze and Khera 2017. On the progress of child development indicators between 2005–6 and 2013–14, see Sinha 2015, and also section 4 of this book.

6

EMPLOYMENT GUARANTEE

INDIA'S NATIONAL RURAL EMPLOYMENT Guarantee Act (NREGA) builds on the simple idea that people who have no better means of livelihood should have a right to be employed on local public works at a minimum wage. Other important entitlements under the act include payment within fifteen days, basic worksite facilities, and an unemployment allowance if work is not provided. The act can serve many useful objectives: enhancing economic security, empowering rural women, activating gram sabhas, protecting the environment, restraining distress migration, creating productive assets, and promoting social equity, among others.

The early years of NREGA were a time of hope and progress. Within a few months of the programme being launched (on 2 February 2006), millions of workers found employment at NREGA worksites. Women who had never earned an income of their own got a chance to work for the minimum wage at their doorstep. Gram sabhas gradually came to life in areas where they had rarely been seen before. Thousands of NGOs started awareness campaigns, social audits, and other NREGA-related activities. Corruption was fought step by step. Slowly but – it seemed – surely, things improved year after year, sustaining the hope.

Five years on, it looked like NREGA could claim some real achievements. The scale of employment was staggering: 219 crore person-days in 2011–12, according to official data, largely reflected in independent survey data for the same year.[1] The majority of NREGA workers were women (who have a very low share of employment in the economy as a whole), and more than half were Dalits or Adivasis. Further, the programme helped rural workers in general, by putting some upward pressure on market wages. Much good also happened, and continues to happen, in terms of the other objectives mentioned earlier.

Even as these low-hanging (and some medium-height) fruits were being reaped, however, it became clear that NREGA still had a long way to go in "creating accountability", as the first essay in this section puts it – accountability of the state to rural workers. One symptom of this was the routine violation of workers' entitlements, from work-on-demand to timely payment. Many other implementation problems, such as continued corruption and the poor quality of NREGA assets, can also be seen as a consequence of this lack of accountability.

The latter, in turn, reflects a deep contradiction or at least tension with NREGA: it is a pro-worker law implemented by an anti-worker system – a system pervaded by indifference if not hostility towards marginalised people in general and rural workers in particular. This may sound like a harsh statement. There are, of course, many committed individuals at all levels of the Indian administration. In general, however, a huge social distance separates government officials from NREGA workers. A junior engineer, say, is far more likely to seek ways of siphoning off NREGA funds than to work overtime for the benefit of NREGA workers. The resilient problem of delayed wage payments also relates to this feature of the system: the hardships endured by the victims are of little consequence to those who might be able to speed up the payments – the panchayat secretary, the block development officer, and so on.

[1] See the last essay in this section. Official employment figures have remained above 200 crore person-days per year ever since (except in 2014–15, when they declined sharply due to budget caps), but the latest independent estimates at the time of writing go back to 2011–12.

A number of accountability provisions were included in the act, such as the unemployment allowance, a penalty clause, and compensation for delayed payments. These provisions, however, remain under the control of the government, so they have been quietly ignored or disabled. The legal system (one possible means of grievance redressal) is of little help, inaccessible as it tends to be to ordinary workers. Indeed, it is a remarkable fact that ten years after NREGA came into force, not a single worker has gone to court to claim his or her rights under the act.

When the act was framed, it was expected that workers' organisations would help to create accountability. This organisational process, however, has proved slow and sporadic. One reason for this is that NREGA workers, unlike formal-sector workers, have no real bargaining power. Without that, it is difficult to organise. And without collective organisation, NREGA workers remain at the mercy of the state. There is quite a vicious circle here.

This fundamental issue of low accountability, and its multiple manifestations, continue to haunt NREGA today. Meanwhile, the central government has tried to address implementation problems mainly through top-down technological fixes: digitisation, e-muster rolls, Aadhaar-enabled payments, geo-tagging, and so on. The jury is out on their effectiveness, but personally I am a little sceptical. In fact, I would not be surprised if some of them had led to a revival of corruption (largely removed from NREGA by 2011–12, at least in the wage component of expenditure) in recent years. The growing centralisation and complexity of NREGA are creating their own problems. These new challenges are not covered in this book, but they loom large over the future of NREGA.

Ten years after the act came into force, there is no reason to give up the basic idea that people without an adequate means of livelihood can be helpfully employed on local public works. The experience so far shows that effective implementation of NREGA has wide-ranging benefits, well beyond poverty alleviation. However, realising this potential (especially in the poorer states) poses huge organisational and political challenges. Much remains to be done to achieve the initial vision of the act.

The essays that follow only scratch the surface of this vast canvas, and all I can hope is that they will motivate further reading. I take this opportunity to clarify that my role as a so-called architect of NREGA has been greatly exaggerated by the Indian media. Journalists like to single someone out, but the thinking behind NREGA was really a collective effort. If there was an architect at all, it was Nikhil Dey, who had most of the law worked out in his head, though I did help him to put it in writing. We took Maharashtra's Employment Guarantee Act (which goes back to the early 1970s) as a starting point, updated and adapted it as an enabling national law, and circulated a draft. The draft then went through a long process of discussion and revision – first among concerned citizens, then in the National Advisory Council, and after that through various ministries and finally in parliament. The final version, naturally, was very different from the first draft – mostly for the better.

Employment as a
Social Responsibility*

The draft National Rural Employment Guarantee Act has recently entered national policy debates like a wet dog at a glamorous party. The demand for an employment guarantee act is not new, but a series of unlikely events has catapulted it from obscurity to the top of the political agenda.

The proposed act gives a legal guarantee of employment in rural areas to anyone who is willing to do casual manual labour at the statutory minimum wage. Any adult who applies for work under the act is entitled to being employed on local public works within fifteen days. Failing that, an unemployment allowance has to be paid. The guarantee is subject to an initial limit of hundred days of work per household a year.

The need for an act has been questioned. Why is it not enough to initiate massive employment schemes? The main answer is that an act places an enforceable obligation on the state and gives bargaining power to labourers. It creates accountability. By contrast, a scheme leaves labourers at the mercy of government officials.

There is another major difference between a scheme and an act. Schemes come and go, but laws are more durable. A scheme can be trimmed or even cancelled by a bureaucrat, whereas changing a law requires an amendment in parliament. If an Employment Guarantee Act (EGA) is passed, labourers will have durable legal entitlements. Over time, they are likely to become aware of their rights and learn how to defend them.

*November 2004.

Opposition to an EGA often arises from a failure to appreciate its far-reaching economic, social, and political significance. To start with, an EGA would go a long way towards protecting rural households from poverty and hunger. In fact, a full-fledged EGA would enable most poor households in rural India to cross the poverty line. Second, it would lead to a sharp reduction of rural–urban migration: if work is available in the village, many rural families will stop heading for the cities during the slack season.

Third, guaranteed employment would be a major source of empowerment for women. A large proportion of labourers employed under an EGA are likely to be women, and guaranteed employment will give them some economic independence. Fourth, an EGA is an opportunity to create useful assets in rural areas. In particular, there is a massive potential for labour-intensive public works in the field of environmental protection: watershed development, land regeneration, prevention of soil erosion, restoration of tanks, protection of forests, and related activities.

Fifth, guaranteed employment is likely to change power equations in rural society, and to foster a more equitable social order. Finally, an EGA is a unique opportunity to activate and empower panchayati raj institutions, including gram panchayats and gram sabhas. It will give them a new purpose, backed with substantial financial resources.

Having said this, an EGA would not come cheap. Even those who are otherwise sympathetic to the idea often wonder whether it is affordable. It is interesting that similar concerns have seldom been raised with respect to the "interlinking of rivers" project. The cost of this project is far greater, and its benefits (if any) far more speculative, than those of an EGA. Yet the project easily mustered support from some of the country's most prestigious institutions and personalities, based on the flimsiest possible arguments. It would be surprising if this had nothing to do with the fact that the interlinking project is a potential bonanza for the corporate sector.

Be that as it may, the economic viability of employment guarantee needs to be examined in its own terms, and not by comparison with extravagant projects. In the note on this issue prepared by the National Advisory Council, the cost of employment guarantee is anticipated to rise from 0.5 per cent of GDP in 2005–6 to 1 per cent of GDP in 2008–9. This is based on the assumption that the scheme is gradually extended to the whole of India within four years, starting with the 150 poorest districts.

The anticipated cost of 1 per cent of GDP is a financial cost. It is arguable that the "real" cost would be much lower. For instance, the financial cost of employing a labourer on public works is the statutory minimum wage, but the economic cost (the real resources foregone) may not be so high if the labourer is otherwise unemployed. However, even if the real cost of employment guarantee is as high as 1 per cent of GDP, there is no cause for panic.

The challenge of financing employment guarantee has to be seen in the light of the fact that India's tax–GDP ratio is very low from an international perspective: about 15 per cent (for the centre and the states combined) compared with, say, 37 per cent in OECD countries. Further, India's tax–GDP ratio has declined in recent years. For instance, the ratio of central taxes to GDP was only 9.3 per cent in 2003–4, compared with 10.6 per cent in 1987–8. These are some indications, among others, suggesting there is much scope for raising India's tax–GDP ratio to finance employment guarantee and related social programmes.

On the nuts and bolts of enhancing tax revenue, there are useful hints in the recent "Kelkar 2" report submitted to the ministry of finance. Some aspects of this report are questionable, including its fixation with uniform taxes and its touching faith in the scope for raising revenue by lowering tax rates. Nevertheless, the report also suggests many sensible ways of raising the tax–GDP ratio, such as introducing value-added taxes, extending taxation to most services, using information technology to broaden the tax net, eliminating arbitrary exemptions, and (last but not least) fighting tax evasion. If these opportunities are well utilised, Plan expenditure can be raised by much more than 1 per cent of India's GDP.

Further, there is no need to stop at "Kelkar 2". Many other financing options can be considered. For instance, a recent World Bank study estimates that lifting the anachronistic cap on the Professions Tax would enable state governments to collect additional tax revenue to the tune of 0.9 per cent of GDP.

Similarly, much revenue could be generated from "green taxes" on environmentally harmful consumption, or more generally on anti-social activities. There is also much scope for pruning unnecessary public expenditure, starting with military expenditure and subsidies for the rich – there are many. In short, the fundamental ability of the Indian economy to sustain employment guarantee is not in doubt. What is required is imagination and commitment in tapping that potential.

Some of these proposals are likely to be opposed by those who stand to gain from the status quo, as happened with the introduction of VAT as well as with the "capital transactions" tax. One way around it is to link tax reforms more clearly with positive initiatives such as the EGA. Instead of piecemeal reforms, often derailed by vested interests, the need of the hour is for a comprehensive "new deal", involving a higher tax–GDP ratio but also better use of tax revenue. A package of this kind has a greater chance of success than piecemeal reform.

"Tax the rich" would be a useful guiding principle for this package. During the last twenty years or so, the so-called middle class (i.e. the top 5 per cent or so of the income distribution) has become rich beyond its wildest dreams. It has literally transplanted itself to the first world without even applying for a visa. The time to share is long overdue.

The onset of cold weather in the capital is a good time to ponder over these matters. This year again, thousands of people are going to die in agony because they do not possess as much as a blanket to cover their emaciated bodies at night. The slaughter will be attributed to a "cold wave" but the real issue is the dreadful poverty in which people have been allowed to live decade after decade. This is not just a tragedy for the victims, but also a deep scar on the national fabric.

It affects everything, from the self-respect of the nation to the quality of democracy.

To put it differently, there are two ways of thinking about the proposed EGA. One is to see it as a pitched battle between the working class and the privileged classes. Another is to regard it as a national endeavour – a visionary initiative in which most citizens have a stake in one way or another. There is some truth in both perceptions, but so far the first one has dominated public debates. Better recognition of the wide-ranging social benefits of an EGA is likely to put the issue in a different light.

Employment Guarantee and
Its Discontents*

In *Manufacturing Consent* and other writings, Noam Chomsky presents an illuminating analysis of propaganda techniques in democratic societies. One of these techniques is "flak" – a barrage of attacks on ideas that challenge the interests of established power. The Employment Guarantee Act (EGA), no doubt a "dangerous" idea, has been the target of two waves of flak in recent months. The first occurred around December 2004, when the National Rural Employment Guarantee Bill was tabled in parliament. The second started earlier this month, just after the political leadership of the United Progressive Alliance (UPA) government threw its weight behind some key recommendations of the parliament's Standing Committee on Rural Development.

Unseemly Arguments

As Chomsky observes, flak often involves personal attacks, and that certainly applies in this case. Dr Surjit Bhalla, for instance, attacked the so-called "leaders" of the pro-EGA campaign as "liars" and also accused them of being "arrogant", "ignorant", and "brazen", among other colourful epithets (*Business Standard*, 25 December 2004 and 8 January 2005). Swapan Dasgupta called some of us "jholawala economists", as if there was something indecent about an economist carrying a jhola instead of a corporate briefcase. Tavleen Singh used the same term (no copyright it seems), and extended it to the entire

*August 2005.

National Advisory Council, dismissed as "a bunch of jholewalas with their hearts in the right place but their worn out sandals walking the wrong way" (*Indian Express*, 6 February 2005). She argued that instead of these jholewalas, the National Advisory Council needed "people like Sam Pitroda", apparently forgetting that Sam Pitroda was in the NAC at the time.

Even fratricide has figured in this merciless crusade. Jairam Ramesh, otherwise known as the "poster boy of economic reforms", was recently called a "turncoat" in the business media for support- ing EGA and related ideas (*DNA*, 7 August 2005). "What is he smoking these days?", asked an aghast member of the pro-reform brotherhood quoted in the article.

Aside from personal attacks, deceptive statistics played a major role in this propaganda operation. Surjit Bhalla deployed some of his most spectacular hat-tricks to rubbish the Employment Guaran- tee Act. He even managed to show, based on a creative reading of National Sample Survey data, that "poor agricultural workers had an unemployment rate of only 1 per cent" (*Business Standard*, 25 December 2004). Ergo, the Employment Guarantee Act is not required. As the late Sudhir Mulji soberly observed: "That the magni- tude of unemployment is substantially higher than one per cent inferred by analysts of NSS data is obvious to even casual observers if not to skilled statisticians" (*Business Standard*, 20 January 2005). It is worth adding that Dr Bhalla's figures do not stand the scrutiny of serious "analysts of NSS data".

In a related genre, statistical hyperbole has been widely used to produce scary estimates of the cost of an Employment Guarantee Act. Bibek Debroy, for instance, came up with a figure of Rs 208,000 crores per year (*Indian Express*, 23 October 2004). In per capita terms, this is almost twenty times as much as the cost of Maharashtra's Employ- ment Guarantee Act, which is more liberal than the proposed National Rural Employment Guarantee Bill.

It is also interesting to consider the alternatives that have been proposed by these and other opponents of EGA. The first prize for creativity goes to Swaminathan Aiyar, who suggested dropping cash from helicopters instead of asking people to work for wages (*Times of India*, 19 December 2004). Shankar Acharya argued that "the first best option would be to do nothing" (*Business Standard*, 30 November 2004). Bibek Debroy tersely said that it would be "better to have unemployment insurance alone, without the employment guarantee" (*Indian Express*, 13 October 2004), without explaining how a universal unemployment insurance scheme could possibly work in rural India. T.C.A. Srinivasa-Raghavan suggested taking refuge in Section 80G of the Income Tax Act, which allows donations to charity to be deducted from tax: "re-examine 80G, tighten it, and direct it for rural employment creation" (*Business Standard*, 19 December 2004).

For once, Surjit Bhalla was the least unreasonable: he suggested universal cash transfers as an alternative to EGA. I leave it to the reader to guess whether this is a serious proposal, or just another stick with which to beat the act. Be that as it may, the proposal can easily be accommodated. All one has to do is to insert a clause in the act stating that if the government prefers to pay the equivalent of a hundred days' wages to every household in a particular district, instead of organising public works, it is free to do so.

Fireworks aside, is there any substance in this chorus of protest against the EGA? I believe there is. As Anatol Rapoport pointed out in his illuminating work on ethical debate, even the most outlandish statements often have their "domain of validity". For instance, the statement "black is white" makes sense in the limited circumstance where one is looking at the negative of a photograph. Similarly, there is an important message in these shrill interventions – more on this below.

Employment and Empowerment

The proposed Employment Guarantee Act has found wide support among political parties, social movements, and the public at large.

This broad support is reflected in the recent report of the Standing Committee on Rural Development, aptly described by the finance minister as a "microcosm of Parliament".

Opposition to the act has come chiefly from a small but powerful section of the corporate sector and its allies in government. It tends to be rooted in a "minimalist" view of the role of the state in the social sector. In an article with a transparent title ("Can the State Really Help the Poor?"), T.C.A. Srinivasa-Raghavan clearly articulated the main argument of the minimalists: "those who think that the money will reach the intended beneficiaries are living in a fool's paradise" (*Business Standard*, 19 December 2004). Similar statements can be found in most of the writings cited earlier.

This argument should not be lightly dismissed. The record of anti-poverty programmes in India is far from encouraging. Early feedback on the National Food For Work Programme (NFFWP), from a recent survey conducted by students from Delhi University and Jawaharlal Nehru University, is also sobering. The survey suggests that the programme is a potential lifeline for the rural poor, and also has many other positive effects, from slowing down rural–urban migration to the creation of useful assets. However, much of this potential has been wasted due to widespread corruption.

The issue is whether this situation is immutable, or whether corruption can be eradicated from public works programmes. The minimalists feel that corruption is an intrinsic feature of these programmes, but recent experience suggests otherwise.

One development of interest is the cleaning of "muster rolls" (work attendance sheets) in Rajasthan. Fudging muster rolls is the principal method through which public funds are siphoned off from rural employment programmes. For instance, unscrupulous officials enter fake names in the muster rolls and appropriate the wages of the fictitious labourers. This has been going on for decades all over India. In Rajasthan, however, this practice has been significantly curtailed, at least in areas where active use has been made of the state's Right to Information Act. This is largely a reflection not only of the accessibility of the muster rolls under the act, but also of the culture of public vigilance and bureaucratic accountability that has started spreading in Rajasthan in the wake of the right to information movement.

The NFFWP survey mentioned earlier confirms that Rajasthan is different from other states in this respect. In each of the other five sampled states (Chhattisgarh, Jharkhand, Madhya Pradesh, Uttar Pradesh, West Bengal), the muster rolls were virtually impossible to trace. In rare cases where they could be traced, simple verification exercises uncovered massive fudging. In Rajasthan, however, the muster rolls were easy to obtain and were, by and large, accurate.

There is much to learn from this experience. First, corruption is not an immutable feature of rural development programmes. Second, the best way to fight corruption in public works is to empower the victims of fraud and embezzlement – starting with the labourers, for whom it is a matter of life and death. Third, the right to information is a powerful tool of empowerment. The national Right to Information Act, which is due to come into force next month, is a major breakthrough in this respect. Fourth, a law is not enough – legal rights have to be combined with a process of public mobilisation that enables people to exercise those rights.

The Employment Guarantee Act is an opportunity to take this process much further than it has gone in Rajasthan. Like the Right to Information Act, the EGA is an important tool of empowerment. It puts in place legal safeguards and accountability mechanisms that strengthen the bargaining power of labourers: job cards for all workers, pro-active disclosure of muster rolls, mandatory social audits by gram sabhas, penalties for any violation of the law, among others. The act will also give labourers a new opportunity to organise. This feature of Maharashtra's EGA is well conveyed in a recent study by Anuradha Joshi, who says a strong national EGA is likely to lead to "a flourishing of activist organisations that would help mobilise the poor in their interests".

Thus, while the EGA is widely regarded as a potential fountain of corruption, it can also be seen (along with the Right to Information

Act) as an integral part of the battle for restoring accountability in rural development programmes. There is a possible meeting ground here for the "minimalists" and their opponents.

The premise of the Employment Guarantee Act is that every adult has a right to basic employment opportunities at the statutory minimum wage. It is a political initiative based on the state's responsibility to protect the right to work. The existence of corruption should not be used as an excuse to abdicate this responsibility – it can and must be fought.

Myths and Reality of Corruption*
(with Reetika Khera and Siddhartha)

The National Rural Employment Guarantee Act (NREGA), launched two years ago in 200 districts, is going through a critical learning phase. During this period, there are bound to be many procedural problems, all the more so as the NREGA guidelines are very exacting. This does not detract from the fundamentally positive nature of the initiative, or from the possibility of making it a success. But it did give the Comptroller and Auditor General (CAG) good reasons to demand remedial action when the programme came under its redoubtable scanner.

Contrary to media reports, the draft CAG report on NREGA does not present much evidence of large-scale embezzlement of funds, nor does it conclude that NREGA is "a failure". The report focuses mainly on procedural lapses, and constructive ways to address them. This is a useful wake-up call, just a few weeks ahead of the extension of NREGA to the whole country.

The question remains whether NREGA funds actually reach the poor. In this connection, we report here some findings of recent "muster roll verification exercises" initiated by the G.B. Pant Social Science Institute, Allahabad. The survey teams consisted of carefully trained students from Delhi University and elsewhere. The muster rolls were selected through random sampling and obtained just before the survey, leaving little scope for window dressing. The investigators

*January 2008.

interviewed the labourers listed in a particular muster roll and asked them to confirm the details of days worked and wages earned.

The methodology of muster roll verification was developed in Rajasthan in the context of the right to information movement. This learning process was also an opportunity to develop a range of transparency safeguards for public works schemes (such as the proactive disclosure of muster rolls, regular maintenance of job cards, and social audits). Many of them have been incorporated in the operational guidelines of NREGA, and even in the act itself. There is a good deal of informal evidence from Rajasthan that these safeguards can go a long way in preventing corruption. We have reported some of our own observations on this elsewhere (*The Hindu*, 13 July 2007).

This new series of verification exercises started in May–June 2007 in Jharkhand and Chhattisgarh, in areas where we had found evidence of large-scale corruption just two years earlier, under the National Food For Work Programme (NFFWP). For instance, in Surguja district of Chhattisgarh there was virtually no check on the embezzlement of NFFWP funds at the time. The situation was so bad that one of us was constrained to describe the NFFWP as a "Loot For Work Programme" (*Times of India*, 2 July 2005). In the same district, we were interested to hear this year, from a wide range of sources, that the enactment of NREGA had led to a steep decline in the incidence of corruption. This was borne out by the muster roll verification exercises: in a random sample of nine works implemented by gram panchayats, we found that 95 per cent of the wages that had been paid according to the muster rolls had actually reached the concerned labourers. A similar exercise conducted in Koriya, the neighbouring district, led to similar estimates of leakages in the labour component of NREGA – only 5 per cent or so.

In Jharkhand, detailed muster roll verification of NREGA works in five randomly selected gram panchayats of Ranchi district suggested leakages of around 33 per cent. Clearly, this is totally unacceptable, but even this high figure (one of the highest we found anywhere, outside Orissa) would not justify the claim that the bulk of NREGA funds fail to reach the poor. Further, in Jharkhand too there was evidence of a gradual retreat of corruption compared with earlier years, when it was not uncommon to find that entire muster rolls had been manufactured from top to bottom.

Next we went to Tamil Nadu to participate in a social audit of NREGA in Villupuram district, conducted in July–August 2007. There we found much evidence of serious efforts to prevent the spread of corruption in NREGA. For instance, the Government of Tamil Nadu has initiated an imaginative system of muster roll maintenance, whereby each labourer has to enter her signature or thumbprint in the muster roll every day by way of marking attendance. This ensures not only that the muster roll is available for public scrutiny at the worksite, as required by the NREGA guidelines, but also that large numbers of people actually see it every day. In this and other ways, much progress had evidently been made towards a corruption-proof system. Unfortunately, it was not possible to quantify the leakages, as the Villupuram social audit did not include systematic muster roll verification exercises.

A brief follow-up visit to Andhra Pradesh enabled us to observe and appreciate various initiatives to prevent corruption in NREGA. For instance, the Government of Andhra Pradesh has taken the bold step of paying all NREGA wages through post offices. This is an example of the "separation of payment agencies from implementing agencies" recommended in the NREGA guidelines. This system virtually removes any incentive the implementing agencies have to fudge muster rolls, since the payments are beyond their reach. In addition, Andhra Pradesh has put in place a system of institutionalised social audits, involving routine verification of NREGA records through participatory processes. Judging from our brief visit, and from the social audit reports, these safeguards are quite effective. While various forms of petty corruption (such as postmasters demanding bribes) have emerged from the social audits, there is no evidence of the sort of large-scale fraud that plagued public works schemes in Andhra Pradesh just a few years ago.

After these relatively upbeat discoveries, we had a rude shock in Orissa, where muster roll verification exercises were conducted in October 2007 for thirty randomly selected worksites spread over three districts (Bolangir, Boudh, and Kalahandi). The findings of this investigation have been reported elsewhere (*The Hindu*, 20 November 2007). Briefly, we found that Orissa had barely begun the transition from the traditional system of corruption in public works schemes (involving private contractors, mass fudging of muster rolls, and institutionalised kickbacks) towards a transparent and accountable system. The transparency safeguards had been sabotaged by vested interests and the system was virtually unverifiable. In Bolangir and Kalahandi, the infamous "PC system" (whereby various functionaries demand fixed percentages of scheme funds) continued and seemed to absorb around 22 per cent of NREGA funds. The silver lining is that even in this corruption-ridden region there were many indications of positive change. As checks and balances are put in place, the system is becoming harder for vested interests to manipulate, and corruption is declining. The clampdown on corruption has recently intensified, after Orissa earned a bad name for mass corruption in NREGA.

After this, it was refreshing (literally) to head for the hills of Himachal Pradesh in December 2007. A sharp contrast emerged there between the two survey districts – Kangra and Sirmaur. In Kangra, we found a remarkable culture of transparency in public records, including NREGA. The muster rolls and other NREGA records were usually available for public scrutiny at the gram panchayat office, often in computerised form. Further, with one major exception (Minta gram panchayat), there was an almost perfect match between the muster rolls and workers' testimonies. In Sirmaur, however, there was evidence of significant fudging of muster rolls. In some cases, this had been done (illegally) to augment the material component of the scheme, without appropriating any funds, but there were also cases of embezzlement.

More extensive investigations are required to consolidate these findings, but even small-scale surveys of this kind yield rich insights.

All the relevant information, including muster rolls and verification sheets, is available on request. These records would be useful reading for those who believe that NREGA funds are systematically going down the drain. Equally enlightening are people's testimonies. No sensitive person can fail to be moved by the words they have used to describe how NREGA employment helps them to live with dignity, feed their children, and send them to school.

Behind the diversity of these findings is one overarching lesson. Corruption can be eradicated from NREGA, and the way to do it is to enforce the transparency safeguards that are built into the act and the guidelines. Along with this, swift action needs to be taken whenever corruption is exposed. This is not the time for a loss of nerve.

Employment Guarantee or
Slave Labour?*

Reports of long delays in NREGA wage payments have been pouring in from all over the country in recent months. The reports are truly alarming, with delays of several months becoming the norm in entire districts and even states. Worse, there are worksites where labourers have lost hope of being paid at all (we found some in Khunti district, Jharkhand). This is not very different from slave labour.

Under the National Rural Employment Guarantee Act (NREGA), workers must be paid within fifteen days. Failing that, they are entitled to compensation based on the norms of the Payment of Wages Act – up to Rs 3000 per aggrieved worker. However, except for one isolated instance in Jharkhand, compensation has never been paid.

Even small delays often cause enormous hardship for workers who live on the margins of subsistence. How are they supposed to feed their families as they wait day after day for their wages, clueless as to how long it will take and powerless to do anything about it? A recent investigation of hunger deaths in Baran district, Rajasthan, found that delays in NREGA wage payments were partly responsible for these tragedies. Timely payment is, literally, a matter of life and death – all the more so in a drought year.

It is often argued, especially by government officials, that the main reason for the delays is the inability of banks and post offices to handle mass payments of NREGA wages. There is a grain of truth in this, but as a diagnosis of the problem, it is quite misleading. First,

*September 2009.

the current jam in the banking system is the central government's own doing. It reflects the hasty and top-down manner in which the switch to bank payments was imposed about a year ago. As early as October 2007, members of the Central Employment Guarantee Council had warned against this, and advocated a gradual transition, starting with villages that are relatively close to the nearest bank.

Second, the delays in banks and post offices are by no means immutable. In fact, the main obstacle (opening millions of accounts in a short time) is already behind us. In a few states, like Rajasthan, the volume of NREGA payments is certainly a continuing challenge. But in most states, NREGA payments would be quite manageable with suitable arrangements on the part of banks and post offices. In Khunti district, we found that bank payments were easy to expedite, with a little help from trained volunteers who accompanied workers to the banks. In Andhra Pradesh, there is a clear protocol for wage payments through post offices, with strict timelines and constant monitoring. According to this monitoring system, I am told, 70 per cent of the wages are paid within fifteen days.

Thirdly, the delays are not confined to the banking system. Very often, it takes more than fifteen days for "payment orders" to be issued to the banks by the implementing agencies (e.g. the gram panchayat). Thus, there are lapses outside the banking system too. For the local administration, blaming the banks is a convenient way of passing the buck.

On closer examination, various hurdles appear to contribute to the delays. These include delays in work measurement (themselves linked to the tyrannical behaviour of the engineering staff), bottlenecks in the flow of funds (sometimes bringing NREGA to a halt in entire blocks), irresponsible record-keeping (such as non-maintenance of muster rolls and job cards), and, yes, hurdles related to bank payments. But I venture to suggest that behind these specific hurdles is a deeper backlash against NREGA in many areas. With bank payments making it much harder to embezzle NREGA funds, the whole programme is now seen as a headache by many government functionaries: the workload remains, but not the inducements. Aside from the possibility of some general foot-dragging, slowing down wage payments is a convenient way of sabotaging NREGA, because it makes *workers themselves* turn against the programme. That was certainly the situation we found a few months ago in Khunti district, where workers had started deserting NREGA worksites. This backlash, I surmise, is the real reason why massive delays have emerged around the same time as the transition to bank payments. Seen in this light, the delays are not just operational hurdles – they reflect a deliberate attack on NREGA.

The central and state governments, for their part, seem to be in denial. In Delhi, the ministry of rural development has a vague awareness of the delays, but little to show by way of factual evidence or remedial action. When the ministry's attention was drawn to the morass of wage payments in Khunti district, the district collector was asked to take action and certify that no wages were pending. She sent the certificate (in writing) within a few days. It turned out to be based on nothing more than empty assurances from block development officers, who have no credible data on wage dues. A recent social audit in Khunti district showed that rampant delays persist to this day. Ostriches are alive and well in Jharkhand.

Instead of addressing this emergency, the ministry is lost in a maze of confused proposals about "NREGA-2". The real meaning of this term became clear on 20 August 2009, when the ministry was expected to unfurl the NREGA-2 blueprint on the occasion of Rajiv Gandhi's birthday. This blueprint boiled down to an architectural sketch (hastily prepared by the School of Planning and Architecture) for "Rajiv Gandhi Seva Kendras", to be built in all gram panchayats as one of the core activities under NREGA. This is a strange idea, especially in a drought year – pacca (brick) buildings are not even on the list of permissible works. Perhaps someone thought that putting the Gandhi tag on NREGA across the country would please the political bosses and help the ruling party to reclaim the programme. The recent rearrangement of the Central Employment

Guarantee Council, with some very able members being shown the door to make room for Congress MPs and friends, was in the same genre. A better way of winning credit for NREGA would be to make it work, starting with timely wage payments.

In so far as the central government has any answer to the problem, it seems to be based on the "business correspondent" model, whereby bank agents will be going around villages to make cash payments recorded through hand-held electronic gadgets. This solution, however, is based on a wrong diagnosis – that the main problem is the distance that separates many villages from the nearest bank. Distance is certainly an issue in some areas, but it has little to do with the delays. In any case, the need of the hour in a drought situation is not for futuristic experiments but for an immediate acceleration of payments.

Ending the delays is not a simple matter. The first point to note is that, as things stand, there is no in-built alert in the event of delays, let alone any in-built pressure to act. Programme officers at the block level typically have no data on delays in wage payments. The workers, for their part, have no way of airing their grievances. This is one aspect of the general lack of grievance redressal provisions in NREGA; or rather, of the sidelining of these provisions on the part of central and state governments – in this case by ignoring the compensation clause. Activating this clause (along with section 25 of NREGA, which provides for penalties on anyone who does not do his or her duty under the law) would be of great help in accelerating wage payments.

Aside from this, other effective measures can be taken. Piece-rate work could be replaced with daily-wage work in drought-affected areas, to dispense with the cumbersome process of work measurement. In any case, wages could be paid on the basis of attendance wherever work measurement is not completed within, say, seven days. Buffer funds can be provided to gram panchayats and post offices, to avoid bottlenecks in the flow of funds. Clear timelines are required at every step of the payment process, along with close co-ordination of the

NREGA machinery with banks and post offices. Job-card entries need to be made at the worksite, so that workers have a proof that wages are due. Partial advances on wage payments, in cash at the worksite, could also be considered. And of course, wage payments need to be meticulously tracked.

These are just a few examples of possible steps to reduce delays in wage payments. The first step, however, is to recognise the problem and give it overwhelming priority. That is the big stumbling block today.

Guaranteeing
Productive Work*

Few social programmes in India attract more resentment from the corporate sector than the National Rural Employment Guarantee Act (NREGA). This is easy to understand, since NREGA is partly aimed at empowering workers and reducing their dependence on private employers. Many employers see this as a potential threat to the availability of cheap and docile labour.

Playing With Mud?

This resentment tends to generate a steady stream of critical reports and editorials in the corporate-sponsored media. Going by these reports, one would think that public works initiated under NREGA are wholly useless. As one recent editorial put it, "in most places across the country, this [NREGA] meant digging up trenches for no purpose whatsoever and then filling them up." The editor provided no evidence for this sweeping statement.

During the last few years, I have seen hundreds of NREGA works, and I do not remember a single case that resembled digging trenches and filling them up. I have certainly seen some useless NREGA works (like a pond being built at the top of a hill in Sonebhadra district, Uttar Pradesh), but also many useful ones. For lack of careful studies of the productive value of NREGA works, the larger picture is not very clear. But some recent studies suggest that the view of NREGA as a makeshift work programme is far off the mark.

*August 2014 and July 2015.

Among them is an insightful study by Dr Sudha Narayanan and her colleagues at the Indira Gandhi Institute of Development Research, who examined 4100 NREGA assets scattered over 100 villages of Maharashtra. Among the sample works, 87 per cent were functional and 75 per cent contributed directly or indirectly to better agriculture. An overwhelming majority (90 per cent) of the users of these NREGA works considered them "very useful" or "somewhat useful". As the principal author notes, NREGA workers in Maharashtra have "replaced scrublands with forests, built earthen structures for impounding water and preventing soil erosion, cleared lands and levelled them to make them cultivable", among other activities. This is hardly "playing with mud", to quote another disparaging view of NREGA work from the mainstream media.

While the Maharashtra study focuses mainly on people's perceptions, another recent study (by Anjor Bhaskar and Pankaj Yadav at the Institute for Human Development) looks at objective measures of economic returns on NREGA works in Jharkhand. This study inspected nearly 1000 randomly selected dug wells constructed under NREGA in the last few years. Interestingly, the proportion of completed wells in the sample (70 to 80 per cent depending on whether one insists on the construction of a parapet) was not very different from official estimates for the same gram panchayats. Further, most of the completed structures were very well used – especially to grow vegetables and other high-value crops, but also to bathe, water domestic animals, and even keep fish, among other possible uses. Looking just at the impact on agricultural productivity, the authors estimate (from a sub-sample of about 100 randomly selected wells) that NREGA wells have a financial rate of return of 6 per cent or so in real terms. This is a respectable rate of return, on par with many industrial projects. Despite considerable difficulties at the construction stage, sometimes even leading them to sell some property, almost all the well owners were glad they had built a well.

These findings are consistent with those of other recent studies in the same vein, notably by the Indian Institute of Science, the International Water Management Institute, and the University of Allahabad. More evidence is certainly needed to form a clear view of the productive value of NREGA works in general, but as things stand there is no reason for despondency.

Recent research also suggests that the central government has a misguided view of how to make NREGA works more productive. The basic assumption tends to be that the best way to enhance the productivity of NREGA works is to raise the material–labour ratio. In fact, there is no evidence that material-intensive works (e.g. building pacca structures) are generally more productive than labour-intensive works (e.g. levelling land or digging ponds). Most states today have an average material–labour ratio below the stipulated maximum of 40:60, and there is no obvious reason why this upper limit should be raised. A more effective step would be to improve technical support and supervision for all NREGA works, irrespective of the material–labour ratio. This would also be a good opportunity to enhance the skill-building role of NREGA.

It is often said that NREGA should be reoriented towards skill formation instead of casual labour. This overlooks the fact that NREGA is already one of the largest skill-building programmes of the central government. Lakhs of women and men are learning technical, administrative, and social skills as Gram Rozgar Sevaks, programme officers, worksite mates, barefoot engineers, data entry operators, and social auditors under NREGA. Since NREGA functionaries are mainly contract workers, many of them eventually move on and make use of these skills in the private sector. Building up these skill formation activities, as an integral component of NREGA, would be an excellent way of taking the entire programme forward.

Learning from NREGA

Another neglected aspect of the usefulness of NREGA relates to the process aspects of the programme. In the process of planning works, organising employment, paying wages, or fighting corruption, many valuable activities take place: gram sabhas are held, workers agitate for their rights, social audits are conducted, technical assistants are trained, administrators find out how to speed up wage payments, and so on. These activities, aside from being valuable in themselves, are also a great opportunity to learn.

One productive area of learning has been the prevention of corruption. The principal method of embezzlement in labour-intensive public works programmes is well known: muster rolls are inflated and middlemen pocket the difference. Before the Right to Information Act came into force, muster rolls were beyond public scrutiny and the crooks had a field day. Things improved after muster rolls were placed in the public domain, and even displayed page by page on the internet. Even then, an enterprising middleman might fudge the muster rolls and hope that no-one would bother to verify them. Over time, further safeguards were introduced.

One major breakthrough was the transition to bank (or post-office) payments of NREGA wages. This was a painful affair – the system was not ready for it and the overload led to long delays in payments. Five years later, banks and (especially) post offices are still not equal to the task. For the prevention of corruption, however, this was a step forward: the new system makes it much harder to embezzle NREGA funds since the money now goes directly to workers' accounts.

One major qualification is that village post offices are still vulnerable to capture by powerful middlemen. Extracting money from someone else's bank account without his or her knowledge is difficult, because banks have strict norms of identity verification. For a suitable commission, however, a village postmaster can often be persuaded to use the accounts of illiterate workers as a conduit to siphon off NREGA money. Over time, workers learn to collect their wages in person from the post office and verify the passbook entries. But it will take a while for many of them to protect their account from fraud. And the crook's next refuge is to involve workers themselves in the scam.

How much progress has been made in this step-by-step battle against corruption? The second India Human Development Survey (IHDS), conducted in 2011–12, provides a tentative answer. Early tabulations of IHDS data, kindly shared by project director Sonalde Desai, suggest that 25 per cent of all rural households did some NREGA work in 2011–12. The average number of days of NREGA work was 49 per employed household, or 2.53 days per person for the whole sample. Multiplying this by the rural population total from the 2011 census yields an estimate of 210 crore person-days of NREGA employment in 2011–12. This compares with 219 crore person-days of employment being generated by NREGA in 2011–12 according to the ministry of rural development. In other words, the bulk of official NREGA wage expenditure is fully reflected in this independent household survey.

One survey is not conclusive evidence, but it certainly gives some reason for hope. As it happens, the IHDS findings are consistent with those of another recent survey – the Public Evaluation of Entitlement Programmes (PEEP) survey. This was a relatively small survey (about 2000 households), conducted in May–June 2013 in ten states: Bihar, Chhattisgarh, Himachal Pradesh, Jharkhand, Madhya Pradesh, Maharashtra, Odisha, Rajasthan, Tamil Nadu, and Uttar Pradesh. In this survey, too, the number of days of NREGA work reported by the respondents (twenty-two days on average, in 2012–13) was very close to the corresponding average for the same households (twenty-four days) from official records.

The picture emerging from National Sample Survey (NSS) data is a little different. According to recent estimates by Clément Imbert of Oxford University, 68 to 78 per cent of official NREGA person-days of work are reflected in NSS data for 2011–12. The corresponding estimates for 2007–8 (prior to the introduction of bank payments of NREGA wages) are much lower: 42 to 56 per cent. Thus, NSS-based estimates of NREGA employment are consistently lower than the official figures, but the gap is narrowing over time. I suspect that the IHDS figures on NREGA employment are more accurate than NSS data, because the collection of social statistics is one of the primary objectives of the IHDS survey, but not of NSS surveys (there are precedents of patchy collection of social statistics in NSS surveys, e.g. gross underestimation of the coverage of midday meals). The good news is that each of these three surveys points to a sharp reduction in the extent of embezzlement of NREGA funds in recent years, at least in the wage component of the programme.

Much remains to be done to ensure that NREGA is corruption-proof – not just the wage component but also the material component. Meanwhile, the transparency safeguards that have been painstakingly built into NREGA are crying to be extended to other domains. In this and other respects, the programme is a great learning tool. This process aspect of NREGA deserves more recognition than it has received so far.

Notes

Employment as a Social Responsibility

This essay was written just before the National Rural Employment Guarantee Bill was tabled in parliament, in December 2004. The bill turned out to be a severely diluted version of the draft prepared by the National Advisory Council – so diluted that it virtually defeated the purpose of an employment guarantee (see Drèze 2004). Many of the essential safeguards, however, were reinstated by the time the National Rural Employment Guarantee Act was passed, in August 2005.

The NAC estimates of anticipated cost of NREGA were summarised in a note on "Financial Implications of an Employment Guarantee Act", posted on the NAC website (the site, however, is no longer accessible). For the "Kelkar-2" report, see Government of India 2004. On the potential revenue from an enhanced professions tax, see World Bank 2004. The tax-GDP ratio figures are based on the Kelkar-2 report and *World Development Indicators*.

As anticipated, women's participation in NREGA has been high from the beginning: their share of total NREGA person-days rose from around 40 per cent in 2006–7 to nearly 60 per cent or so today.

Employment Guarantee and Its Discontents

August 2005 was a time of huge suspense, with the government trying to redeem its high-stake promise to enact a rural employment guarantee act, the Left parties (which supported the government from outside) bargaining hard for some final amendments, and the business media doing its best to disparage the entire project. This essay was part of a stream of articles written at that time by supporters and critics of the proposed act.

On ethical debate, see Rapoport (1960). The Anuradha Joshi quote is taken from her article "For Effective Employment Guarantee", *The Hindu*, 8 February 2005. The comments on the National Food For Work Programme (NFFWP, a precursor of the NREGA), and on muster rolls in Rajasthan, are based on a quick survey of the NFFWP conducted with student volunteers in the summer of 2005, in association with the Centre for Equity Studies and the Centre for Development Economics at the Delhi School of Economics.

Myths and Reality of Corruption

This essay is based on a series of social audits of NREGA initiated in collaboration with the G.B. Pant Social Science Institute, Allahabad. For further discussion of the CAG report on NREGA, see Siddhartha and Vanaik 2008. For an update on corruption in NREGA, see the last essay in this section.

Employment Guarantee or Slave Labour?

This article was a sort of wake-up call, written soon after the central government made it mandatory for NREGA wages to be paid through bank or post-office accounts. For further discussion of this difficult transition, see Adhikari and Bhatia 2010. After a long phase of apathy towards delayed wage payments, the central government initiated some serious steps towards more effective payment systems. Unfortunately, the repeated and drastic changes in payment systems (e.g. from post offices to bank cheques and then to electronic payments, e-FMS, p-FMS and finally "Aadhaar-enabled" payments) kept creating new problems even as some of the old ones were solved. Eight years after this article was written, the system is still unequal to the task of paying NREGA wages within fifteen days, as required under the law.

Guaranteeing Productive Work

The initial quote on NREGA serving no purpose is from an editorial in *The Pioneer*, 21 May 2015. The findings of the Maharashtra study, by Sudha Narayanan and colleagues, are presented in Ranaware, *et al.* 2015. On wells in Jharkhand, see Bhaskar, Gupta, and Yadav 2016. For further details of the Indian Institute of Science study and "other recent studies", see Drèze and Sen 2013, chapter 7.

The calculations based on "early tabulations of IHDS data" can now be replicated quite easily from the IHDS report on NREGA (Desai, *et al.* 2015). The Imbert estimates are based on a draft version of Imbert and Papp 2015. On the PEEP survey, see Drèze and Khera with the PEEP team 2014.

7

FOOD SECURITY AND
THE PUBLIC DISTRIBUTION
SYSTEM

INDIA'S PUBLIC DISTRIBUTION SYSTEM (PDS) used to have a very bad name among economists, and is still viewed with suspicion today. The main reason is that "leakages" were very high, making the PDS an expensive way of helping poor households. About ten years ago, the proportion of PDS grain (rice and wheat) diverted by corrupt middlemen was probably around 50 per cent at the all-India level, rising to 80 or even 90 per cent in states like Bihar and Jharkhand. Only a few states, such as Tamil Nadu (and to some extent, other southern states), had a well-functioning PDS.

From the mid 2000s on, however, serious PDS reforms were initiated in many of the lagging states. Chhattisgarh was the first to show the possibility of turning the PDS around. This is an achievement of much interest, because Chhattisgarh's PDS used to be as bad as that of any of the BIMARU states (see "The Right to Food and Public Accountability" in section 1). As recently as 2005, Harsh Mander, who had worked in Chhattisgarh for many years as a senior Indian Administrative Service officer, told us that "one thing that will never improve in Chhattisgarh is the PDS". Speaking from experience, he felt that the nexus of corrupt middlemen that had grown around the PDS was too powerful to be broken. This pessimism was proved wrong within two years, as Chhattisgarh's political leadership made up its mind to take on that nexus and make the PDS work – not out of charity, but as an electoral pitch. The pitch, it seems, succeeded: Raman Singh, then chief minister of Chhattisgarh, earned the nickname of "chawal baba" (rice daddy) and is still the chief minister today.

The nuts and bolts of Chhattisgarh's PDS reforms are discussed in the second essay in this section. Chhattisgarh's experience later inspired analogous reforms in many other states, with similar – though less spectacular – results. It also influenced the National Food Security Act (NFSA), which includes an important section on PDS reforms. The other essays in this section are contributions to the debates that have surrounded the act in the last few years. They engage with successive drafts of the act, from the lame initial version prepared by an empowered group of ministers in 2010 to the final version.

The ambit of the NFSA is not restricted to the PDS. It also includes important provisions related to child nutrition programmes and maternity entitlements, often overlooked in public debates on the act. In this section, too, the main focus is on the PDS, but mainly because child nutrition and (to a lesser extent) maternity entitlements are discussed elsewhere in the book.

The NFSA had a long and difficult birth. The draft of the act took four years, from 2009 on, to wind its way through the National Advisory Council, the prime minister's office, various ministries, a parliamentary standing committee, and the Lok Sabha. It raised complex issues, relating for instance to the mandatory coverage of the PDS and the selection of eligible households.[1] The financial implications, of course, were also substantial (though not as daunting as the opponents claimed), and the government seemed a little half-hearted about it. The final version of the act, passed by the Indian parliament

---

[1] The initial plan was for the act to prescribe that eligible households should be identified using the "exclusion approach" (see section 2), based on Socio-Economic and Caste Census (SECC) data. However, the release of SECC data was delayed by several years. As a fallback, the act left it to the states to identify eligible households in their own way.

in August 2013, had a more limited scope than the initial drafts (for instance, it excluded social security pensions and community kitchens). It also had some important flaws, including weak provisions for grievance redressal.

Nevertheless, in the years that followed, the NFSA led to some positive developments, especially in the poorer states. PDS reforms gathered further momentum, exclusion errors were greatly reduced, and food security became a lively political issue in many states. (Some of this progress, unfortunately, is now in danger of being undone by the imposition of Aadhaar-based biometric authentication in the PDS – see section 8.) Children's right to nutritious midday meals, already upheld by supreme court orders, became a permanent legal entitlement. Last but not least, the NFSA affirmed the principle of universal maternity entitlements, albeit at a low initial level (Rs 6000 per child). Women's right to maternity entitlements under the NFSA has been quietly ignored by the central government for the last three years, but is finally being recognised – and acted on – as this book goes to press.

The essays that follow reflect a position of critical support for the NFSA. At times I have taken issue with the flaws and limitations of the act, at other times I found myself defending it against those who wanted no act at all. In a democratic system, progress towards our goals and visions generally proceeds in steps (and not always forward). The NFSA, I believe, was a step in the right direction, but the goal of good nutrition for all is still far from being realised.

Food Security Act:
Indecent Proposal?*

When I first visited Surguja district in Chhattisgarh, nearly ten years ago, it was one of those areas where the public distribution system (PDS) was virtually non-functional. I even felt constrained to write, at that time, that "the whole system looks like it has been designed to fail". Ration shops were in the hands of corrupt private dealers, who made money by selling PDS grain in the open market. People were powerless to argue when the local dealer told them that, for no fault of his own, his stocks were bare. Hunger haunted the land.

Ten years later, the PDS has experienced a remarkable turnaround. One hesitates to give any good marks to the Government of Chhattisgarh these days, given its objectionable actions in other domains – the sell-out to mining companies, its backing of the unofficial vigilante militia Salwa Judum, and its suppression of human rights, to mention a few. Still, the revival of the PDS in Chhattisgarh is a major achievement, of interest to the whole country.

I had an enlightening view of this revival in Surguja itself a few weeks ago. Today, almost every household in this area is entitled to 35 kg of grain every month, at one or two rupees per kg (depending on the type of ration card). What is more, the system is working – everywhere we went, we found that people were getting 35 kg of grain on time every month. For people who live on the margin of subsistence, this is a dream.

The forthcoming National Food Security Act presents a unique opportunity to achieve similar gains across the country. However,

*July 2010.

the current draft, prepared by an empowered group of ministers, is a non-starter in this respect. Indeed, the food guarantee is restricted to 25 kg of grain (at an unspecified price!) to BPL households – less than their existing entitlements. In response to recent agitations, the government seems willing to raise the poverty line a few notches, so that more households are included. Even then, a targeted PDS is not the way to guarantee the right to food.

The main problem with targeting is that it is both unreliable and divisive. The first point is evident from many investigations of the distribution of BPL cards. The exclusion errors are enormous. For instance, among all rural households falling below the poverty line according to National Sample Survey data, almost half did not have a BPL card in 2004–5. Similar findings emerge from National Family Health Survey data.

Perhaps exclusion errors can be reduced with better BPL identification methods. The N.C. Saxena Committee has made valuable suggestions in this respect. But the fact remains that there is no reliable way of identifying poor households based on proxy indicators – it is bound to be a hit-or-miss exercise. A landless household, for instance, may or may not be poor, and similarly with a scheduled caste or female-headed household. The fact that a household may be well-off today but poor tomorrow (due, say, to illness, displacement or unemployment) does not help matters. And the power equations in rural areas are such that any BPL survey is vulnerable to manipulation. There is no reason to expect the next BPL survey to be more reliable than the last one.

Targeting is also divisive: it prevents the emergence of a cohesive public demand for a functional PDS. And vocal demand is very important for the success of the PDS. This is one reason why the PDS works much better in Tamil Nadu than elsewhere: everyone has a stake in it. Chhattisgarh's recent success builds on the same principle – about 80 per cent of the rural population is covered.

In short, targeting is an ugly business, and it would be particularly dangerous to freeze the BPL – APL distinction into a law. This would amount to converting a purely statistical benchmark, the poverty line, into a permanent social division.

For all these reasons, serious consideration must be given to the obvious alternative – a universal public distribution system, at least in rural areas and urban slums. Imagine the potential benefits first: every family would have assured food in the house, month after month. Gone would be the days of cold hearths and empty stomachs. For those at risk of hunger, the PDS would be a lifeline. For others, it would be a form of income support and economic security – a valuable thing to have, even when you are not hungry. The case for universalisation builds on this dual purpose of the PDS – food security and income support.

The nutrition impact of the PDS, one may argue, is likely to be limited even in the universal version. This may well be true. One reason is that the PDS may not do much for young children – the crucial age group as far as nutrition is concerned. What most children need is not more foodgrains, but more nutritious food (including animal protein), better breastfeeding practices, health care, and related support. They also need to be heavier and healthier at birth, which requires further interventions (important in their own right) related to women's health and maternal entitlements. Special programmes are also needed for marginalised groups such as the urban homeless. The PDS is only one part of an effective system of food and nutrition security.

This is not likely to come cheap. Tentative calculations suggest that a comprehensive Food Security Act may cost something like one lakh crore of rupees per year. This may sound like a mind-boggling price tag, but it is not. For one thing, in a country where half the children are undernourished, there is no quick fix – any serious attempt to deal with mass undernourishment is bound to be expensive. For another, one lakh crore of rupees is just about 1.5 per cent of India's GDP – is that an excessive price to pay to protect everyone from hunger?

Incidentally, India already spends more than that on things that are rather trivial compared with the right to food. I am not just thinking of military expenditure, which could do with some pruning, especially when it is used for internal repression. The fertiliser subsidy is also in the range of one lakh crore of rupees a year, with doubtful social benefits, not to speak of the environmental damage. And the annual "revenue foregone" on account of tax exemptions is more than *five* lakh crores of rupees, according to the finance minister's own "foregone revenue statement". This includes about Rs 80,000 crores of corporate income tax foregone (some of it "on account of contributions to political parties") and nearly Rs 40,000 crores of foregone customs duties on "vegetables, fruits, cereals and edible oils".

The food subsidy itself is already around Rs 70,000 crores. The problem is not so much that this subsidy is too low, but that it is badly used. A telling symptom of this today is the mindless accumulation of nearly 60 million tonnes of grain in government warehouses. Instead of whining about food inflation, and blaming "hoarders" for it, the government would do well to release some of these gigantic food stocks.

This is not to dismiss the resource constraints. One way ahead would be to introduce the universal PDS, say, in the poorest 200 districts, and extend it gradually to the whole country, at least in rural areas – much as happened with the National Rural Employment Guarantee Act. Today's excess stocks would be of great help in the initial phase of this transition. Five years from now, the cost of a comprehensive food security system will be closer to 1 than 1.5 per cent of GDP, if current growth rates continue. Meanwhile there would be enough time to enhance food procurement and mobilise extra funds. The roadmap is clear: promote local procurement and tax the rich.

None of this, of course, would be of much use unless the PDS can be made to work. Expanding the coverage of the PDS will help in that respect, as argued earlier. But systemic reforms of the PDS are also required, building on the wealth of insights that have been gained from recent initiatives to restore transparency and accountability in various domains. If Chhattisgarh can turn the PDS around, why not other states?

The National Food Security Act is not going to eliminate malnutrition in one go. But it could be the end of hunger, and the beginning of a new movement for the realisation of everyone's right to good nutrition. This is worth pondering before the idea is dismissed as unaffordable.

The PDS Turnaround in Chhattisgarh*

(with Reetika Khera)

India's public distribution system (PDS) has been in bad shape for decades, so much so that it is often thought to be beyond repair. Recent experience, however, suggests otherwise. The amazing revival of the PDS in Chhattisgarh is of special interest in this respect.

First Steps: Checking the Middlemen

We had an interesting view of this turnaround a few months ago in Lakhanpur block (Surguja district), on the sidelines of a survey of NREGA in the area. Everyone we spoke to, across the block, said that they were receiving their full quota of 35 kg of grain each month, and at the correct price – one or two rupees per kg, according to the ration card. The stocks apparently reach the village on time, on the seventh day of each month, and are promptly distributed. There were no complaints of cheating. This is no mean achievement in an area where the PDS was severely dysfunctional just a few years ago.

Other reports from Chhattisgarh suggest that this is not an isolated success. One survey of food-related schemes, conducted in September–November 2009 in eight blocks spread over the state, found that 85 per cent of the cardholders were getting their full 35 kg of grain every month from the PDS (others were getting at least 25 kg). Only 2 per cent of the entries in the ration cards were found to be fake.

*November 2010.

One of the early steps towards PDS reform was the "de-privatisation" of ration shops. In Chhattisgarh, private dealers were allowed to get licences for PDS shops from 2001 onwards (before that, PDS shops were run by the state co-operatives network). This measure allowed the network of ration shops to widen, but also created a new nexus of corrupt players whereby dealers paid politicians to get licences as well as protection when they indulged in corrupt practices. In 2004, the government reversed this order (despite fierce opposition from the dealers) and put gram panchayats, self-help groups, van suraksha samitis (forest protection committees), and other community institutions in charge of the ration shops. Aside from bringing ration shops closer to people's homes, this helped impart some accountability in the PDS. When people run their own ration shop, there is little incentive to cheat, since that would be like cheating themselves. Community institutions such as gram panchayats are not necessarily "people's institutions", but nevertheless, they are easier for people to influence than corrupt middlemen or the government's bureaucratic juggernaut.

Another major reform was to ensure "doorstep delivery" of the PDS grain. This means that grain is delivered by state agencies to the ration shop each month, instead of dealers having to lift their quotas from the nearest godown. How does this help? It is well known that corrupt dealers have a tendency to give reduced quantities to their customers and sell the difference in the open market. What is less well understood is that the diversion often happens *before* supplies reach the village. Dealers get away with this by putting their hands up helplessly and telling their customers that "*picche se kam aya hai*" (there was a shortfall at the godown). When the grain is delivered to the ration shop, in the village, it is much harder for the dealers to siphon it off without opposition. Truck movements from the godowns to the ration shops are carefully monitored, and if a transporter cheats the dealers have an incentive to mobilise local support to complain, as we found had happened in one village.

These two measures (de-privatisation of ration shops and doorstep delivery) were accompanied by rigorous monitoring, often helped by creative uses of technology. For instance, a system of SMS alerts was launched to inform interested citizens (more than 15,000 have already registered) of grain movements, and all records pertaining to supplies, sales, timelines, etc. were computerised. This involved much learning-by-doing. For instance, at one point the state government tried distributing pre-packed sacks of 35 kg to prevent cheating, but the practice had to be discontinued as it was found that the sacks were being tampered with too. Therefore, in recent months, a move towards electronic weighing machines has been initiated.

Perhaps the most important step was improved grievance redressal, based for instance on active helplines. Apparently the helplines are often used by cardholders, and if a complaint is lodged there is a good chance of timely response. Further, action is not confined to enquiries – in many cases, FIRs have been lodged against corrupt middlemen and it is not uncommon for them to land in jail (there was at least one recent case in Lakhanpur itself). Grain has also been recovered from trucks that were caught offloading their stocks at unintended destinations.

People-friendly Transparency

Greater transparency is an important step towards corruption-free administration. This is one important lesson from the National Rural Employment Guarantee Act (NREGA). "Information walls" in Rajasthan, whereby the names and employment details of all job-card holders in a village are painted on the walls of the gram panchayat office, can help prevent the fudging of muster rolls. The NREGA's monitoring and information system (MIS), which computerises all records and makes them available on the internet, is another important transparency measure which people are slowly learning to use.

Along similar lines, simple transparency measures have been introduced in Chhattisgarh to eliminate bogus ration cards. For instance, every house in Lakhanpur had a large round sign, painted next to the door, displaying the type of ration card held by that household and the corresponding entitlements (price and quantity). This serves the dual purpose of generating awareness about entitlements and of "naming and shaming" those who possess a ration card (e.g. an Antyodaya card) for which they are not eligible.

Enhancing Voice

Turning to the demand side of the story, the most significant step in Chhattisgarh was a major expansion in the coverage of the PDS. In what is widely seen now as a shrewd political move, Raman Singh (BJP leader and current chief minister) revamped the PDS ahead of the 2007 state elections. Today, close to 80 per cent of the rural population – including all scheduled caste and scheduled tribe households – is entitled to PDS grain at one or two rupees per kg. The fact that most rural households have a strong stake in the PDS has generated immense pressure on the system (ration shops in particular) to deliver.

Expanded PDS coverage and lower issue prices have both contributed to enhancing the voice of otherwise poor and disempowered rural cardholders. As Rajeev Jaiswal (Joint Director, Food and Civil Supplies) put it: "At the moment we are only using the voice of 80 per cent of the rural community. When the PDS is universalised, the entire community including the better educated and more vocal sections will start putting pressure on the system."

A Political Move

Ultimately, however, it is political will that seems to matter most. Somehow, the PDS became a political priority in Chhattisgarh and a decision was made to turn it around, instead of siding with the corrupt dealers who were milking the system. When political bosses firmly direct the bureaucracy to fix a dysfunctional system, things begin to change.

The fact that government functionaries were under enormous pressure to make the PDS work was evident in Lakhanpur. For instance, monitoring grain movements had become one of the top priorities of the patwaris (land-record officers) and tehsildars (revenue officers). The tehsildar mentioned that the PDS was the first agenda item whenever meetings were held at the district level. The political pressure was also manifest in their willingness to stand up to vested interests, e.g. by arresting corrupt middlemen and sending them to jail if need be.

It would be naïve to think that the revival of the PDS in Chhattisgarh reflects the kind-heartedness of the state government, especially in the light of its contempt for people's rights in other contexts. It was a political calculation, nothing more. But it worked, and can be made to work elsewhere as well.

Rural Poverty and the Public
Distribution System*
(with Reetika Khera)

In earlier writings, we have drawn attention to the quiet revival of the public distribution system (PDS) in many Indian states during the last few years. Market prices of PDS commodities – mainly rice and wheat – have increased sharply, giving people a much greater stake in the system. In response to this, or for other reasons, many states have initiated bold PDS reforms. The combination of increased public pressure and greater political commitment to the PDS has led to major improvements, including more regular distribution and reduced leakages.

Inclusive PDS

Many states have also moved towards a more inclusive PDS. Restricting the PDS to "below poverty line" (BPL) households has proved very problematic: there is no reliable way of identifying BPL households, exclusion errors are massive, and targeting is also very divisive. There is, therefore, growing pressure for a different approach, where the PDS covers a large majority of the population. Tamil Nadu has gone all the way to a universal PDS: every household there is entitled to 20 kg of rice every month, free of cost. Other states that have made significant moves towards a universal or near-universal PDS (at least in rural areas) include Andhra Pradesh, Chhattisgarh, Himachal Pradesh, Kerala, Odisha, and Rajasthan. This approach has helped not only to

*September 2012.

avoid exclusion errors but also to ensure that the PDS works: a more inclusive PDS is under much greater pressure to function.

In some states, such as Odisha and Rajasthan, these changes are very recent. In others, notably Chhattisgarh and of course Tamil Nadu, they were initiated several years ago. National Sample Survey (NSS) data for 2009–10 provide a useful opportunity to look for early signs of the results.

One interesting development is a major increase in PDS purchases: between 2004–5 (the previous "thick round" of the NSS) and 2009–10, household purchases of wheat and rice from the PDS increased by 50 per cent in quantity terms. The proportion of households purchasing at least some rice or wheat from the PDS increased from 27 per cent in 2004–5 to 45 per cent in 2009–10. This quantitative expansion is one important aspect of the recent revival of the PDS in large parts of India.

Further, in value terms, PDS entitlements are now quite substantial in many states. The implicit income subsidy from the PDS can be calculated as the difference between PDS price and market price, multiplied by quantity purchased, and summed over wheat and rice. There are different ways of estimating this, since there is more than one way of identifying the relevant market price. Using the median market price, state-wise, as a benchmark, the average implicit subsidy (for rural households that purchased at least some grain from the PDS) was around Rs 250 per month in 2009–10. Over the year, this is equivalent to the earnings of a whole month's work under the National Rural Employment Guarantee Act – without having to work. In absolute terms, it is not much, but for people who are constantly struggling to make ends meet, it does help. The implicit subsidy would be larger, of course, if the PDS worked well across the country.

Impact on Poverty

Based on these implicit subsidy calculations, it is possible to estimate the impact of the PDS on rural poverty – by adding the implicit subsidy to the explicit NSS estimate of monthly per capita expenditure (MPCE) for each sample household. To illustrate, consider the following exercise. Suppose we define the "Tendulkar poverty gap" as the aggregate MPCE shortfall from the Tendulkar poverty line (the sum, over all poor rural households, of the difference between the poverty line and their actual MPCE). How far does the PDS reduce the Tendulkar poverty gap? In other words, how much smaller is the poverty gap (in rural areas) when the implicit PDS subsidy is added to the standard components of MPCE?

Using NSS data for 2009–10, it turns out that the PDS (more precisely, the foodgrain component of the PDS) reduces the Tendulkar poverty gap by around 18 per cent at the national level. This is a moderate achievement, but what is more interesting than the national average is the contrast between states. In Tamil Nadu, the PDS reduces the Tendulkar poverty gap by more than 50 per cent. Other states where the PDS has a large impact on rural poverty include Chhattisgarh and Andhra Pradesh (about 40 per cent), and also Himachal Pradesh and Kerala (around 35 per cent). By contrast, the poverty impact is below 15 per cent in Bihar, Jharkhand, Madhya Pradesh, Punjab, Rajasthan, Uttar Pradesh, and West Bengal. As it happens, all the states in the high-impact list have a relatively inclusive PDS, whereas all those in the low-impact list were still clinging to BPL targeting at that time (Rajasthan did expand the coverage of the PDS after 2009–10). A more inclusive approach seems to give better results not only in terms of the general functioning of the PDS, but also in terms of its impact on poverty.

These figures are illustrative, since (as mentioned earlier) there are various ways of going about these calculations. All of them, however, point to the same basic conclusion: the PDS is now having a substantial impact on rural poverty in states where it is broad-based and functions relatively well.

So far, we have looked at the PDS as an implicit income transfer. Aside from transfer benefits, however, the PDS is likely to have important "stabilisation benefits", in so far as it brings some security in people's lives. It is a little bit like having an additional source of income, and a stable one too; this can be very important for those who depend on a single and meagre source of income (such as casual labour) for their survival. The PDS may also have a positive impact on food consumption patterns (e.g. by enabling households to spend more on nutritious food items), although this is somewhat speculative. More likely, the PDS will start having a significant impact on nutrition when commodities other than rice and wheat (e.g. pulses, edible oil, and millets), with a higher nutrition value, are included in it. This has already happened in some states, such as Tamil Nadu (where a wide range of food commodities are included in the PDS), Andhra Pradesh, and Himachal Pradesh. The provision of nutritious foods that are badly lacking in the diets of poor households is an important future possibility for the PDS.

Lessons for the Food Security Bill

These findings have an important bearing on the National Food Security Bill. The bill is a great opportunity to complete the transition towards a functional and inclusive PDS across the country, and put an end to food insecurity. In its present form, however, the bill is likely to undermine instead of facilitating this transition. This is because it seeks to impose a rigid targeting formula, based on a complicated division of the population into three groups (priority, general, and excluded), without any clarity as to how each group is to be identified. Given the failure of numerous expert committees and advisory groups to come up with any reliable targeting method, the idea of a universal PDS – at least in rural areas – looks more sensible than ever.

Various proposals have also been made for an intermediate approach (sometimes called the "exclusion approach"), whereby all households would have common minimum entitlements except those who meet reasonable and well-specified exclusion criteria. However, the government is turning these proposals into a reductionist version of the bill, which would amount to little more than a reshuffling of existing PDS allocations, without any justiciable entitlements being created for anyone. Further, under the abominable formula proposed by the food ministry, whereby – roughly speaking – 33 per cent of the population would be excluded from the PDS across the board (in every state, in rural as well as urban areas), the reshuffling would favour the richer states at the expense of the poorer states. Punjab and Haryana would be the biggest gainers, while Odisha stays in place. This makes no sense, and defeats the purpose of the bill.

These and other flaws of the bill (including a gradual trimming of many entitlements) derive partly from misplaced fears about the foodgrain requirements. Meanwhile, procurement has crossed 70 million tonnes per year, distribution is not keeping up, and excess stocks are growing. Never in history has so much undernutrition coexisted with so much food hoarded. The government is desperately trying to export the surplus stocks, or simply allowing them to pile up unprotected. Reviving and revamping the food security bill sounds like a better idea.

The Food Security Debate
in India*

The right to food is finally becoming a lively political issue in India. Aware of the forthcoming national elections in 2014, political parties are competing to demonstrate – or at least proclaim – their commitment to food security. In a country where endemic undernutrition has been accepted for too long as natural, this is a breakthrough of sorts.

The rhetoric, however, is not always matched by understanding, let alone action. The National Food Security Bill tabled in parliament on 22 December 2011 in pursuance of electoral promises made by India's governing coalition, the United Progressive Alliance, is at the heart of the current debate over food security. The bill was to be put to vote during the last session of parliament, along with a series of amendments based on the report of a parliamentary standing committee. Opposition parties, however, continuously disrupted the proceedings under one pretext or another.

Exasperated by this obstruction, and quite possibly hoping to win votes, the government recently promulgated the National Food Security Ordinance 2013. The ordinance effectively activates the bill, but it must be ratified by parliament within six weeks of its first sitting or else the bill will lapse. The use of emergency powers to promulgate this ordinance is being criticised as undemocratic, and rightly so, but most political parties bear some responsibility for this outcome.

*July 2013. Unlike other essays in this book, this one (posted at *India Ink*, a *New York Times* blog at that time) was written for an international audience, as a sort of overview of the Indian debate on food security. Minor repetitions with earlier essays have been retained, to avoid gaps in the overview.

The bill is a modest initiative. It consolidates various food-related programmes and entitlements that have made gradual headway during the last decade. Provisions of the bill dealing with foodgrain entitlements under the public distribution system have grabbed most of the attention. Children's entitlements, however, are possibly more important. These include cooked midday meals for all schoolgoing children and nutritious food (either a cooked meal or a take-home ration) for all children below the age of six years. These child nutrition programmes are already in place; they are mandatory under supreme court orders. Permanent legal entitlements could strengthen and energise these initiatives.

The bill also provides for maternity benefits – Rs 6000 per child for all pregnant women (except those already covered by maternity benefit schemes in the formal sector). This is a small step, and since the benefits are not indexed to inflation, their real value could erode very quickly. Nevertheless, the principle of universal maternity benefits is important and provides a useful foothold for further action.

The bill is effectively what remains of bolder proposals initially discussed at the National Advisory Council. The council's early drafts of the bill included many provisions that were quietly dropped, one by one, first by the council itself and later by the government: social security pensions, special entitlements for vulnerable groups, community kitchens, and strong accountability measures, among others.

Ironically, even as the central government pruned and diluted the council's proposals, the eastern state of Chhattisgarh, ruled by the Bharatiya Janata Party (the main opposition party), built on them and prepared its own Chhattisgarh Food Security Act, enacted in December 2012. Chhattisgarh's much stronger legislation is in place and a recent survey by the Indian Institute of Technology in Delhi suggests that food-related programmes in Chhattisgarh are quite effective. This experience in one of India's poorest states helps to dispel the notion that the food security proposals are impractical or unaffordable.

Some provisions in the bill are based on considerable experience and evidence. The value and effectiveness of India's school-meal programme, for instance, are reasonably well established. The programme, inspired by Tamil Nadu's pioneering initiatives, covers more than 100 million children and has steadily improved over time. In several states, for instance, the school-meal menu now includes eggs, a very valuable source of animal protein for growing children. In Tamil Nadu, schoolchildren get an egg every day. This is not a trivial matter in a country where millions of poor children rarely get the chance to eat an egg.

Several studies have documented the wide-ranging benefits of school meals in India, from higher school attendance and better child nutrition to remunerative employment for rural women and the erosion of caste barriers. The case for a permanent school-meal programme under the law is widely accepted.

The controversial parts of the bill relate to the public distribution system (PDS). Food commodities, mainly rice and wheat, have been distributed at subsidised prices for a long time to Indian households, according to the type of ration card they possess: APL (above poverty line) and BPL (below poverty line). The bulk of food subsidies are meant to reach households in the latter category, which comprises about one-third of the population. But the process of targeting these households has proved very cumbersome, unreliable, and divisive. At least three national surveys show that about half of all poor households in rural India do not have a BPL card. Further, as Richard Titmuss pointed out nearly fifty years ago, "services for the poor will always be poor services". This is one reason why the performance of the PDS has been far from satisfactory in many states.

Other states, however, have dropped the distinction between households above and below the poverty line and moved toward a more inclusive approach. In Tamil Nadu, the food distribution system covers everyone and works very well. Other states that have also moved toward a more inclusive system in recent years include Andhra Pradesh, Chhattisgarh, Himachal Pradesh, and Odisha, among others.

All of them have combined this move with other reforms of the PDS, and the results have been impressive. There is a crucial lesson here for the National Food Security Bill.

Indeed, the bill can be seen as an opportunity to extend these achievements across the country. Under the bill, 75 per cent of the rural population and 50 per cent of the urban population will be entitled to five kg of foodgrains (rice, wheat, or millets) per person per month at a nominal price. This means that about half of the recipients' grain requirements will be taken care of by the PDS. Further, the roadmap for PDS reforms that has emerged from recent experience is partly included in the bill.

However, the bill has many flaws as far as the PDS is concerned. For instance, the identification of eligible households is left to the discretion of the government. In the absence of clear eligibility criteria, no-one is really entitled to anything as a matter of right; this defeats the purpose of having a law. Similarly, the overnight imposition of per capita food entitlements on a system that is currently based on household entitlements is likely to be disruptive. The promulgation of an ordinance, unfortunately, severely constricts (without precluding) further discussion of these and related issues in parliament.

Media reports give the impression that the bill involves a major expansion of the PDS. In fact, it is more a restructuring than an expansion, as aggregate foodgrain allocations will remain much the same. The distribution, however, will change, with poorer states getting more and poor households being at much lower risk of exclusion. And the current foodgrain quota for households above the poverty line, which has become a huge, corruption-ridden dumping ground for excess food stocks in recent years, will be much better utilised.

Some of the criticisms of the bill are a trifle ill-informed. Many critics cite wildly exaggerated estimates of the costs of the bill and barely consider the economic benefits. Others cite a Planning Commission report to the effect that more than half of PDS foodgrains end up in the open market. That particular report was published in 2005 and is based on data collected in the late 1990s. Much has changed in the meantime, even if corruption in the PDS remains an important issue.

A more pertinent criticism is that the PDS is expensive and that cash transfers would serve much the same purpose at lower cost. In some circumstances, cash transfers are certainly appropriate. For instance, cash-based social security pensions for widows and the elderly are doing relatively well in India and deserve to be expanded.

However, there are many good reasons to be sceptical of a hasty transition from food subsidies to cash transfers. The infrastructure required for mass transfers in cash would take a long time to build. The PDS, on the other hand, is in place, and huge foodgrain stocks – more than 80 million tonnes and growing – are available, so why not make good use of them without delay?

In any case, the bill does not preclude a transition to cash transfers if and when they prove to work better than food subsidies – not just in theory but also on the ground. The immediate issue is not "cash versus food", but to put in place an effective system of income support and social security. Leaving poor people to their own devices is neither socially just nor smart economic policy.

The biggest challenge is to build a serious political backing for food security, as has already happened to a limited extent in specific states. Under the cover of supporting the bill, opposition parties seem to be trying to scuttle it, out of fear that it will help the United Progressive Alliance to stay in power in the next national elections. The government's own commitment to the bill is not entirely clear. A section of the governing coalition certainly wants it, as seen in the ordinance approved last week, but four years of dilly-dallying are hard to understand without an element of internal resistance.

Finally, the food security bill is a fraction of what is required to tackle India's enormous nutrition problems. The battle for the right to food is far from over.

Poor States Catch Up*

Dhobargram is a small Santhal village of Bankura district in West Bengal, with a hundred or so households. Most of them are poor, or even very poor, by any plausible standard. There are also some relatively well-off households – they are not rich, but they have things like concrete houses and motorcycles, often thanks to a permanent job in the public sector.

Should this small minority of better-off households be excluded from the public distribution system (PDS)? Including them costs public money, and they are not at risk of undernourishment. On the other hand, weeding them out is a major headache, as West Bengal and neighbouring states are discovering in the course of implementing the National Food Security Act (NFSA). Also, excluding them creates a small but powerful group of disgruntled people who may be tempted to sabotage the PDS in one way or another. When they are included, there is greater pressure on the system to work.

Improved Framework

A house-to-house survey conducted in Dhobargram last month confirmed something we had already noticed: West Bengal's PDS is based on a restrictive, outdated, and faulty list of "below poverty line" (BPL) households. Out of 105 households, only 29 had a BPL card or an Antyodaya card (meant for the poorest of the poor). The rest had an APL (above poverty line) card, or no card at all – both ways, they were excluded from the PDS except possibly for kerosene rations. By

*January 2016.

contrast, 78 per cent of Dhobargram's households are on the new list of NFSA ration cards, which are to be distributed this month. Further, we found that most of the remaining 22 per cent were households that met the official exclusion criteria, such as having a government job or a pacca (brick) house with at least three rooms. The new list (based on the Socio-Economic and Caste Census 2011) is not only more inclusive than the BPL list, it is also more reliable.

This is just one village (selected at random), but Dhobargram illustrates the major gains that are possible if the NFSA is well implemented in the poorer states. These gains are amplified by PDS reforms, a mandatory adjunct of the act. The PDS in West Bengal has been one of the worst in the country for a long time. Today, it is undergoing reforms similar to those that have been so successful in Chhattisgarh and were also adopted with good effect by neighbouring states such as Odisha and Madhya Pradesh. Hopefully, they will work in West Bengal too.

None of this is to say that all is well in West Bengal, or even just in Dhobargram. Some poor households in Dhobargram are off the list of ration cards, possibly because the Socio-Economic and Caste Census (SECC) missed them, or because they were formed after 2011, or for some other reason. There are many cases of ration cards with missing household members (this matters since PDS entitlements are defined in per-capita terms under the NFSA). Also, the new list of ration cards includes fewer Antyodaya households than the old list, a problem that has also emerged in other states. It will take skilful revision of the NFSA list to resolve these problems. But at least the NFSA has created a relatively sound framework within which this can be done.

Winds of Change

Judging from brief enquiries in Jharkhand and Odisha, which are also in the process of rolling out the NFSA, similar developments have taken place there. The biggest challenge, responsible for the delayed rollout of the NFSA in many states, is to identify eligible households. Even with near-universal coverage (86 per cent in rural Jharkhand and

82 per cent in rural Odisha), this is a daunting task. Jharkhand adopted much the same approach as West Bengal: an initial list of ration cards was prepared from SECC data (by removing better-off households), and later revised based on people's complaints. The main problem with this approach is exclusion errors: there are gaps and mistakes in the SECC data, not always corrected by the complaints process. Odisha followed a different approach, based on self-declaration: ration card applicants had to certify that they met the eligibility criteria, and local functionaries were asked to verify their declarations. The main problem here seems to be inclusion errors: well-off households often get away with claiming that they meet the criteria. The self-declaration approach also requires a reliable administrative machinery – I doubt that it would have worked in Bihar or Jharkhand.

It is too early to tell which of these approaches is preferable. There are also alternatives, such as Madhya Pradesh's pioneering attempt to link the PDS with a database of local residents (the Samagra register) maintained by gram panchayat functionaries. And, of course, one can take the view that it is simply not worth taking all this trouble to exclude 10 or 20 per cent of rural households – universalisation is best, at least in the poorer states. What is clear is that we can do much better today than in the old days of BPL surveys. Among other remarkable improvements is the transparency of the entire process. Even in Jharkhand, the list of NFSA ration cards is available on the net in a reader-friendly format, with all requisite details. That makes it a lot harder to cheat – gone are the days when the village head quietly gave BPL cards to his or her friends without any risk of scrutiny.

The effects of PDS reforms have also started showing in the poorer states. Recent surveys in Bihar and Madhya Pradesh point to remarkable improvements in the last few years. There is no reason why the NFSA latecomers (Jharkhand, West Bengal, Assam, among others) should fail to bring about similar change. Some of them, notably Odisha, actually initiated the process of PDS reform much before rolling out the NFSA, with very positive results. The laggards have their work cut out.

Looking Forward

The picture emerging from recent research is quite different from the impression conveyed by media reports. The latter tend to focus on abuses and irregularities: for instance, the story of a wealthy mayor in Odisha who bagged a ration card, or of someone in Jharkhand who found that 366 ration cards had "inadvertently" been printed in his name. It is certainly part of the media's job to highlight these anomalies, but the larger picture tends to get lost in the process. There is an urgent need for careful evaluations of the impact of NFSA in different states.

Looking ahead, all eyes are on Uttar Pradesh, one of the last states to implement the NFSA. With a foodgrain allocation of 10 million tonnes or so, and a very restrictive PDS under the old system, Uttar Pradesh has more to gain from the NFSA than any other state. But it is also one of India's worst-governed states, if not the worst. Tremendous resolve will be required to break the nexus of corrupt middlemen who have milked the PDS in Uttar Pradesh for so many years (mainly under the APL quota, which is all set to be phased out). As election time approaches, it may just happen – that would be a victory of sorts, not only for food security but also for the larger battle against corruption.

Finally, it is important to remember that the National Food Security Act is not restricted to the PDS. Other critical components include maternity entitlements, brazenly ignored by the central government ever since the act came into force. The PDS itself need not be confined to NFSA entitlements: in several states, some households are now eligible for subsidised pulses and edible oil as well. Perhaps for the first time, there are real possibilities of ensuring a modicum of nutritional support and economic security to all vulnerable households.

Notes

Much of this section draws on collaborative work with Reetika Khera. See particularly Khera 2011b, Drèze and Khera 2010, 2013, 2015a, 2015b, Drèze, Khera and Pudussery 2015, Drèze, et al. 2016.

Food Security Act: Indecent Proposal?

The draft of the National Food Security Act, prepared by an empowered group of ministers (EGoM) in mid 2010, was the first of a series of drafts that followed each other from then until 2013. The ambit of the EGoM draft was restricted to the public distribution system – child nutrition programmes and maternity entitlements came later.

The Saxena Committee report (Government of India 2009b), heavily influenced by an earlier proposal from Harsh Mander and Santosh Mehrotra in 2009, generated considerable debate about possible methodologies for the next BPL census, even within the committee (comments and reservations of nine out of seventeen members are appended to the report). On related matters, see also Drèze and Khera 2010.

Meanwhile, alarming evidence of high exclusion errors in the previous BPL census had emerged from three national household surveys conducted around 2005: the 61st Round of the National Sample Survey (2004–5), the first India Human Development Survey (2004–5), and the third National Family Health Survey (2005–6); on this see also section 2.

The NFSA cost calculations presented in this essay are probably on the high side: there is no reason to count the entire producer-subsidy component of India's "food subsidy" as a cost of NFSA, if subsidised procurement is happening in any case under pressure from farmers' organisations.

The finance minister's annual "revenue foregone" statement is normally included in the budget papers.

The PDS Turnaround in Chhattisgarh

Aside from survey data, this essay benefited from detailed discussions with Samir Garg, Biraj Patnaik, Gangabhai Paikra, and Alok Shukla. Considerable further research is available today on PDS reforms in Chhattisgarh; see e.g. Khera 2011, Puri 2012, and Garg 2013. The findings of the September–November 2009 survey are discussed in Garg 2013.

Rural Poverty and the Public Distribution System

For further details of this analysis, see Drèze and Khera 2013.

The Food Security Debate in India

This article is largely based on evidence mentioned in earlier essays. The findings of the IIT survey cited in the text are presented in Khera 2011b.

Government of India 2005 is the widely-quoted Planning Commission
report on PDS leakages, with 1997–2001 as the reference period; note that
food distribution to non-BPL households is counted as a "leakage" in that
report. For more recent and reliable estimates of PDS leakages, see Drèze
and Khera 2015a.

Poor States Catch Up

This essay is based on a house-to-house survey of Dhobargram village
(Bankura district), conducted with Swagata Nandi and Mukhlesur Rahaman
Gain of the Pratichi Trust, West Bengal. It was part of a series of quick
surveys completed in 2014–16 in the poorer states to assess the status of
the National Food Security Act. The "recent surveys in Bihar and Madhya
Pradesh" are discussed in Drèze, Khera, and Pudussery 2015, and Drèze and
Khera 2015b, respectively. For an update, see p. 225, and also Drèze, Gupta,
Khera, and Pimenta 2016.

8

CORPORATE POWER AND TECHNOCRACY

Among other major developments in Indian society and politics during the last twenty-five years or so is the steady growth of corporate power. It is not that corporate interests were devoid of influence earlier – India's leading business houses, like the Tatas and Birlas, have had a cosy relationship with the government for a long time. Even Dhirubhai Ambani, the icon of Indian entrepreneurs, made his fortune on the back of the Licence Raj (e.g. by getting hold of valuable import permits), with a little help from pliable bureaucrats and politicians.[1] In those days, however, there were some boundaries – real or pretended – between the corporate sector and state policy, and the state sometimes took decisive action (for better or worse) against corporate interests, such as the nationalisation of banks and the coal industry. Further, the concentration of wealth was still at an early stage.

Today, corporate power has not only grown to unprecedented levels, its muscular arms also reach far and wide. Representatives of private businesses sit on all sorts of government committees, oblivious of conflicts of interest. The Sensex, tensely watched by the finance ministry, pronounces instant verdicts on economic policy. State

---

[1] See McDonald 1998. The Ambani family scuttled the publication of this book in India, by threatening legal action (Ghosh and Guha Thakurta 2016). However, the book was published in Australia and is available worldwide.

governments are competing to enhance their ranking in terms of the "ease of doing business". Public–private partnerships give private business wide powers to invade the earlier realm of the public sector with full state support. The magnitude of corporate scams (such as the 2G scam or the coal scam) keeps breaking new records. India's largest corporate houses are also bankrupting its public sector banks by saddling them with billions of rupees of "non-performing assets". The largest of them all, Reliance (headed by Dhirubhai Ambani's sons, Mukesh and Anil), has so much power that, as *India Today* puts it, "when they don't like policy, they change it". Corporate interests increasingly drive not only the traditional areas of business but also urban planning, academic research, communications, sports, entertainment, the mass media, and much more. India is in danger of becoming a "business-driven society", as Noam Chomsky aptly describes the United States.

We had a bitter taste of the invasion of public policy by corporate interests in the context of child nutrition programmes, especially school meals and the Integrated Child Development Services (ICDS). With millions of children covered, a contract to supply ready-to-eat food to them under these programmes, instead of cooked food prepared by local women, can be very lucrative. India's food industry has not lost sight of this business opportunity, and has persistently lobbied for the replacement of cooked food with branded products in the midday meal scheme and ICDS. One example of these efforts, involving the biscuit industry, is discussed in the first essay in this section. That particular attempt was defeated, but there have been many others since, and some of them have succeeded, at the state level if not at the national level.

The hold of corporate power on public policy in India has many other manifestations, from the plunder of public sector banks to the appropriation of land, water, minerals, and (until recently) spectrum at throwaway prices. Another example is technocracy, in the broad sense of an over-influence of technology experts on public policy. Technological innovation, of course, is very important and has often made major contributions to more effective social policies. For instance, the NREGA's web-based monitoring and information system (MIS) has become a model of pro-active information disclosure for all government programmes in India. Sometimes, however, technology seems to become an end in itself, driven by hidden interests at the expense of the public.

There is a strong element of technocracy in India's unique identity (UID) project, also known as Aadhaar. The project was sold to the public by claiming, firstly, that Aadhaar was a "voluntary facility", and secondly, that its main purpose was to remove corruption from social programmes. This was a brilliant act of what the leading lights of Aadhaar call "smart demand evangelisation". The claim that Aadhaar was voluntary defused criticism from libertarians, despite Aadhaar representing a real threat to privacy, civil liberties, and the right to dissent. The swift linkage of social programmes like the NREGA to Aadhaar helped to herd people en masse towards UID enrolment centres. Later on, it became clear that the voluntary nature of Aadhaar was a fiction, and that the real purpose of the project had little to do with social policy. Rather, the project seems to be driven by a convergence of corporate interests (from the biometric industry, software companies, finance-technology developers, and so on) and state interests (related inter alia to the value of Aadhaar as a tool of surveillance). The last three essays in this section were written in response to the relentless propaganda that surrounded Aadhaar from the beginning.

The Aadhaar juggernaut, however, rolls on. In fact, as this book goes to press, the coercive nature of the project is reaching new levels with notifications making Aadhaar compulsory for children who wish to benefit from the midday meal scheme. No Aadhaar, no food. This is being projected as an anti-corruption measure, but the real purpose is clear: forcing parents to get their children enrolled under Aadhaar (the bulk of the shortfall from universal enrolment is among children). It would be more honest for the government to admit that Aadhaar is compulsory, and to make the case for compulsion.

Glucose for the Lok Sabha?*

(with Reetika Khera)

Anyone who has illusions about the influence of corporate interests on public policy in India, or about the priorities of elected representatives, would do well to read the recent correspondence between the "Biscuit Manufacturers Association", members of parliament, and various ministries. The main issue in this correspondence is a proposal to replace cooked midday meals in primary schools with biscuits.

The trail begins with a letter from the Biscuit Manufacturers Association (BMA) to MPs, signed by the president of the BMA, who is also a senior executive at Parle Products. The letter makes an elaborate plea for biscuits as an "alternative" for cooked midday meals in primary schools. There is a specific pitch for the Rs 3.75 glucose biscuit packet, which allegedly contains all the required nutrients and costs much the same as a cooked midday meal under current norms. As it happens, the biggest manufacturer of these glucose biscuit packets is none other than Parle Products.

Among other arguments, the letter mentions that biscuits have "higher recall". This is an interesting hint about the BMA's real motives. In the business world, recall means the proportion of people who remember a particular brand, and recall data are used to track the effectiveness of advertisements. It is not difficult to imagine that an advertisement campaign based on giving every child the same packet of biscuits every day (at the government's expense) would have high "recall".

*April 2008.

It is perhaps not surprising that biscuit manufacturers, like other businesses, should use their influence to sell their products. As Milton Friedman famously said, "the business of business is business". What is more disturbing is the way MPs reacted to this lobbying operation. How many of them received the BMA letter is not known, but what is known is that at least twenty-nine of them wrote personally to Shri Arjun Singh, the minister for human resource development, and urged him to consider the biscuits proposal. Quite likely, this is just a partial count, as the ministry was "flooded with such letters", according to one senior official.

These twenty-nine letters, obtained by the commissioners of the supreme court in the right to food case, are quite edifying. The signatories include members of most major political parties (Congress, Bharatiya Janata Party, Rashtriya Janata Dal, Samajwadi Party, and so on), except for the Bahujan Samaj Party and the Left parties. Nine of them represent constituencies located in Maharashtra (which has a thriving biscuit industry), and six belong to the Shiv Sena. Familiar names in the list include K. Natwar Singh (Congress), Ramdas Athawale (Republican Party), Syed Shahnawaz Hussain (BJP), and Susheela Laxman Bangaru (BJP). What is interesting is that the letters read much the same across authors and political parties. For instance, the letters signed by Natwar Singh and Ramdas Athawale are almost identical from top to bottom. Similarly, several MPs confidently argue for biscuits on the grounds that "the ratio of carbohydrates, proteins, fats and glucose is quite balanced and beneficial to human health of all age group especially for children" (*sic*).

The clue to this telepathy is not far to seek: most of these statements are lifted straight from the BMA promotion material. In other words, these enterprising MPs saw nothing wrong in rehashing the BMA letter and forwarding it to the minister under their own signature. All this, of course, is done in the name of the welfare of children.

To be fair, some of these MPs may genuinely feel (despite much evidence to the contrary) that schoolchildren would be better off with biscuits than with cooked meals. Even then, troubling questions remain. For instance, did they form this view on the basis of serious enquiry, or were they swayed by the BMA's tutorial? If it was based on serious enquiry, why did they need to cut and paste from the BMA's letter to make their case? And is this kind of lifting appropriate in any case?

The letters also reveal the central role played in this campaign by Abu Asim Azmi, a Samajwadi Party MP from Maharashtra. Aside from contributing one of the gems sent to the ministry, Mr Azmi wrote similar letters to other ministries, seeking appointments with a host of bureaucrats and ministers. These letters repeatedly state that the BMA has presented "the merits of substituting biscuits with the existing pre-cooked meal". This sentence, aside from exposing Mr Azmi's innocence of the matter (there is no such thing as an "existing pre-cooked meal"), is one indication – among many – that the intention is to *replace* cooked meals with biscuits, and not just *add* biscuits to the menu.

It is not the first time that Mr Azmi bravely risks his reputation. During the last few years, he has battled a spate of allegations about his role in recent incidents of communal violence in Mumbai, including an affidavit filed in 1997 by the then Bombay police commissioner claiming that he had links with Dawood Ibrahim. He has also been chargesheeted by the Economic Offences Wing for siphoning off government funds in the multi-crore cobbler scam of 1995. Whatever the truth of these allegations (the system often confuses victim with criminal), Mr Azmi seems to live dangerously.

The silver lining is that the biscuit lobby received a fitting reply from the ministry of human resource development (MoHRD). The response was well formulated, coming as it did after a round of consultations with state governments. Most of them shot down the proposal for replacing cooked meals with biscuits. So did nutrition experts such as Dr B. Sesikeran (Director, National Institute of Nutrition), who clearly stated that the midday meal scheme "is supposed to provide one wholesome meal to schoolchildren and biscuits cannot replace it." Following on this, Arjun Singh sent a strong rejection letter to the BMA. Similarly, when this issue came up in the Lok Sabha on 26 February 2008, Md Ali Ashraf Fatmi, minister of state for human resource development, clarified that the biscuit approach does not "fulfill the nutritional norms, dietary requirement and satiety of children and further it also deprives many intrinsic benefits that are being derived through present pattern of implementation."

All is well that ends well in this case. It is worth mentioning, however, that this is not an isolated attack on cooked midday meals for Indian children. Just to cite another example, Real Contracts Private Limited recently approached the MoHRD with a proposal to replace freshly cooked midday meals with "Ready to Cook and Serve Hot" meals – dehydrated food that would just require boiling before serving. As Arjun Singh himself put it in a recent letter to Smt Mayawati (chief minister of Uttar Pradesh) on this issue: "We are, indeed, dismayed at the growing requests for introduction of pre-cooked foods, emanating largely from suppliers/marketers of packaged foods, and aimed essentially at penetrating and deepening the market for such foods."

According to recent media reports, the BMA has not given up. Undeterred by the rebuttal on midday meals, the association has now written to Ms Renuka Chowdhury, minister of state for women and child development, with a similar proposal for supplying biscuits to children below the age of six years under the Integrated Child Development Services (ICDS). It remains to be seen whether Ms Chowdhury will deliver them as straight an arrow as did the fearless Arjun.

Nehruvian Budget in the Corporate Age*

Once upon a time, around the end of the Second World War, there was a naïve view in development economics that growth was mainly a matter of capital investment – building dams, roads, factories, and so on. Further, since the private sector was not equal to the task, the state had to take the lead. So India's early five-year plans were largely about state investment in infrastructure. Human capital, as economists call it, was badly neglected.

This development strategy had little to do with Nehru – it was common around the world at that time and almost unanimously supported by economists, including many who are now ferocious critics of so-called Nehruvian socialism. Anyway, it had some results: prolonged economic stagnation under the Raj gave way to the so-called "Hindu rate of growth" (about 3.5 per cent per year) of the 1950s and 1960s. But clearly, something was missing.

Among early voices of dissent was none other than Milton Friedman, who came to India in 1955 and submitted an enlightening "memorandum to the Government of India" where he warned against "policies that increase physical investment at the expense of investment in human capital". Some Indian economists were on the same wavelength, notably B.V. Krishnamurthi, who wrote a sharp note of dissent on education policy in the same year, where he castigated the government for applying "the calculus of the private grocery merchant to a matter like education". Another dissident, from a very different point of view, was Dr Ambedkar, who saw mass education as essential

*March 2015.

for the liberation of the oppressed. The critics, however, were sidelined and India is still paying a heavy price for it today.

Later, further advances in development economics vindicated these critical thinkers. Needless to say, physical capital is important for growth. But so is human capital, along with related factors such as economic institutions and social norms. Further, growth is not the same as development, in the broad sense of improvements in the quality of life. Growth can be an important tool of development, but the extent to which growth translates into development depends both on the character of the growth process and on various forms of public action.

Oddly, the NDA government's recent budget junks these insights and goes back to the days of Jawaharlal Nehru, when growth and development sounded synonymous, physical capital was thought to be the key, and human capital took the back seat. Growth, we are told, is the overriding objective of public policy – the rest will follow. And the key to growth is "infrastructure" – or rather, a certain kind of infrastructure that the corporate sector favours. Further, infrastructural investment has to be done mainly by the government. So public investment in infrastructure (mainly roads and railways, à la Nehru) gets huge funds, and everything else gets squeezed with the notable exception of defence. Health and education, in particular, receive unprecedented shock treatment.

The revived emphasis on infrastructure is not the NDA's idea. Montek Singh Ahluwalia, the one-man pillar of economic policy under the UPA government, already had grand plans for infrastructural investment – one trillion dollars of it, no less, over five years. What is new is the idea that infrastructure should come from public investment. Unlike Nehru, Ahluwalia wanted a large part of infrastructural investment to be made by the private sector under public–private partnerships (PPPs). But now it's all about public investment again. That sounds a little odd, considering that the public sector is disparaged to no end in the business media. So where does that come from?

The answer is given with great clarity in the finance ministry's "Mid-Year Economic Analysis 2014–15", authored by Chief Economic Advisor Arvind Subramanian. The report candidly states that "the banking sector is increasingly unable and unwilling to lend to the real sector", because its balance sheets have been ruined by Rs 18 lakh crores of failed or stalled projects – mainly infrastructure projects in the PPP mode. "In this context", says the report, "it is imperative to consider the case for reviving public investment as one of the key engines of growth." In other words, after raiding public sector banks and leaving it to the taxpayers to clean the mess of "non-performing assets", the corporate sector is now counting on the public sector to provide it with world-class highways and airports – at the expense of the taxpayer once again.

Raghuram Rajan, no-nonsense governor of the Reserve Bank of India, had some strong words on this state of affairs in recent months. In a lecture at the Institute of Rural Management (IRMA) on 25 November 2014, he pointed out that the Indian corporate sector enjoyed something approaching "riskless capitalism", and appealed for "a change of mindset, where the wilful or non-cooperative defaulter is not lionised as a captain of industry, but justly chastised as a freeloader on the hard-working people of this country." The finance minister, however, is more sympathetic to corporate interests. Not only is he obliging the corporate sector's demand for world-class infrastructure at public expense, his budget speech also calls for a new PPP model of infrastructure development with a "rebalancing of risk", where "the sovereign [i.e. the government] will have to bear a major part of the risk".

Predictably enough, corporates were falling over each other to praise the budget. The fallout for the social sector, however, is deeply worrying. For the first time ever, critical social programmes like school meals and the Integrated Child Development Services (ICDS) are facing deep budget cuts. The gap is to be filled, we are told, by state governments using their enhanced share of the divisible pool of taxes. Anyone with a minimal understanding of centre–state relations is likely to hear alarm bells. Why the axe fell so heavily on children is also unclear.

Another serious victim of this budget squeeze is the health sector. As is well known, public spending on health is lower in India than in almost any other country, as a proportion of GDP. This year, it may go down not only as a proportion of GDP, or in real terms, but even – for the first time – in money terms. Incidentally, in the previous budget, Finance Minister Arun Jaitley announced a grand plan for "universal health assurance". There is not a word of it in last week's budget speech. Instead, the finance minister now promises a new grand plan for "universal social security". As before, there are no specifics, no timelines, and no budgetary commitments worth the name.

The most worrying aspect of this squeeze is that it was greeted with glee in the mainstream media. It signals, we are told, a welcome shift of emphasis from "handouts" to productive investment. But the big-ticket handouts, like subsidies for the privileged, actually remain. Social programmes that can make a real contribution to people's well-being and productive capacity, on the other hand, face severe budget cuts. Welcome back to the Third World.

Unique Identity Dilemma*

It is easy to see why the Unique Identity (UID) project, also known as Aadhaar, has caught the imagination of many administrators, economists, and policy-makers. Identity verification is a common problem in India and Aadhaar sounds like a foolproof solution to it. The idea is really smart and the technology is cutting-edge. After the initial hurdle of universal enrolment, numerous applications are possible: monitoring the attendance of government employees, linking multiple databases, fighting tax evasion, facilitating the portability of social benefits, and much more. When ace promoter Nandan Nilekani was appointed to lead the project, the happy fate of Aadhaar appeared to be sealed.

And yet, Nilekani's sales pitch left one question unanswered: is Aadhaar voluntary or compulsory? The initial claim was that Aadhaar is a voluntary facility. In fact, this is how many sceptics (like business guru Jaithirth Rao, a committed libertarian) were swayed. Yet this claim was clearly hollow: how could Nilekani, or the Unique Identification Authority of India (UIDAI), assure us that Aadhaar was voluntary when they had no control over its applications? The UIDAI's real position was: "we provide the number, it is up to the government to decide what to do with it".

This raised the possibility that Aadhaar would become mandatory for various social programmes such as the National Rural Employment Guarantee Act (NREGA) and the public distribution system. In fact, it quickly became clear that the central government was keen

*March 2015.

to impose Aadhaar on a whole series of schemes – almost anything that involved identify verification. That suited the UIDAI very well, since it led people to rush to Aadhaar enrolment centres. Indeed, the UIDAI's claim that Aadhaar was a voluntary facility posed a problem – how would enrolment be fast-tracked? The government's imposition of UID as an eligibility condition of social benefits provided a neat answer.

And so, a tacit understanding quickly emerged that while Aadhaar was voluntary in principle, it was due to become essential for anyone who wanted to function – get a driving licence, transfer property, have a civil marriage, or just get paid as an NREGA worker. In short, frankly speaking, it was compulsory.

This should have called for a reassessment of the whole project, because there is a world of difference between a voluntary Aadhaar and a compulsory Aadhaar. Providing Indian residents with a convenient way of identifying themselves would certainly be doing a great service to millions of people who lack adequate identity documents. But imposing Aadhaar as an all-purpose identity proof is a very different idea. It carries at least four dangers.

First, Aadhaar creates a vast infrastructure of social control that could be misused. This may sound like paranoia – after all, India is a democracy of sorts. Yet it is a democracy where abuses of state power, from petty harassment all the way to torture, are a harsh reality for large sections of the population. In any case, principled resistance to the growth of state power is important for the healthy survival of democracy everywhere.

Second, the entire project is being rolled out without any legal framework. While Aadhaar is effectively being made compulsory, no law defines or protects the rights of the subjects of this compulsion. Further, in the absence of any privacy laws worth the name, people have no protection against possible abuses of the data they part with – including biometrics – at the time of UID enrolment. Privacy is not only an important liberty in its own right, it is also essential for the exercise of other liberties such as freedom to dissent.

Third, Aadhaar is not always an appropriate technology. Even in the best circumstances, it is not foolproof. In areas with a weak infrastructure (e.g. poor connectivity or power supply), it can cause havoc. Indeed, Aadhaar authentication requires four imperfect technologies to work together: biometrics, computers, mobiles, and the internet. Even a small risk of one of them being out of order can lead to considerable hardship for the users.

Finally, the coverage of Aadhaar is still far from complete, and it could take years to become universal. The enrolment agencies, paid on piece rates, have drained the more accessible ponds, but those who fell through the net will be harder to catch. Even if enrolment centres are created, say, in every block, some people may find it difficult to get there and meet the requirements. As a recent World Bank study notes, identification systems can easily turn into a source of social exclusion.

Confronted with evidence of UID compulsion, the supreme court took a strong stand on this in two successive orders, dated September 2013 and March 2014. The latter clearly states that no-one should be deprived, for want of Aadhaar, of any services to which he or she is otherwise entitled. This order has far-reaching implications since it effectively bans most compulsory applications of UID (with some exceptions, e.g. monitoring office attendance in the public sector).

Interestingly, however, there is no sign of the government having taken any notice of these orders. On the contrary, the UID drive continues, as more and more compulsory applications of Aadhaar are being forced on the public.

The central government's latest move is to make UID mandatory for all NREGA wage payments in 300 districts from 1 April 2015. The ministry of rural development recently sent stern orders to this effect to the state governments. All NREGA workers without a UID are supposed to be "escorted" (*sic*) to enrolment centres, and after that to the bank so that their Aadhaar number can be seeded into their bank account. Everyone knows that it is impossible to do this by 31 March, and that NREGA workers without a UID will effectively be deprived of their right to work from then on – but who cares? Even those with a UID are likely to face serious hardships as the system adjusts to this new and daunting imposition from the centre. Little has been learnt from earlier experiences of similar top-down orders, such as the abrupt switch to bank payments of NREGA wages in mid 2008, which caused prolonged chaos and confusion.

There is another danger on the horizon: the possible reinvention of UID as a security project. After all, it is none other than former Intelligence Bureau chief Ajit Doval who candidly explained, in 2009, that the original idea of a unique identity was "to wash out aliens and unauthorised people", though the project was later "projected as a development-oriented initiative, lest it ruffle any feathers". As National Security Advisor to the prime minister, Mr Doval is dangerously well placed to revive the original idea. Libertarians, left or right, please take note.

The Aadhaar Coup*

The Aadhaar project was sold to the public based on the claim that enrolment was "voluntary". This basically meant that there was no legal compulsion to enrol. The government and the Unique Identification Authority of India (UIDAI), however, worked overtime to create a practical compulsion to enrol: Aadhaar was made mandatory for an ever-widening range of facilities and services. It became clear that life without Aadhaar would soon be very difficult. In these circumstances, saying that Aadhaar is voluntary is like saying that breathing or eating is voluntary. Legal or practical, compulsion is compulsion.

Sweeping Powers

It took the supreme court to put an end to this doublespeak. In March 2014, the court ruled that "no person shall be deprived of any service for want of Aadhaar number in case he/she is otherwise eligible/entitled". This was a very sensible interpretation of what it would really mean for Aadhaar to be voluntary. Throughout the proceedings, incidentally, the central government stood by the claim that Aadhaar was a voluntary facility. The supreme court did nothing more than to clarify the implications of that claim.

It is important to note that Aadhaar could work wonders as a voluntary facility. A certified, verifiable, all-purpose identity card would be a valuable document for many people. But the UIDAI has never shown much interest in the Aadhaar card, or in developing

*March 2016.

voluntary applications of Aadhaar. Instead, it has relentlessly pushed for Aadhaar being used as a mandatory identification number in multiple contexts, and for biometric authentication with a centralised database over the internet. That is a very different ballgame.

The supreme court order caused consternation in official circles, since it ruled out most of the planned applications of Aadhaar. The Aadhaar bill, tabled last week in the Lok Sabha, is the central government's counter-attack. Under section 7, the bill gives the government sweeping powers to make Aadhaar mandatory for a wide range of facilities and services. Further, section 57 enables the government to impose Aadhaar identification in virtually any other context, subject to the same safeguards as those applying to section 7.

In concrete terms, the bill allows the government to make Aadhaar authentication compulsory for salary payments, old-age pensions, school enrolment, train bookings, marriage certificates, getting a driving licence, buying a SIM card, using a cybercafé – virtually anything. Judging from the experience of the last few years, the government will exercise these powers with abandon and extend Aadhaar's grip to ever more imaginative domains. Indeed, Aadhaar was always intended to be "ubiquitous", as Nandan Nilekani himself puts it.

Mass Surveillance

Why is this problematic? Various concerns have been raised, from the unreliability of biometrics to possible breaches of confidentiality. But the main danger is that Aadhaar opens the door to mass surveillance. Most of the "Aadhaar-enabled" databases will be accessible to the government, even without invoking the special powers available under the bill, such as the blanket "national security" clause. It will be child's play for intelligence agencies to track anyone and everyone – where we live, when we move, which events we attend, whom we marry or meet or talk to on the phone. No other country, and certainly no democratic country, has ever held its own citizens hostage to such a powerful infrastructure of surveillance.

If this sounds like paranoia, think again. Total surveillance is the dream of intelligence agencies, as we know from Edward Snowden and other insiders. The Indian government's own inclination to watch and control dissenters of all hues has been amply demonstrated in recent years. For every person who is targeted or harassed, one thousand fall in line. The right to privacy is an essential foundation of the freedom to dissent.

Mass surveillance threatens to halt the historic expansion of civil liberties and personal freedom. For centuries, ordinary people have lived under the tyranny of oppressive governments. Compulsion, arrests, executions, torture were the accepted means of ensuring their submission to authority. It took long and harsh struggles to win the freedoms that we enjoy and take for granted today – the freedom to move about as we wish, associate with whoever we like, speak up without fear. No doubt these freedoms are still elusive for large sections of the population, especially Dalits and those who live under the boot of the security forces. But that is a case for expansion, not restriction, of the freedoms we already have.

The Aadhaar bill asks us to forget these historic struggles and repose our faith in the benevolence of the government. Of course, there is no immediate danger of democracy being subverted or civil liberties being suspended. Only an innocent, however, would fail to anticipate Aadhaar being used as a tool of mass surveillance. And mass surveillance per se is an infringement of democracy and civil liberties, even if the government does not act on it. As Glenn Greenwald aptly puts it in his book *No Place to Hide*, "history shows that the mere existence of a mass surveillance apparatus, regardless of how it is used, is in itself sufficient to stifle dissent."

Uncertain Benefits

The champions of the Aadhaar bill downplay these concerns for the sake of enabling the government to save some money. Wild claims are being made about Aadhaar's power to plug leakages. In reality,

Aadhaar can only help to plug specific types of leakages, such as those related to duplication in beneficiary lists. It will be virtually useless to plug leakages in, say, the public distribution system (PDS), which have little to do with identity fraud. On the other hand, recent experience has shown that Aadhaar could easily play havoc with the PDS. Wherever Aadhaar authentication has been imposed on the PDS, there have been complaints of delays, authentication failures, connectivity problems, and more. The poorer states, where the PDS is most needed, are least prepared for this sort of technology. There are better ways of reforming the PDS. Similar remarks apply to the National Rural Employment Guarantee Act (NREGA).

I have seen some of this damage at close range in Jharkhand, where Aadhaar was supposed to prove its mettle. Aadhaar applications (in the PDS, NREGA, and even the banking system) have had poor results in Jharkhand, and caused much disruption. For instance, NREGA functionaries have cancelled job cards on a large scale for the sake of achieving "100 per cent Aadhaar seeding" of the job-cards database. NREGA workers have been offloaded by rural banks on Aadhaar-enabled "business correspondents" who proved unable to pay them due to poor connectivity. And the proposed imposition of biometric authentication at ration shops threatens to disrupt recent progress with PDS reforms in Jharkhand.

Seven years after it was formed, the UIDAI has failed to produce significant evidence of Aadhaar having benefits that would justify the risks. Instead, it has shown a disturbing tendency to rely on public relations, sponsored studies, and creative estimates (including the much-cited figure of Rs 12,700 crore for annual savings on the LPG subsidy). To my knowledge, there has been no serious evaluation of any of the Aadhaar applications so far. Worse, some failed experiments have been projected as successes through sheer propaganda – business correspondents in Ratu (Jharkhand) and "direct benefit transfer" of kerosene subsidies in Kotkasim (Rajasthan) are just two examples.

No doubt Aadhaar, if justified, could have some useful applications. Given the risks, however, the core principle should be "minimum use, maximum safeguards". The government has shown its preference for the opposite – maximum use, minimum safeguards. The Aadhaar bill includes some helpful safeguards, but it does nothing to restrain the use of Aadhaar or prevent its misuse as a tool of mass surveillance. And even the safeguards protect the UIDAI more than the public.

The wizards of Aadhaar are fond of telling us that we are on the threshold of a "revolution". With due respect for their zeal, a coup would be a more appropriate term. The Aadhaar bill enables the government to evade the supreme court orders and build an infrastructure of social control. Further, it does so by masquerading as a money bill, pre-empting any serious discussion of these issues. This undemocratic process reinforces the case for worrying about Aadhaar.

Dark Clouds over the PDS*

State governments are under growing pressure from the central government to introduce compulsory biometric authentication of all cardholders in the public distribution system (PDS). This top-down imposition threatens to disrupt recent progress with PDS reforms. It also deprives millions of people of their food entitlements.

PDS Reforms

India's PDS has improved steadily during the last ten years (see section 7). The system used to be most ineffective and corruption-ridden, with leakages of around 50 per cent at the national level, going up to 80 or 90 per cent in some states. Around 2007, Chhattisgarh took the lead in reforming the PDS – making it more inclusive, methodical, and transparent. Within a few years, the system was overhauled. Later, it turned out that the Chhattisgarh model (so to speak) was replicable. Odisha was among the first states to emulate Chhattisgarh's experience, with similar results. Many other states also initiated Chhattisgarh-style PDS reforms: broad coverage, clear entitlements, the de-privatisation of PDS shops, the separation of transport agencies from distribution agencies, computerisation, fixed distribution schedules, tight monitoring, active grievance redressal, and more.

In 2011, a survey of the PDS (initiated by the Indian Institute of Technology, Delhi) was conducted by student volunteers in nine

*September 2016.

states: Andhra Pradesh, Bihar, Chhattisgarh, Himachal Pradesh, Jharkhand, Odisha, Rajasthan, Tamil Nadu, and Uttar Pradesh. It emerged that the system was working reasonably well for "below poverty line" (BPL) households: on average, they were receiving 84 per cent of their foodgrain entitlements from the PDS. A similar picture emerged from a follow-up survey in 2013. However, high leakages continued in the "above poverty line" (APL) quota, which tended to be used by the central government, at that time, as a dumping ground for excess food stocks.

The National Food Security Act (NFSA), enacted three years ago, was – and still is – a chance to complete the process of PDS reform and ensure a modicum of food security for everyone. Under the NFSA, the APL category is abolished and eligible households come under two well-defined categories: Priority households, entitled to 5 kg of foodgrains per person per month at nominal prices, and Antyodaya households (the poorest), entitled to 35 kg per household per month. The PDS is to cover at least 75 per cent of rural households at the national level, rising to 80–90 per cent in the poorest states.

In June this year, we went back to six of India's poorest states (Bihar, Chhattisgarh, Jharkhand, Madhya Pradesh, Odisha, and West Bengal) for an update. We found that four out of six had a fairly good PDS, with most NFSA cardholders receiving the bulk of their entitlements every month and relatively low exclusion errors. The last two, Jharkhand and (especially) Bihar, still have a long way to go. Even there, however, the situation is much better than a few years ago. In Jharkhand, for instance, the transparency of the system has vastly improved, and the official NFSA website is among the best in the country.

Impending Setback

Recent progress, however, is in danger of being undone soon due to the central government's counterproductive push for Aadhaar-based biometric authentication (ABBA) in the PDS. This involves installing point of sale (PoS) machines at PDS shops, and verifying the identity of cardholders by matching their fingerprints against the Aadhaar database over the internet every time they buy their food rations.

This system requires multiple fragile technologies to work at the same time: the PoS machine, the biometrics, the internet connection, remote servers, and often other elements such as the local mobile network. Further, it requires at least some household members to have an Aadhaar number, correctly seeded in the PDS database.

This is a wholly inappropriate technology for rural India, especially in the poorest states. Even in state capitals, network failures and other glitches routinely disable this sort of technology. In villages with poor connectivity, it is a recipe for chaos. Note that internet dependence is inherent to Aadhaar, since there is no question of downloading the biometrics.

Recent developments in Rajasthan illustrate the dangers of impos-ing biometric authentication on the PDS. During the last few months, the Government of Rajasthan has tried hard to enforce the system. The use of PoS machines is compulsory and every PDS shop has one. Yet, according to official data compiled by Nikhil Dey, only 61 per cent of Rajasthan's foodgrain allocation found its way through the PoS system in July 2016, with a similar figure (63 per cent) for August. The rest is either siphoned off or delivered using the old "register" system – which of the two is hard to say since utter confusion prevails about the permissibility of using registers as a fallback option.

Further evidence comes from Ranchi district in Jharkhand, where the PoS system is also mandatory. In July 2016, NFSA cardholders in Ranchi district received less than half their foodgrain entitlements through that system, according to the model website mentioned earlier. The situation was much the same in August.

As in Rajasthan, it is not clear whether those for whom the PoS system does not work in Ranchi are getting any grain through the old register system. Officially, that is not allowed, according to local PDS dealers and officials (indeed, some dealers have been suspended for using this fallback option). Even if it happens unofficially, this dual system, where the PDS grain goes partly through the PoS system and partly through the fallback register system, is the worst. The reason is that only PDS dealers know whether and when the register system is permissible, and they have no incentive to share that information with the cardholders. Quite likely, the new system is *reviving* PDS corruption in Jharkhand, reversing a healthy trend towards lower leakages in recent years.

A short visit to a PDS shop just outside Ranchi quickly brings out the multiple vulnerabilities of the new system. Within minutes, we met many people who had been deprived of their food rations for months because they had no Aadhaar number, or because their Aadhaar number had not been correctly seeded, or because their biometrics did not work, or simply because the PoS machine returned various error messages.

Even those for whom the system works face huge inconvenience. Often they have to make repeated trips to the PDS shop, or send different members in turn, until the machine co-operates. Sometimes schoolchildren are asked to skip classes and try their luck at the PDS shop. This unreliable system causes a colossal waste of time for everyone.

By the way, all this is one year after I was told by the food department's upbeat consultants that "the PoS system is functional throughout Ranchi district".

The Aadhaar Juggernaut

In spite of ample warnings, the central government continues to push for compulsory Aadhaar-based biometric authentication in the PDS. Incidentally, this is a violation of supreme court orders. The court did allow the *use* of Aadhaar in the PDS, but not its *imposition* for PDS users. Nor can the government invoke the Aadhaar act to justify this move: the relevant sections of the act are yet to be notified.

ABBA seems to be expected to ensure a corruption-free PDS. This expectation, however, builds on a misunderstanding of PDS leakages.

The main vulnerability today, at least in Jharkhand, is not identity fraud (e.g. bogus cards), but quantity fraud: PDS dealers often give people less than what they are entitled to, and pocket the rest. ABBA is powerless to prevent quantity fraud. Biometrics may help to reduce identity fraud, such as it is, but that does not justify depriving people of their food entitlements when the technology fails.

As with many other applications of Aadhaar, this one is proceeding like a juggernaut, without paying serious attention to the collateral damage. Instead, the central government peddles bogus figures of Aadhaar-enabled financial savings (often relayed by unsuspecting columnists or economists) to justify further imposition of the technology. It is only when concerned journalists, activists, or researchers make enquiries from the victims that we learn about the adverse effects of Aadhaar on the PDS.

The central government and its advisors pride themselves on their commitment to "evidence-based policy", but this is a case where evidence is being systematically ignored to press on with technological solutions based on blind faith (handsomely nurtured by commercial interests). The drive to impose biometric authentication on the PDS must stop immediately to avoid further damage. There are better ways of plugging last-mile leakages, including simpler technologies not dependent on the internet. Imposing a technology that does not work on people who depend on it for their survival is a grave injustice.

Notes

Glucose for the Lok Sabha?

This article is largely based on correspondence obtained from the ministry of human resource development, under the Right to Information Act, by the office of the commissioners of the supreme court in the right to food case. Thanks are due to Biraj Patnaik for sharing this information.

Nehruvian Budget in the Corporate Age

This essay was written immediately after the finance minister's 28 February 2015 budget speech, and draws on the budget papers 2015–16. The initial social-sector cuts in 2015–16 were so shocking (e.g. around 50 per cent for ICDS and 36 per cent for midday meals) that some of them had to be partly reversed later in the year. On the so-called Hindu rate of growth, Friedman's 1955 memorandum, and related matters, see Drèze and Sen 2013. On the "wilful or non-cooperative defaulter" and the dangers of "riskless capitalism", see Rajan 2014. B.V. Krishnamurthi's 1955 note of dissent on education is reprinted in Balasubramanyam 2001.

Unique Identity Dilemma

The supreme court orders mentioned in the text were reiterated several times. For instance, an order dated 15 October 2015 states that "the Aadhaar card scheme is purely voluntary and it cannot be made mandatory till the matter is finally decided by this Court one way or the other." Significantly, a further order of 14 September 2016 makes it clear that the Aadhaar Act, passed in March 2016, does not supersede these orders.

The statement by Ajit Doval was made in an interview to *Tehelka*, reported by Tusha Mittal in "Falling between the Barcodes" (*Tehelka*, 22 August 2009). On the World Bank's warnings that "identification systems don't always serve the bottom 40%", see Brewer, *et al.* 2015.

The Aadhaar Coup

This essay was written just after the Aadhaar Act was passed by the Indian parliament, under the garb of a money bill, obviating the need for the assent of the Rajya Sabha (upper house). The same tactic was used by the central government the following year, in 2017, to pass a series of sweeping legislative amendments. The ruling Bharatiya Janata Party has a majority in the Lok Sabha (lower house) but not in the Rajya Sabha – at least not yet.

Dark Clouds over the PDS

The findings of the 2011 PDS survey are presented in Khera 2011b. A preview of the findings of the 2016 follow-up survey in six states is available in Drèze, *et al.* 2016. The problem of high leakages in the APL quota is discussed in Drèze and Khera 2015a. On these matters, see also section 7.

The comments on Aadhaar-based biometric authentication in Jharkhand are based on enquiries conducted with Sneha Menon in Ranchi district; see also Drèze 2017b. The comparison of actual distribution with entitlements is based on official data from the Jharkhand government's PDS website (http://aahar.jharkhand.gov.in).

9

WAR AND PEACE

THE USE OF VIOLENCE is not a very sensible way of settling conflicts. The balance of brute force between two sides generally bears no relation to the merits of the case, so the outcome tends to be arbitrary. Meanwhile, extreme pain may be inflicted on one side or both. Surely, there are more rational methods of conflict resolution.

This is not to say that all violence is wrong. Here it may be useful to distinguish between pacifism and abolitionism.[1] A pacifist considers all violence immoral. That position is difficult to sustain: it is easy to imagine situations where a little violence would be justified (perhaps to prevent greater violence). Also, it is an uncomfortable fact that we owe the freedoms we enjoy today to courageous people who fought against oppression and injustice in earlier generations. None of this, however, detracts from the fact that it is possible to abolish violence (or, at the very least, war and armed conflicts) from human affairs, just as slavery has been abolished. That is, it is possible to build social

---

[1] I use "abolitionism" not in its traditional connection with the abolition of slavery, but in connection with nonviolence. The distinction between pacifism and abolitionism is borrowed from Anatol Rapoport 1992, 1997, though he used it in a slightly different sense. In Rapoport's approach, both pacifists and abolitionists believe in the elimination of war, but pacifists (like, say, Tolstoy or the Quakers) see that as a question of change in personal ethics or morality, while abolitionists (including Rapoport himself) focus on war as a social institution.

institutions and social norms that make violence unnecessary and repulsive. Such is the endeavour of the abolitionist.

The abolition of nuclear weapons would be a good start. Indeed, along with climate change, nuclear war remains a big threat to the survival of humanity. Even if humanity survives it, the consequences of a possible nuclear war are too horrible to contemplate.

There is an interesting contrast between what the public is told about nuclear strategy and the professional literature on this subject. The public is led to believe, firstly, that "nuclear deterrence" has a defensive purpose (pre-empting attacks); secondly, that "mutually assured destruction" is safe; and thirdly, that India is a "responsible nuclear power". In the professional literature, nuclear deterrence has a different meaning – it refers to the use (or, more likely, threat of use) of nuclear weapons to achieve political objectives. Further, it is well understood that nuclear games, so to speak, are risky and unpredictable. Nuclear war, if it ever occurs, is likely to happen by escalation, as the culmination of a series of intensifying hostilities. The dangers are all the more serious when nuclear adversaries are very close to each other and often engage in military skirmishes, as applies to India and Pakistan. Bearing in mind the fundamentally perilous nature of nuclear deterrence, the notion that India is a "responsible nuclear power" gives a false sense of security.

Four of the six essays in this section deal with nuclear deterrence and related matters. The overarching theme is that nuclear weapons are not only immoral but also fundamentally unsafe. It seems to me that unless we get rid of them, it is only a matter of time until nuclear war breaks out somewhere on the planet – quite possibly in South Asia.

The remaining essays focus on Kashmir – not as a possible nuclear flashpoint, though that is an issue too, but as the site of a territorial dispute and popular uprising. One was written in 2000, when I visited Kashmir (more precisely, the Kashmir Valley) for the first time. It was a moving experience. I was overwhelmed not only by Kashmir's legendary beauty, but also by its relatively egalitarian society, prosperous economy, and tolerant culture. Coming from

Uttar Pradesh or even Delhi, it was a refreshing experience in many ways. I also had a taste, of course, of the intense popular aspiration for azadi – freedom from what is widely perceived there as military occupation by a foreign country. Almost every family I met had a personal experience of relatives, friends, or neighbours being victim of the brutality of the security forces in one way or another – search, arrest, interrogation, beating, or even torture.

The aspiration for freedom was intact sixteen years later, when I visited Kashmir again. In the intervening period, the situation was supposed to have been "normalised" to a large extent, from the point of view of the Indian authorities. Estimates of the number of armed militants in Kashmir had sharply declined (partly reflecting an extended ceasefire with Pakistan and the construction of a fence along the Line of Control), and people's participation in elections was read as a sign of loyalty to Indian democracy. The decline of armed struggle, however, took place along with the growth of mass action, best known in the form of stone-pelting, but also involving a range of nonviolent protests or attempted protests. These events go virtually unreported in the Indian media, so I decided to see the situation for myself in October 2016. The last article in this section tries to convey my impressions of the latest popular uprising in Kashmir.

Nuclear Deterrence: From MAD to Worse*

If Hiroshima has become a symbol of the horror of nuclear war, the perils of nuclear deterrence are best illustrated by the Cuban missile crisis of 1962. The recent publication of *The Kennedy Tapes* (transcripts of Oval Office conversations between President Kennedy and his advisers during the crisis) sheds new light on this event. The lessons are enduring, despite subsequent changes in world politics and military technology.

The background is well known. In Washington, following the Bay of Pigs fiasco, covert operations to overthrow Fidel Castro (codenamed "Operation Mongoose") were being planned. Fearing an attack, or for other reasons, Cuba started installing Soviet nuclear missiles on its territory. Kennedy demanded their removal, and obtained it after a series of threats, counter-threats, incidents and accidents that took the world closer to nuclear war than it has ever been.

Deterrence and Credibility

Chilling as they are, the transcripts contain useful insights on the logic of nuclear deterrence. To start with, the 1962 crisis clearly illustrates the real function of nuclear weapons. While the public is told that nuclear weapons are here to protect us from enemy attacks, strategists see a much broader role for them: enhancing the coercive powers of the state for political purposes. In this case, neither Cuba nor the Soviet Union were about to attack the US, yet the threat of nuclear

*August 1999.

war was used to persuade them to dismantle the missiles. Implicit or explicit threats of using nuclear weapons (or, more precisely, of unleashing a sequence of events that might lead to nuclear war) have been made on other occasions in a similar manner. Such threats, for instance, were instrumental in settling the status of West Berlin in the 1960s, in keeping the Soviet Union out of the Yom Kippur war in 1973, and in dissuading Saddam Hussein from using chemical weapons during the Gulf War. The common statement that "nuclear weapons have never been used since Hiroshima" is misleading: they have been used several times, for bargaining purposes if not (at least not yet) as explosive devices.

The Cuba crisis also highlights a fundamental problem with the idea of using nuclear threats for political purposes: the threat of unleashing nuclear weapons against a nuclear state is not "credible", since acting on it would lead to mutual destruction. And if the threat is not credible, the opponent may simply ignore it. This credibility problem, lucidly discussed forty years ago by Thomas Schelling in his classic *Strategy of Conflict*, has haunted nuclear strategists ever since. Rivers of ink down the line, no convincing answer has been found.

One alleged solution, made famous by the movie *Dr Strangelove*, is to install a device of *automatic* nuclear retaliation in the event where the enemy takes a certain hostile step. But politicians seem to lack the nerve to install this "doomsday machine", though there are rumours that the Soviet Union used to have a device of such inspiration. In any case, real-world contingencies are too diverse and complex to be pre-programmed in this way. Mutually assured destruction (MAD) is not as simple as it sounds.

Escalation Games

The correct theoretical answer to the credibility problem is illustrated, yet again, by the Cuba missile crisis. In a nutshell, the answer is that while the threat of a deliberate, full-scale nuclear attack is not credible, one may credibly threaten to create a situation where hostilities *might escalate* into a nuclear exchange. This is what Kennedy did: he felt that the stakes were high enough to justify the risk of a game of brinkmanship which could very well end – intentionally or accidentally – in nuclear war. As it turns out, last-minute concessions on both sides resolved the crisis. But an intrinsic feature of the scenario is that it *may not* have had this happy ending. Kennedy himself considered that the odds of nuclear war had been "between one out of three and even".

Several variants of this general tactic of "risking escalation" have been developed by nuclear strategists. Schelling himself is credited, in *The Kennedy Tapes*, with the "ingenious" (*sic*) idea of "replying to a Soviet move against Berlin with a demonstration drop on a Hiroshima-sized Soviet city". In strategic Newspeak, this is called "limited retaliation" (a shot in the air, as it were). The idea is to show that you mean business, and thereby enhance the credibility of further threats. Another variant is to create a deliberate risk of the situation getting out of hand. To quote Schelling again, "what can make it [the threat of war] exceedingly credible to the Russians . . . is that the triggering of a general war can occur whether we intend it or not."

The basic principle, in each case, is to take a calculated risk that hostilities will escalate. In practice, however, calculated risk is an elusive concept. Even in the sanitised world of game theory, a rational way of handling the risks involved in "escalation games" may not exist. In the real world, mishandling of risks is all the more likely due to faulty information, mutual misperceptions, emotional responses, and a host of decision-making pathologies. Putting the nuclear trigger in the hands of leaders who have problems of self-delusion or alcohol addiction (there are precedents) does not help either.

Kennedy's advisers were not drunkards, yet their ability to analyse the situation was far from impressive. As the editors of *The Kennedy Tapes* note, "critical meetings had an inherently disorderly character", and at least one key adviser broke down under the stress. Some of the advice was frankly vulgar, as when General David Shoup summed up the situation as follows: "You can't fiddle around with the [missile] sites. You got to go in and take out the goddamn thing that's going to stop you from doing your job." The job, presumably, was the overthrow of Fidel Castro. Shoup's advice, like that of other military commanders, was a recipe for nuclear war. Fortunately, Kennedy ignored it.

Responsible Leaders?

Is nuclear brinkmanship a thing of the past? According to K. Subrahmanyam, India's leading strategic analyst, the foolish nuclear games of Western strategists came to a halt in 1986, when Reagan and Gorbachev declared from Reykjavik that "nuclear wars cannot be won and should not be fought." This rhetorical statement was certainly made, but with little effect on nuclear strategies on either side. Indeed, it is beside the point: today, as in 1962, the *threat* of using nuclear weapons can be effective even if full-scale nuclear war is a mutual disaster. As a leading US strategist clearly reiterated years after the supposed Reykjavik turnaround, "creating a situation in which total war can result although neither side wants it is an important tool of statecraft in an era in which military victory is impossible."

The preceding statement is typical of the "crackpot realism" (as C. Wright Mills called it) of US strategists, and Subrahmanyam has argued that Indian and Pakistani leaders are more responsible. No doubt they are. The notion that nuclear threats have political uses, however, is not foreign to them. Is it an accident, for instance, that the idea of "hot pursuits" beyond the Line of Control was floated soon after the Pokhran explosions of May 1998? And is it inconceivable that Pakistan might take a leaf from Schelling's book and plan, say, "a demonstration drop on a Hiroshima-sized Indian city" in the event where India does engage in hot pursuits across the Line of Control? This scenario may sound far-fetched, but it is the stuff that nuclear strategy is made of.

The central problem with nuclear deterrence is that it is intrinsically based on escalation risk. No matter how responsible the leaders, the risks involved are intolerable. Even if the risk of escalation in a single crisis is small, the long-run odds of nuclear war through repeated gambles are bound to be high. The only possible guarantee that nuclear weapons will not be used is to get rid of them – everywhere.

The Future of
War in Retrospect*

One hundred years ago, a world peace conference was convened at The Hague at the initiative of Nicholas II, Czar of Russia. The object of the conference, as described in the czar's invitation, was to seek "the most effective means of ensuring to all peoples the benefits of a real and lasting peace, and above all of limiting the progressive development of existing armaments". The sincerity of the czar's intentions was not entirely clear, considering that he had a vested interest in the limitation of armaments, especially Germany and France's awesome "field artillery capable of firing six rounds a minute". Nevertheless, his appeal was well received by the European public, including millions of women from eighteen countries who signed a petition for peace. The reaction of statesmen was another matter. The German kaiser publicly described the czar's proposal as "the most interesting and surprising of this century", but privately disparaged it. The Prince of Wales, for his part, called it "the greatest rubbish and nonsense I have heard of". The conference, held in October 1899, was described by one participant as "a thieves' supper". A few years later, the thieves in question hurled their gigantic armies at each other for no other reason than mutual fear. The rest is history.

One century down the line, the human toll of militarism is staggering. At least 250 wars have been fought in the twentieth century, with more than a hundred million casualties. As the century comes to an end, the destruction continues, much in contrast with earlier hopes of a "peace dividend" after the Cold War. There has been a

*January 2000.

peace dividend of sorts, in the form of a marked decline in worldwide military expenditure in the 1990s. But this has failed to translate either in a reduction of conflict incidence or in a major expansion of social expenditures. In the 1990s, about half of the world population lived in a country at war in an average year. Further, recent conflicts perpetuate the exceptional brutality of contemporary wars. The main victims are civilians, who accounted for over 80 per cent of war casualties in the 1990s (the proportion of civilian casualties was typically much lower at the beginning of the twentieth century).

The human toll of militarism also includes its adverse long-term effects on development and the quality of life. At the risk of simplifying, it can be said that development trends in the second half of the twentieth century reflect two contrasting tendencies. The first is a sustained improvement in living conditions in many countries, discernible for instance in declining mortality rates, rising per capita incomes, better nutrition, improved education levels and an expansion of civil liberties. The second tendency consists of the periodic wrecking of these achievements in specific countries as a consequence of armed conflict. Afghanistan, Angola, Cambodia, Congo, El Salvador, Guatemala, Iraq, Lebanon, Sierra Leone, Somalia, Sri Lanka, Vietnam, and the former Yugoslavia are some examples – among many – of countries where armed conflicts have played havoc with social progress, leaving behind them a long trail of violence, destruction, and misery.

India, for its part, has been relatively successful, so far, in avoiding the ravages of militarism. Yet the danger is always present. Indeed, the events that have followed nuclear tests in India and Pakistan in May 1998 provide a stark illustration of the adverse effects of militarism on development and democracy. First, military expenditure has sharply risen, with prospects of further increases in the near future. This is bound to reduce the scope for the rapid expansion of public expenditure on basic services such as health and education.

Second, the nuclear tests have led to the intensification of a costly and dangerous arms race in the region. Some luminaries in the "strategic community" apparently look forward to this arms race as a way of breaking Pakistan's back, much as happened with the Soviet Union at the end of the Cold War. It would be wiser to build on Pakistan's desire to avoid an arms race as an opportunity to contain defence spending on both sides, to the mutual benefit of both countries.

Third, war broke out within twelve months of the tests, disproving the claim (often made at that time) that nuclear deterrence had made war impossible. In fact, nuclear weapons are no protection against limited aggression, since nuclear retaliation is not a credible response in such situations: nuclear deterrence did not prevent Argentina from taking over the Falklands in 1982, or Iraq from firing Scud missiles at Israel in 1991. Further, even minor conflicts between nuclear states are extremely dangerous, since the risk of escalation is always present. The first world war is a prime example of this danger.

Fourth, there has been a consolidation of anti-democratic tendencies in both countries. In Pakistan, democracy has collapsed – an ominous development for the entire region. In India, the rising influence of the security establishment has affected the quality of democracy. For instance, the Kargil incident was a period of sustained national-ist propaganda. As one expert on military intelligence aptly put it, "media management has been the buzzword in the Army in recent years" (*Hindustan Times*, 3 August 1999). Similarly, alleged threats to national security are frequently invoked to justify repressive measures (such as the revamping of TADA), not only in conflict areas such as Kashmir and the North East but across the country.

Finally, recent events have led to a massive displacement of deve-lopment concerns by "security" concerns. This point can be illustrated with reference to the extent of media coverage of defence issues *vis-à-vis* development issues. In 1996 and 1997 (before the tests), defence-related and development-related issues received more or less equal front-page coverage in English-medium dailies. Last year, front-page coverage of defence-related issues was about four times as high as that of development-related issues. A similar trend can be seen on editorial pages: between April 1998 and March 1999, as many as 1375 defence-related opinion articles were published in a sample of seventeen English-medium dailies. There is a startling contrast here with the very limited editorial coverage of health-related matters, discussed in section 4.

Among the participants at the world peace conference in 1899 was a Polish economist, Ivan Bloch, author of a six-volume study, *The Future of War*. The book's predictions, considered extravagant at the time (e.g. "the day of the bayonet is over"), turned out to be correct in many cases. Bloch's main thesis was that new developments in the technology of war, such as "the introduction of the magazine rifle", had made war "impossible, now that it is clear that war means suicide". However, he added that "until mankind has made experience of the deadliness of its weapons, there will be terrible bloodshed." One hundred years later, the "terrible bloodshed" has occurred, but war is no more impossible than it was in Bloch's days. Nations continue to seek security in the unilateral accumulation of ever more terrifying weapons, in spite of the proven failure of this approach. The case for a different approach, based on détente and co-operation, is overwhelming.

Kashmir: Manufacturing Ethnic Conflict*

Kashmir has often been described as a paradise, and the term strikes the visitor as appropriate in more ways than one. The description usually refers to the landscape, which is indeed stunning, especially the panoramic view of the Himalayas in their full glory. On a less predictable note, Kashmir looks refreshingly prosperous and civilised compared with other parts of North India.

The Valley, where the majority of the Kashmiri population lives, boasts a vibrant rural economy based on wide-ranging farm products (rice, apples, vegetables, saffron, milk, meat, fish) as well as a diversity of manufactures, from carpets to cricket bats. Living conditions are good by Indian standards, and so is the public infrastructure. What is more, most families own at least some land, so that extreme poverty is rare. "*Yahan roti, kapada aur makaan sab ke paas hai*" (Here everyone has food, clothes, and housing), I was often told in the villages, and the statement has a ring of truth. It is all the more tragic that economic development in Kashmir is now stifled by armed conflict.

On a similar note, Kashmiri society and culture look anything but "backward" (as often implied in the Indian media). One gets the impression of a relatively well-integrated society with a fine blend of tradition and modernity. Most villages have a mosque as well as an "English-medium" school. Kashmiri women seem to enjoy a higher social status than their North Indian counterparts, in many respects. Of course, gender relations in Kashmir are quite conservative, with clearly demarcated gender roles and little participation of women in

*March 2000.

public institutions. However, they are less oppressive than elsewhere in some important ways: purdah is uncommon, female infanticide and bride-burning are virtually unknown, married women retain a strong bond with their parents and siblings, widow remarriage is viewed in a positive light, and sexual harassment in public places is regarded as a serious matter. There also seems to be a positive attitude towards girls' education.

Such are the initial impressions I formed of Kashmir when I visited it for the first time last month. Curious to learn more, I hired a bicycle in Srinagar and spent a few days riding around the Valley and talking with local residents. My initial purpose was to study the schooling situation, but it turned out to be difficult not to focus on people's overwhelming concern: the endless zulm (repression) unleashed by the security forces.

The security forces were rarely out of sight, even in remote villages. As far as the local population is concerned, Kashmir is occupied by a foreign army. Everywhere I went, there were sobering tales of harassment at the hands of the Indian army and para-military forces: curfews, searches, interrogations, killings of suspected militants, and accidental as well as intentional killings of innocent civilians, to mention a few complaints. In one village, I was told that a father and son had recently been shot in the knee before being pushed into a house in flames. In several villages, shops and houses had recently been burnt in retaliation against recent killings of army personnel – a prime example of "collective punishment", proscribed by international conventions. Physical hardships are compounded by constant humiliation. "Imagine how we feel when a Bihari or a Madrasi asks us for our identity card in our own country, when *we* should be asking them for their papers", said one. In a similar vein, a middle-class woman in Srinagar complained that her house had recently been searched by a "*Chambal ka daku*" (Chambal dacoit) in uniform.

Most people trace the beginning of this nightmare to 1989, when violence first spread in the Valley. The situation that has prevailed since then is referred to as "militancy". This does not mean that people hold militants – local or foreign – responsible for the problem. "Militancy" is simply the situation. As for the militants, they seem to enjoy varying degrees of popular support, partly due to their decent behaviour towards the people (often contrasted with the brutality of the security forces), partly because they are seen to be upholding the common cause – azadi.

Azadi (freedom) has come to be identified with an independent state, but the main concern of ordinary people is to be able to lead their life without harassment, and to be free from Delhi's yoke. Interestingly, one person said that "before 1989, there was azadi". He added, however, that things have come to a point where azadi cannot be achieved short of an independent state. It is possible that most people would, in fact, be willing to accept a compromise, for the sake of ending the repression, if it involves the substantive freedoms they aspire to. Those who are unlikely to compromise are the hard-core militants, whose power and influence has been greatly enhanced by the Indian government's iron-fist approach to the situation.

Asked whether the ongoing conflict was in part a Hindu–Muslim conflict, people emphatically said "no". Some respondents even had difficulty understanding the question: it simply had not occurred to them to think in those terms. They insisted that it was simply "*azadi ki ladai*" (a freedom struggle). Considering that this is a situation where, effectively, a predominantly Muslim population is brutally policed by a predominantly Hindu army (which takes its orders from a BJP-led government), it is remarkable that the conflict has not taken a more communal turn. Asked about the flight of Kashmiri pandits in 1990, most people said, "*Jagmohan ne unko bhaga diya*" (Jagmohan drove them away). This is probably a mixture of truth and propaganda, but the perception is interesting. In one remote village, I met Hindu and Sikh families; they were quite happy there and felt secure.

Kashmiris come across as peace-loving people, and they are even said to take pride in their non-violent nature. "People here used to hate guns", one teacher told me. Folklore has it that Kashmiri men used to be capable of little more violence than throwing their kangris (fire-pots) at each other. While these clichés should not be taken literally, there is at least one tangible indication that they contain a grain of truth: Kashmir used to have one of the lowest murder rates in India.

The non-communal and peace-loving outlook of the Kashmiri people, however, is in danger of subsiding as army repression pushes some of them into the hands of foreign-sponsored extremists. Soon after I returned to Delhi, news came of the massacre of thirty-five Sikhs in Chani Singhpore. No doubt this incident will be seen by some as a confirmation that the Kashmir conflict is rooted in ethnic hatred. It is possible to take the opposite view: that ethnic animosity in Kashmir is so weak that the most gruesome provocations are needed to incite communities against each other. The incident reminded me of a comment made a few years ago by a bemused resident of war-torn Bosnia: "The war had to be so bloody because the ties between us were so strong."

On the train back to Delhi, I talked with members of the Border Security Force who were going home for Holi. In Kashmir, I had often felt sorry for the jawans, seeing how they had to stand for hours in the biting cold, bored to death, looking nervous if not frightened. Asked about army brutality, one of them said, "We don't like to beat them up, but they don't talk straight, so we have to do it."

There is no simple solution to the Kashmir conflict. What seems clear is that the present stand of the Indian government is a trifle contradictory. In international fora, mediation is rejected on the grounds that Pakistan and India have agreed to resolve the Kashmir dispute bilaterally. When Pakistan approaches India for talks, it is told that Kashmir is an internal matter (despite India's own claim to "Pakistan-occupied Kashmir"). Within India, however, Kashmir is treated like a colony, unworthy of democratic rights. It is no wonder that the Indian government's attempt to entice the state into the national fold has failed to strike a chord with the Kashmiri people.

The Warped Logic of
Nuclear Gambles*

It is difficult to attribute a shred of rationality to the war preparations that are taking place in India. Aside from being ethically objectionable, they serve no useful purpose.

The impulse behind these war preparations is easy to understand. As the Indian leadership sees it, cross-border terrorism cannot be allowed to continue. Sooner or later, "we have to hit back". Let us for the moment accept this discourse of counter-terrorism, even though it may hide other designs, as discussed below. Where will this reaction lead?

Pakistani leaders have made it clear that if they are pushed to the wall, they may use nuclear weapons. Indian strategists dismiss the threat on the grounds that Pakistan would never dare do that, since it would invite a devastating second strike. This confidence is misplaced, for several reasons.

First, it is far from clear that India would really respond to a Pakistani first strike with a devastating second strike. That would certainly be a foolish thing to do, since India has nothing to gain (and plenty to lose) from a nuclear showdown with Pakistan. Also, international intervention may prevent it. Of course, a second strike cannot be ruled out. The point is that India's response is anyone's guess. The uncertain nature of India's response makes it difficult, in

*May 2002. This article was written at the height of the India–Pakistan military standoff of 2002 (known in India as Operation Parakram), when nuclear war looked like a real possibility.

turn, to rule out a first strike: if the stakes are high enough, Pakistani leaders may take the risk.

Second, even if a second strike is certain, it does not follow that Pakistan would necessarily refrain from a first strike. It would be naïve to expect nuclear decisions in a war situation to be based on a rational assessment of the consequences. Further, suicide is not incompatible with rationality. People often risk or sacrifice their life for what they regard as a higher purpose, and sometimes even for doubtful purposes such as safeguarding personal dignity or national prestige.

Third, nuclear war does not proceed in neat and predictable steps like first strike and second strike. It is more likely to be the outcome of a process of escalating violence. The risky, unpredictable, and even irrational nature of escalatory processes is well understood in the strategic literature. History, too, tells us that massive armed conflicts often begin with trivial skirmishes, initiated on the assumption – or hope – that hostilities will not get out of hand. Even the First World War essentially happened by escalation.

Indian strategists have produced all sorts of warped arguments to convince us that the military option is safe. The most eminent of them all, K. Subrahmanyam, has recently argued that we can sleep in peace because if Pakistani fingers come anywhere near the nuclear button the U.S. army will disable Pakistan's nuclear facilities through surgical strikes. Really? What if this highly speculative reasoning turns out to be mistaken, for whatever reason? What if the U.S. strikes on Pakistan happen a little late – say an hour late, enough for a dozen Pakistani missiles to leave the launch pad? What if some of the U.S. missiles miss their target, leaving enough firepower for Pakistan to nuke a few Indian cities?

The bottom line is inescapable: if India attacks Pakistan, nuclear war cannot be ruled out. In answer to this, many argue that "Pakistan has much more to lose from a nuclear war than we do". Big deal. When Delhi is in flames and Jaipur has been reduced to ashes, the thought that things across the border are "worse" is unlikely to help.

The problem with nuclear war is that grasping its horrors challenges our powers of imagination. That makes it possible to speak of nuclear war as if it were a game. We can discuss the pros and cons of "taking out" enemy cities or "settling scores" with Pakistan with the same detachment as chess players or cricket fans. The cool language of strategic thinking insulates us from the excruciating agony of the victims.

Assuming that we could somehow trust the impending war to be "limited", what would India gain from it? No-one has explained this clearly. It would certainly be childish to expect that a limited war between India and Pakistan would end cross-border terrorism, let alone help to bring peace in Kashmir. On the contrary, there is every chance that the violence would increase.

Even if a war is averted, troubling questions arise about the strategic value of this kind of nuclear bullying (or "coercive diplomacy", as it is called in strategic circles), not to speak of its ethical acceptability. The possible gains are small, and the risks are enormous. The military build-up on the border has effectively put India at the mercy of enterprising terrorists: any loose cannon with a few grenades and some "made in Pakistan" items in his knapsack (maybe chocolates) can potentially trigger a nuclear conflict in the region. The situation has already been skilfully exploited by the perpetrators of the Kaluchak massacre; the military build-up is almost an invitation for further incidents of this kind.

Given the transparently counterproductive nature of war preparations from the point of view of halting cross-border terrorism, we are forced to consider an alternative reading of the whole situation. What if the cross-border terrorism issue is just an excuse for a war many people in positions of power would actually welcome? The BJP hardliners have made no secret of their military ambitions. Their ideological inspiration, the Rashtriya Swayamsevak Sangh (RSS), never gave up its commitment to Akhand Bharat (undivided India), which includes not only "Pakistan-occupied Kashmir" but also the rest of Pakistan.

Further, the Gujarat massacres have made it painfully clear that the Sangh Parivar "means business", if one can use this deplorable expression. Quite likely, many of those who have supported the mass killing, raping, and burning of innocent Muslims in Gujarat would also condone a showdown with Pakistan. In fact, some of them are making no secret of this apocalyptic dream: they are proclaiming it in open meetings, in television interviews, and other public forums. Seen in this light, the main issue is not whether and how India should respond to cross-border terrorism (important as that issue might be). The main issue is to protect the country from the sinister adventurists who are pushing the region towards the nuclear abyss under the cover of patriotism.

What is most distressing in all this is the lack of concern, on all sides, for the people on whose behalf the violence is supposed to be taking place, namely the Kashmiri people. In this respect, official policy on Kashmir is a bundle of contradictions. On the one hand, Kashmir is held to be an inalienable part of India. On the other, Kashmiris are not deemed worthy of the basic human and civil rights owed to all Indian citizens. Until their aspirations are addressed, the iron-fist approach to cross-border terrorism will be futile and the violence will continue.

India and the Deal: Partner
or Pawn?*

Those who applaud India's "nuclear deal" with the United States would do well to read Gopinath Mohanty's beautiful novel *Paraja*, where hapless tribals often make "deals" with the local sahukar (moneylender), who has overwhelming power over them. For instance, young men go to the sahukar when they are in dire need of money to get married (bride-price was customary among the Parajas of Orissa), and agree to work as bonded labourers until the money is repaid. But the sahukar keeps shifting the goalpost: just as the tribals think that they are about to regain their freedom, he fiddles the accounts and tells them that more is due. There is nothing they can do. The "deal" is whatever the sahukar decides.

Another recurring insight is that solidarity among the sahukar's victims is fragile as an egg. Off and on, the tribals resolve to help each other out of his clutches, but it takes little effort for the sahukar to defeat their plans. For instance, at one point Sukru Jani, the central character in the novel, takes the sahukar to court. His friends and neighbours readily agree to act as witnesses, but later turn hostile as the sahukar wields carrot and stick. The old adage "divide and rule" is alive and well.

No doubt those who cherish India's budding superpower status would be hurt to see the country being compared with Mohanty's helpless tribals. But it is hard to deny that the United States has tremendous power in the world today and behaves, in many ways, like the sahukar of the novel. For one thing, the United States government

*September 2007.

makes short shrift of international treaties whenever they stop serving its own designs. In fact, in the very process of signing the nuclear deal with India, the U.S. government is undermining another "deal", the Non-Proliferation Treaty. As the *Financial Times* bureau chief Edward Luce, who can hardly be accused of belonging to the loony left, put it in a recent article: "For India's sake, the U.S. has driven a coach and horses through an international treaty that is a centrepiece of its foreign policy." It is touching to hear that the U.S. is doing this "for India's sake", and I leave it to the reader to speculate on the real motives. Be that as it may, the point is that the U.S. is wrecking one deal to sign another. What, then, is the status of the new one?

Further, the assurances initially given to India in the context of this nuclear deal have already been broken through the Hyde Act. For good measure, the U.S. president went on to reassure India that this act was "not binding" (*sic*), and that he would just treat it as "advice". It seems that the man (the world's super-sahukar) considers himself above the law, and presumably above international treaties – including the nuclear deal – as well. The situation was aptly summed up a few years ago by President George Bush, Sr.: "What we say goes."

Instead of seeing the situation for what it is, the Indian government deludes itself and the public. According to the defence minister, the Hyde Act is "not binding on India". This is beside the point, since the Hyde Act places no obligations on the Indian government. The issue is whether the act is binding on the U.S. government. The defence minister seems to endorse the view that it is not. But if the Hyde Act is not binding, then the nuclear deal is not binding either, since the Hyde Act is the legislation that makes this agreement permissible under U.S. law. And indeed, it is quite correct to say that the deal is not binding, but we are not supposed to know it!

In short, the credibility of this "nuclear deal" is far from clear. Indeed, in the process of signing this agreement with India, the United States government is not only wrecking the Non-Proliferation Treaty, but also violating U.N. Security Resolution 1172 and flouting the directives of the Nuclear Suppliers Group. No doubt it will also shift the goalposts of the nuclear deal whenever required. To say that the deal is "symmetric and reciprocal", as its advocates have claimed, is wishful thinking. It amounts to turning a blind eye to the overwhelming power of the United States *vis-à-vis* India.

All this is a matter of common sense, as is the fact that the nuclear deal is part of an effort to draw India into a strategic alliance geared to U.S. interests. Perhaps the reason why this simple message is falling on deaf ears in the corridors of power is that it comes from the Left parties. Interestingly, however, the U.S. government and its advisers are saying much the same thing. To illustrate, according to Ashley Tellis (an influential U.S. strategic expert and former RAND Corporation analyst), "accommodating India on the issue of nuclear cooperation" would "buttress its potential utility as a hedge against a rising China" and "encourage it to pursue economic and strategic policies aligned with U.S. interests", helping to "shape the Asian environment in a way that suits our interests". Prakash Karat could not have put it more clearly.

Mohanty's novel ends on a dramatic note: pushed to the wall, Sukru Jani crashes his axe on the sahukar's skull and then surrenders to the police. There ends – for better or worse – the scope for parallels with international politics.

Kashmir's Hidden Uprising*

A historic popular uprising is happening in Kashmir, but the Indian public is barely aware of it. I was unaware of it myself before I went there last month (October 2016) and travelled across the Kashmir Valley. I had read, of course, about some sort of "shutdown" happening there since early July, and also about the stone-pelting and pellet guns. But nothing I had read did justice to the situation on the ground.

No Protests Allowed

The first thing that strikes the visitor on entering Kashmir is the massive military presence. Heavily armed soldiers and para-military forces are all over the place. Their number is estimated at 600,000 or so, for a population of seven million – that's nearly one soldier for ten civilians. In "sensitive" areas, such as Sopore, Shopian, and even parts of Srinagar, there is a soldier in front of almost every house, at least on the main roads.

Why are these soldiers there? Clearly, not to repel a possible attack from Pakistan – that would require them to be near the border. Nor are they watching for terrorists: standing at street corners in full battle gear is not the way to hound underground militants. Perhaps the soldiers are there to counter stone-pelters? That makes no sense either, because the simplest way to clear a neighbourhood of stone-pelters is to demilitarise it: the stones are directed at army personnel, not civilians.

*November–December 2016.

We are led to conclude what every Kashmiri knows: the purpose of this massive army presence is to control the civilian population, and especially to prevent any so-called "anti-India protests", however peaceful they may be.

It was a revelation for me to learn that all forms of peaceful protest in Kashmir are banned in one way or another, if there is any hint of a demand for freedom (azadi). The authorities have sweeping powers to prevent protests, not only under the Armed Forces Special Powers Act (AFSPA), but also under Jammu and Kashmir's draconian Public Safety Act. Section 144 of the Criminal Procedure Code, prohibiting assemblies of more than four persons (an old tactic of the British Raj to prevent nationalist protests), is in force throughout the Valley. Assemblies, marches, graffiti, pamphlets, even silent vigils – all these are effectively banned if there is any trace of their being part of a freedom struggle.

Further restrictions on civil liberties ensure that this state of affairs goes unchallenged. Student politics are banned. International human rights organisations such as the United Nations Human Rights Council are not allowed to visit Kashmir. Local human rights activists are also on a short leash – the arbitrary detention of Khurram Parvez during the last two months is the latest warning that they should not go too far. Similarly, when *Kashmir Reader* (one of Kashmir's leading dailies) was banned on 30 September 2016, other media outfits "got the message", to quote a prominent Kashmiri editor. Kashmir, in short, has been turned into a kind of open jail.

General Strike

Despite these restrictions, there have been continuous protests, or attempts at protest, all over the Kashmir Valley ever since Burhan Wani was killed on 8 July 2016. Some of them involved stone-pelting, but the uprising also included a wide range of non-violent activities. In fact, the main protest was a hartal (general strike): during the last four months, shops have been closed in Kashmir, traffic has been halted, and schools have been deserted. This is called a "shutdown" in the Indian media, with calculated ambiguity, and often confused with curfews that have occasionally been imposed by the authorities. But it was actually a general strike. There have been thoughtful exemptions from the strike, say, for street vendors, chemist shops, and specific times of the week. Some public services, notably health care and the public distribution system, were not only allowed but encouraged to keep going. For the rest, the strike brought public life to a halt for months on end. That, at any rate, was the situation until I visited Kashmir in late October.

So far as I can tell from many discussions with students, farmers, workers, businessmen, intellectuals, and others over a whole week, the strike has overwhelming popular support. It is difficult, of course, to believe that public life can be paralysed to this extent without an element of coercion or pressure. Sometimes the pressure is explicit: anyone who drove a car in Kashmir (outside privileged areas of Srinagar) during the last few months ran the risk of a broken windscreen. But this traffic control was not the work of armed squads or anti-social goons. It was the job of local residents and youngsters who support the strike. In any strike, there is a difficult question of how to deal with potential strike-breakers and free-riders.

There is something puzzling about the ability of Kashmir's economy to withstand such a long strike. This was possible for several reasons. First, Kashmir has a vibrant and relatively egalitarian rural economy, a feature that owes much to the land reforms of the 1950s. The strike did not prevent self-employed farmers, artisans, and apple growers from continuing with their work to a large extent. Second, migrant workers from Bihar and elsewhere left Kashmir *en masse* soon after the strike began. Kashmiri workers, therefore, continued to find work, that too at relatively high wages by Indian standards. Third, Kashmir has a strong tradition of mutual support. For instance, neighbour-hood relief committees (often associated with the local mosque) were active after the 2014 floods, and again on this occasion. Indeed, relief work was an integral part of the Hurriyat's "protest calendars" during the strike. Finally, living standards in Kashmir are quite high. Unemployment is certainly an issue, but poverty and hunger are rare, except among migrant workers. Anyone who thinks that the Kashmir problem is due to lack of development is severely deluded.

Along with the strike, a series of protests took place all over Kashmir during this period. A protest calendar was issued every week (with varying effect) by Hurriyat leaders, who seem to have wide popular support. Examples of suggested protests include occupying the roads, freedom marches to the district headquarters, converging to the United Nations office in Srinagar, performing namaz (prayers) on the road, sit-ins in various locations, visiting those injured by pellet guns, boycotting government offices, reading collective pledges, wall-painting, playing resistance songs or music, sending letters to the armed forces, holding conventions on the right to self-determination, displaying banners and placards saying "We Want Freedom", and more. To my knowledge, there are no calls to stone-pelting in the calendars, though it is perhaps taken as read that protests in Kashmir often end up with stone-pelting for one reason or another.

The spirit of these protest calendars was well expressed by Hurriyat leader Mirwaiz Umar Farooq in a "preface" published on 24 August 2016 in *Greater Kashmir*:

> As a war has been waged against us by a mighty force, our only means of resistance against the oppression is peaceful protest. The space for that is also highly constricted. Yet individually and collectively we have to find ways and means of registering our protest. The protest calendar is our collective voice. Each one of us especially our intelligentsia, artists, poets, writers, painters have to come forward and use their skills and creativity to express our pain and sentiment. Every Kashmiri's contribution to the movement counts.

Sledgehammer Response

In the absence of any space for peaceful protest, stone-pelting became the highlight of the uprising. The security forces responded with overwhelming force. More than a hundred civilians (including many children) were killed, at least a thousand were victims of blinding or other eye injuries from pellet guns, and thousands were thrown into jail. Much larger numbers were harassed by the security forces in one way or another.

On 18 October, I joined a fact-finding team of the People's Union for Civil Liberties (PUCL). We visited the family of Faisal Akbar (name changed), a young lecturer who was beaten to death by the Rashtriya Rifles last August. According to witnesses, there was a "crackdown" in the village that evening. This means that soldiers barge into people's homes, beat them up, smash their belongings, and generally spread terror – typically by way of retaliation against stone-pelting. One officer apparently told the terrified villagers, "We know that you are innocent, but if we don't beat you up, you will never learn." Interestingly, the local station house officer (SHO) agreed with their account of the event. Faisal, as he put it, "succumbed to his injuries" – in other words, he was murdered by the army. One rarely hears such consistent accounts of human rights violations from the police and the people. The SHO promised a fair enquiry, but hastened to add that requests for permission to prosecute army personnel were routinely turned down by the home ministry in Delhi.

Every incident of this sort intensifies the rage of the Kashmiri people against the Indian army, and against India itself. This rage, and the passionate desire for azadi, were already evident sixteen years ago, when I visited Kashmir for the first time. They are even stronger today. In fact, the recent uprising, and the repression that followed, have turned almost every Kashmiri into an active participant in the struggle for freedom.

Dead Conscience

The response of the Indian government to this uprising is to stonewall: refuse any concessions (even just a ban on pellet guns), arrest the leaders (Syed Ali Geelani, Mirwaiz Umar Farooq, Yasin Malik, the lot), and wait for people to lose hope. This strategy, however, perpetuates the repression and enhances the yearning for freedom in Kashmir. Nothing unites people like shared persecution.

If the current policy of inflexible suppression persists, the brutality will continue for decades. Continued repression is likely to lead to further alienation of the Kashmiri people from India, and possibly also to a revival of armed resistance in Kashmir and beyond. It would be much wiser to realise the futility of stonewalling, and initiate unconditional talks with all concerned. Atal Bihari Vajpayee (then prime minister of India) had taken significant steps in that direction, and seems to be remembered for it in Kashmir. Today, however, the iron fist is back.

The conformist nature of public opinion in India, when it comes to Kashmir, does not help matters. It is hard to understand how opposition parties, civil society, and social movements have remained silent on Kashmir for so long. There have been no major demonstrations of solidarity with the people of Kashmir anywhere in India during the last few months. Even public discussions of the situation in Kashmir are extremely rare in India. As veteran journalist Kuldip Nayar observed many years ago, "When it comes to Kashmir, the conscience of most in the country becomes dead." If anything, the situation is worse today, as the Indian media further dull our conscience with a barrage of distorted accounts of the situation in Kashmir.

None of this is to say that there is a simple solution to this situation. Any solution would have to address multiple complexities such as the status of Ladakh, the rights of minorities in Kashmir, the injustice done to Kashmiri pandits, how to take Pakistan on board, and more. Perhaps the important thing for now is not to devise a ready-made solution, but to initiate a process that might lead to a solution. The status quo is certainly intolerable.

Notes

For further discussion of many of the issues considered in this section, and details of the original sources, see Drèze 2000.

Nuclear Deterrence: From MAD to Worse

On the Kennedy Tapes, see May and Zelikow 1997. Limited retaliation and related ideas were developed by Thomas Schelling (1960, 1961) in his seminal work on "the strategy of conflict"; the quote on how the threat of nuclear war can be made "exceedingly credible to the Russians" is from Schelling 1962. The pathological nature of escalation games is discussed in Shubik 1971; on related issues, see also Drèze 2016b and the literature cited there. The quote from a "leading US strategist" refers to Robert Jervis 1989, p. 96. On crackpot realism, see Wright Mills 1958. The delusions and illusions of nuclear deterrence, alas, are still alive today.

The Future of War in Retrospect

This essay draws on material presented in Drèze 2000, where original sources are also given. Pakistan was under martial law at that time (starting in 1999, soon after the Kargil incident).

Kashmir: Manufacturing Ethnic Conflict

This essay is based on a visit to Kashmir in March 2000. Murder rates are available from the National Crime Records Bureau. Recent data suggest that even today, murder rates in Jammu and Kashmir are among the lowest in India, e.g. second-lowest (after Kerala) among major Indian states in 2010: Drèze and Sen 2013, table A.3.

The Warped Logic of Nuclear Gambles

The backdrop of this article is the India–Pakistan military standoff that followed a terrorist attack on the Indian parliament on 13 December 2001. Tensions escalated further after 14 May 2002, when thirty-one people were massacred in Kaluchak (Jammu and Kashmir) by three gunmen who, according to the Indian media, had come from Pakistan and had Pakistani chocolates in their pockets. For an enlightening discussion of the RSS's views on Akhand Bharat, see Kulkarni 2016; on this, the statement made by Nathuram Godse in 1948, when he was tried for assassinating M.K. Gandhi, is also illuminating: Godse 2015.

India and the Deal: Partner or Pawn?

This essay was written at a time of intense controversy about the India–US Civil Nuclear Agreement, also known as the "Indo–US nuclear deal". The deal, briefly, involves India separating its military and civilian nuclear facilities and agreeing to place its civilian facilities under international safeguards, in return for the United States agreeing to resume civil nuclear co-operation with India. The deal, however, is contingent on the Hyde Act, the US legislation that modifies certain provisions of the US Atomic Energy Act to make the Indo–US nuclear deal permissible. For instance, the Hyde Act would require the US to terminate civilian nuclear co-operation with India if India conducts further nuclear tests. On US interests in the nuclear deal, see Tellis 2005.

Kashmir's Hidden Uprising

This essay is based on a visit to Kashmir in October 2016. The short film "Tales of Siege", made around the same time by two students from Kashmir University and available on YouTube, powerfully conveys the situation that prevailed then. The Kuldip Nayar quote is from his "Double Standards" (*The Hindu*, 18 November 2000); he was actually referring to both Kashmir and the North-East.

10

TOP-UP

THIS SECTION IS A potpourri of essays that did not fit easily in the earlier sections but do connect, in one way or another, with the themes of this book. For instance, the first essay below is concerned with the living conditions of the urban poor – this fills an important gap in the book, which focuses mainly on rural areas. The essay on caste touches on a central aspect of Indian society, with a bearing on almost all the other issues explored in this book. Similarly, "The Bullet Train Syndrome", though written in a light vein, draws attention to a pervasive feature of public policy in India: the tendency to create separate public facilities for the privileged and the rest, and, quite often, to give priority to the former instead of aiming at decent services for all. This pattern helps to understand India's education system, its health care institutions, and many other aspects of economic and social policy.

The essay on the mythology of social policy also has abiding relevance. A myth is being cultivated, in some sections of the media, that India is a kind of nanny state where social spending has become excessive. In fact, the social sector in India looks very limited in international perspective. There is enormous scope for improving and expanding the better social programmes (along with phasing out some wasteful ones). What is certainly excessive in India is the extent of state support for the privileged, whether in the form of regressive subsidies or tax exemptions or lucrative contracts or licence to plunder the environment.

The same essay ends on a note of uncertainty about the fate of social policy under the new government – the National Democratic Alliance (NDA) government led by Narendra Modi. It was not quite clear, at that time (July 2014, just a few weeks after the new government took charge), which way the Modi government would go in this respect. Today, the picture is much clearer: the central government seems to have washed its hands of social policy and left it to the states to pick up the pieces. This is evident from official speeches and statements, but also, more importantly, from the government's actions. For instance, the NDA government tried to restrict NREGA to selected districts as soon as it came to power, and when that failed it imposed stringent budget caps that led to an unprecedented crash in NREGA employment. The following year, caps were removed and employment picked up, but only to lead to massive arrears in wage payments as the requisite budget allocations had not been made. Similarly, the central government ignored women's right to maternity entitlements under the National Food Security Act for more than three years.[1] Even the ICDS was the target of deep budget cuts (about 50 per cent initially, though that was partly reversed later on), and while the cuts, were sought to be justified on the grounds that states were receiving a higher share of the divisible pool of taxes, there was no reason for the axe to fall so heavily on children. The silver lining is that there is no sign of a similar abdication at the state level – at least not yet. In fact, the slow but steady trend towards more active social policies has continued in many states during the last three years. However, there is a danger that the new outlook at the centre will, in due course, percolate to some state governments as well.

This concluding section also deals with three distractions that have clouded the new government's thinking on social policy: the so-called

---

[1] As this book comes to completion, the central government is finally acting on this: the union budget 2017–18 includes a provision of Rs 2700 crores for maternity entitlements. However, this is barely sufficient to cover one-fourth of all pregnant women, and the government is already talking of restricting maternity entitlements to the first child, that too with conditionalities.

Gujarat model, the "demonetisation" move of November 2016, and universal basic income. As explained in the penultimate essay, I do like the idea of universal basic income in the context of affluent countries, but as far as India is concerned it is a case of premature articulation – there are much better things to do for now with the limited resources available.

I am aware that some readers may be disappointed not to find more discussion of many other issues of critical importance. Examples that come to mind are farmer suicides, gender inequality, and environmental issues (the eternal blind spot in development economics). All I can say in my defence is that these essays were written as stand-alone articles over time, without being meant to constitute a whole. I am not retiring yet, so perhaps there will be an opportunity to fill some of these gaps.

The book ends with a recent essay on "development and public-spiritedness". I felt like using it as the parting essay because too much of this book is about the nitty-gritty of poverty, hunger, and other urgent issues. In this inevitable involvement with the here and now, there is a danger of losing sight of the future, with all its possibilities. Looking ahead, I do believe that changes in human values and social norms are important both to the survival of humanity and to the creation of a society that reconciles liberty and equality. As mentioned in the introduction, ethical progress is an integral part of social development in the full sense of the term.

Rang de Basti*

(with Bela Bhatia)

About two weeks ago, a terse notice appeared here and there on the walls of Sanjay Basti, a squatter settlement in Timarpur, North Delhi. Posted by the Central Public Works Department (CPWD), it directed residents to vacate by 27th April or face demolition soon after. The notice does not explain the purpose of this forcible removal, or specify the area to which the order applies, or mention any relocation plan. Nor does it provide a contact number where further details might be sought – so much for the right to information.

Most of the houses in Sanjay Basti are small, single-room dwellings, with thin brick or mud walls and corrugated sheets on the top. The residents belong to the informal sector of the urban economy: they work as vegetable vendors, domestic helpers, casual labourers, street hawkers, rickshaw pullers, mechanics, painters, drivers, among other occupations. They survive and live without much comfort but protected at least from the deprivations and indignities many of them had endured in the villages before they migrated to Delhi. For the outsider, a basti may seem drab, dirty, and degenerate, a virtual colony of crime and filth. For insiders, trials and tribulations there may well be, but the basti also throbs with a vibrant social life.

In common parlance, Sanjay Basti is a "slum" or "encroachment", but these pejorative terms fail to convey the real nature of this settlement. Most of the residents have been there for twenty years or more, and they have had time to transform their humble dwellings into real homes. Without much help or subsidies, they have made

*May 2007.

thoughtful use of every inch of space to improve their environment, often by recycling middle-class "waste". Their houses are tidy and functional, and what is more, they have character. In this respect, this "slum" compares favourably with the somewhat dull lower-middle-class quarters across the road, built at considerable public expense. As a form of low-cost urban housing, Sanjay Basti is not doing badly.

Ever since the eviction notice came up, people have been worried, fearful, and confused even though their everyday life continues much as before. The notice did not come as a surprise – they have always known that eviction was only a matter of time. There have been many occasions when rumour was rife that the basti was about to be demolished. Yet it survived each time, and even seemed to take root: election cards were made, ration cards were distributed, children were immunised and admitted in local schools. But now, part of Sanjay Basti is already rubble: as a starter towards full demolition, a row of shops and houses (on the edge of the road) was razed to the ground on 6 March 2007. This swift and ruthless operation made it clear that the eviction notice has to be taken seriously.

In principle, Sanjay Basti is well protected from arbitrary demolition under existing policies and laws. The Delhi Laws (Special Provisions) Act 2006 prohibits any slum demolition for the time being unless the land is required for a "specific public project", which is conspicuous by its absence in this case. Indeed, persistent enquiries from countless offices failed to uncover any specific reason for the demolition of Sanjay Basti.

Further, the Delhi Master Plan 2021, which has statutory force, declares and mandates a policy of *in situ* upgradation or relocation as per strict specifications (provided for in the plan itself) of all slums and "jhuggi-jhopri clusters", and a continuance of these settlements in the interim. The impending demolition of Sanjay Basti violates this Master Plan as well as the Delhi Laws (Special Provisions) Act 2006. For good measure, it is also contrary to the slum policy of the Municipal Corporation of Delhi (MCD).

These laws and policies, unfortunately, are being overridden by reckless high court orders aimed at "cleansing" the city from settlements of this kind. Indeed, Sanjay Basti is only the latest target in a long series of slum demolitions carried out under pressure from the Delhi high court and its offshoots – notably the commissioners and monitoring committees appointed to oversee the progress of demolition orders.

These orders are based on the notion that slums are parasitical settlements that tarnish the urban environment. They overlook the fact that slums serve an essential economic purpose: they provide low-cost housing to masses of workers who service the city, and for whom no provision has been made in urban development planning. For many of them, it would be impractical or expensive to commute long distances from the outskirts of the city. For instance, street vendors and roadside workers (barbers, tea-stall owners, cycle mechanics, and so on) need equipment that would be difficult to carry back and forth. Similarly, it is the short distance between work and home that enables many women to work as part-time domestic helpers in the neighbourhood, even as they continue to handle child care and other household tasks.

Slum demolition drives also overlook another important fact about squatter settlements in Delhi: they occupy very little space. Indeed, squatter settlements in Delhi cover barely *1 per cent* of the total land area in the city. This point can also be appreciated by examining Google Earth's high-resolution maps of Delhi. It is a striking fact that slums are virtually invisible on them. The reason is that squatter settlements are tucked away in the nooks and crannies of the city, too small to be visible on today's aerial maps.

On this 1 per cent of the total Delhi area live some three million people who keep the informal economy going and for whom no shelter facilities have been planned. Seen in this light, the case for removal looks much weaker than when slums are regarded as an eyesore and a nuisance. Would it really be unwise to allocate 1 per cent of the land for *in situ* improvement of existing slums, and spare the trauma of forced eviction to millions of people, except possibly when essential public purposes are at stake?

It is interesting to contrast the harsh treatment meted out to "slums" with current policies towards another category of squatters – motorised vehicles. Delhi's private cars alone (there are more than 12 lakh) occupy a larger area, for parking purposes, than all the city's slums. In many neighbourhoods, it has become difficult to move around as public spaces are jammed with private cars. Cars also cause endless noise, pollution, accidents, traffic jams, among other nuisances, rapidly turning the whole city into a living hell. Yet, little is done to stem the runaway growth of vehicular traffic.

This contrast is one symptom, among others, of the class character of urban development in Delhi. The housing needs of the working class are brushed aside, while the city is redesigned to suit the aspirations of the privileged classes. As the Master Plan puts it, the top priority is to convert Delhi into a "world-class city". Here, as in Sanjay Basti, the writing is on the wall.

Voting in Maoist Land*

Latehar district in Jharkhand is one of India's so-called "Maoist-infested" areas, where people are said to live at the mercy of left-wing extremists. On the surface, it is quite peaceful. I have never felt unsafe when I moved about in the rural areas of Latehar over the years. But the calm is deceptive. Over time, one learns to feel the heavy yoke of structural violence under which people live: economic exploitation, social discrimination, police repression, and so on. Most of the time, the violence does not surface, because people learn to stay in their place. But if they step out of line, there is swift repression: beatings, arrests, false cases, even killings if need be. People's main fear is not the Maoist party (at least not among those who lead simple and honest lives), but the traditional upper-caste exploiters, their assorted gangs, and – last but not least – the long arm of the state: the police, the court, the forest officer, state-sponsored anti-Maoist squads, and of course the "security forces".

I was curious to see how voting takes place in these areas, so I spent a day in Latehar on 18 October, the last day of the assembly elections in Jharkhand. I went around half a dozen villages and booths of Manika block, with two accredited observers.

Election day was an occasion of sorts in the area. People headed for the booths in large numbers. The voter turnout rate was around 60 per cent, a respectable figure by international standards. Most people were quite disciplined, and queued patiently at the booths.

Massive security arrangements were in place. On the main road to Daltonganj, for miles on end, there was an army jawan in full gear

*January 2010.

every twenty metres or so. In the interior villages, every booth was heavily guarded. But people were moving about in groups, so they were not afraid of the "forces". Nor did we see any sign of the army or police interfering with the election process.

I was impressed with the administrative preparations that had been made. Voter ID cards (with photograph) had been distributed in advance, and reams of matching identity slips were ready at each booth. The prescribed procedures seemed to be observed. Voters were allowed one at a time into the booth, and the anonymity of their vote was respected. We did not witness any incident of rowdiness or disruptive behaviour.

However, we did observe some serious irregularities. For instance, at one booth (Rankikalan, Booth No. 69) a BJP activist was trying to influence voters before they entered the booth, under the guise of helping them. And we found no active booth after 2 p.m., even though the official timings stretched to 3 p.m. The departing officials claimed that voting was "over", but what about people's right to vote after 2 p.m. if they wished? On my way back to Daltonganj, I also met a young man who claimed that when he reached the polling booth, he was told that someone had already voted under his name. This was an isolated but disturbing sign of the fact that the system may not be as foolproof as it looks. Having said this, considering that this is one of India's most troubled areas, where the local administration is rotten to the core, the entire operation looked reasonably credible.

So much for the good news. On a less cheerful note, most people's vote seemed to be little more than a shot in the dark. At each booth, I asked a few men and women who they had voted for and why. Most of them were quite happy to tell me who they had voted for, but found it difficult to explain why. "Someone told me to vote for the lantern, so I voted for the lantern"; "I always vote for the hand"; and "This candidate is from our area" are some examples of their responses.

Most of the respondents were unable to relate the symbols to political parties. They know about the flower, the lantern, the banana, and so on (there were about twenty different symbols on the machine), but ask them which party the lantern stands for and you are unlikely to get the correct answer. I also noted with interest that the voting machines do not mention any political party. Against each symbol is the name of the candidate, and nothing more. When most people are unable to relate symbols to parties, as seemed to be the case in Latehar, this arrangement reinforces the focus on personalities at the expense of issues.

In larger villages on the main road, the situation was a little different. There, the mainstream parties had conducted intensive campaigns, and people's education levels were also higher. Some voters there refused to tell me who they had voted for, arguing – quite rightly – that it was a private matter. Others did tell me, and were able to associate symbols with parties. Even there, however, I saw no evidence of specific parties being identified with specific issues.

To understand how the poor vote in these areas, we must remember that most of them live in a very hostile environment where the whole system (the contractor, the landlord, the police, the BDO) is against them. So, what people look for is some sort of "strong man" who can help them to get things done and come to their rescue in times of trouble. It may not matter much if that man (or woman) is corrupt, or communal, or an opportunist. And it certainly does not matter much that he or she belongs to the privileged classes. On the contrary, a strong man, by definition, must be rich and powerful.

So how do people pick their preferred "strong man"? It's hard to guess, based on a single day of observation. Some voters may identify with the caste or community of a particular candidate, or with the fact that she is "from our area", as one respondent put it. Some were said to have been given liquor or money to vote for a particular symbol. Some may have gone by rumours that so-and-so was the person or symbol to vote for. And quite likely, many others just followed the advice of someone who matters. It is these influential middlemen, more than the voters themselves, who are wooed by the political parties.

All this helps to explain why Jitendra, a "different" candidate who talks about people's rights and social justice, had a sad face on 18ᵗʰ October. Jitendra looks much like any other villager of the area, and certainly not like an MLA or future MLA (no special outfit, no gizmos, no bodyguards). He took a leading role in a successful struggle against forced displacement in the area, and thought that this would give him a good chance in the assembly elections. Around his own village, Jitendra had a lot of support, and many people were voting for the banana. But beyond that, he didn't seem to count for much. His defeat was assured.

At the end of the day, I wondered why people vote at all. Knowing that their own vote makes no difference, and that the whole system is against them anyway, why do they bother? One answer is that they clutch to the little they have – the faint hope that they can do something to bring change into their circumstances. There are other answers too. To some extent, it may be a form of herd behaviour. Voting is also a social event of sorts – a distraction that brings fleeting excitement in people's monotonous lives.

Yet another answer is that people think of voting as a collective rather than an individual act. When they vote, they feel part of a collective effort to back a particular candidate. This point was vividly conveyed to me last year by a young man in Rewa (Madhya Pradesh), who said: "Had I voted for the flower while others in my village voted for the hand, my vote would have been wasted."

I believe that there is some truth in all these answers. And, in a sense, we don't really need an explanation: voting just requires the sort of minimal public-spiritedness that is readily found among ordinary people in most societies.

What does seem to elude a simple explanation is why people vote for specific parties or leaders, especially in this sort of area. No wonder experts often get it wrong.

The Bribing Game*

In a clever and engaging paper posted on the finance ministry's website, Kaushik Basu (Chief Economic Advisor, Government of India) has argued that the act of bribing should be made legal. Strictly speaking, the argument applies only to what Basu calls "harassment bribes", that is, bribes that people give in order to get something they are entitled to, like a passport or ration card. How the legal system is supposed to distinguish between harassment bribes and other bribes is not discussed. But let us leave that aside and focus on harassment bribes.

The argument is simple enough: if bribe-giving (though not bribe-taking) is made legal, bribe-givers will have an incentive to "blow the whistle" after paying a bribe. Knowing this, bribe-takers will hesitate to take bribes. Note that the paper is boldly prescriptive: "The central message of this paper is that we *should* declare the act of giving a bribe *in all such cases* [of harassment bribes] as legitimate activity . . . this *will cause a sharp decline* in the incidence of bribery" (emphasis added).

The moral acceptability of this proposal has already been questioned by other commentators. However, there is another problem with Basu's paper: the central argument – that the legalisation of bribe-giving "will cause a sharp decline in the incidence of bribery" – is incorrect.

To see this, note that a bribe-giver has three options (not two, such as "bribe" and "don't bribe"): don't pay a bribe; pay a bribe and blow the whistle; and pay a bribe but don't blow the whistle. As Basu correctly points out, the proposal to legalise bribe-giving enhances

*April 2011.

the attractiveness of the second option *vis-à-vis* the first. However, it also makes the *third* option more attractive, in two ways: the bribe-giver is not penalised if caught, and her conscience is also clearer since bribe-giving is not illegal. It is easy to construct examples where the effect of the proposal would be a switch from the first to the third option, leading to an *increase* – not decrease – in the incidence of bribery.

To illustrate, consider someone who is tempted to pay a bribe to get an electricity connection. Suppose that the consequences of blowing the whistle are huge litigation costs, possible harassment, and little chance of getting justice. This is not a far-fetched situation in the Indian context, considering the frequent asymmetry of power between bribe-giver and bribe-taker as well as the nature of the state (issues that receive little attention in Basu's paper). In this situation, "paying a bribe and blowing the whistle" is not much of an option, even if bribe-giving is legal. The real choice is between not paying a bribe, and paying a bribe without blowing the whistle. It is perfectly possible that many people would choose the former if bribing is illegal and punishable, but the latter (paying a bribe) if bribe-giving is legalised. The argument applies even after factoring in the bribe-taker's behaviour, as one must naturally do in the game-theoretic approach adopted by Kaushik Basu.

None of this detracts from the *possibility* that legalising bribe-giving might lead, in some circumstances, to a decline in the incidence of bribing. But Basu's general claim that the proposal guarantees "a sharp decline in the incidence of bribery" does not stand scrutiny.

Basu's argument is all the more puzzling as the paper ends with a plea for acknowledging the role of values and ethics in eradicating corruption: "If we want to really get at corruption, what we need to build up are values of honesty and integrity in society." Well said. But how is the legalisation of bribe-giving supposed to help in building up such values?

In fact, once moral considerations are introduced, the initial argument breaks down once again. Is the legalisation of bribe-giving supposed to make it less immoral? If so, that would tend to encourage, not discourage, bribing. If not, why would anyone blow the whistle after paying a bribe? That would be like drawing attention to one's own immorality. Kaushik Basu suggests bribes be reimbursed to bribe-givers if they blow the whistle. That would indeed give them an incentive to blow the whistle – but this suggestion takes us further and further away from the real world.

It may be argued that paying a harassment bribe is not morally reprehensible in the first place, because the bribe-giver is a victim and the bribe is an act of self-defence. I am not persuaded. When you pay a harassment bribe, you abdicate your duty to use other means to resist the harassment, not only for yourself but also on behalf of others who might face the same situation. You also secure an advantage for yourself *vis-à-vis* others who may not be able or willing to bribe. This does not sound particularly ethical.

If you find all this heavy going, just think about it from a common-sense point of view: does it make sense to fight corruption by making it easier for people to blow the whistle on their own acts of bribe-giving, so that bribe-takers are deterred from asking for a bribe in the first place? Ethical issues aside, this is quite a far-fetched idea, even if it is certainly possible to think of situations where it might work.

Creative and thought-provoking as it may be, Kaushik Basu's paper is symptomatic of a common malady in the economics profession: the tendency to make sweeping policy recommendations based on analytical models that have a very limited domain of validity. In this case, the problem is compounded by analytical flaws as well as tensions between economic arguments and ethical concerns. Basu's proposal is excellent fodder for intellectual debate, but rather misleading as far as real-world policy-making is concerned.

Postscript

I am including this essay with some hesitation, for two reasons. First, while I stand by the claim that Basu's analysis was flawed, his proposal looks less far-fetched to me today than it did at that time. The essay does acknowledge that there are "situations where it might work". One important class of examples arises when people have some sort of principled commitment to the eradication of corruption, and therefore a natural inclination to blow the whistle (this is quite different from Basu's idea of creating whistle-blowing incentives by reimbursing bribes to whistle-blowers). People like that may well find themselves in situations where they are constrained to pay harassment bribes, and in such situations legalising bribe-giving would certainly help them to blow the whistle: failing that, they might fear being penalised. At the time of writing the essay, I felt that situations of this sort were unlikely, but on reflection, that may or may not be the case. Public aversion to corruption, and willingness to expose it, have probably increased in India in recent years, and if so, the domain of validity of Basu's argument must have expanded.

The other reason for my hesitation is that the essay does not discuss the possibility of a modified version of Basu's proposal, whereby giving bribes would generally be illegal but bribe-giving would be exempt from prosecution *if* the bribe-giver reports the bribe. It can be argued that this would be a better formula than Basu's proposal (and also better than punishing all bribe-giving). As it happens, India's Prevention of Corruption Act already includes a provision along those lines, under Section 24. Basu argues that this provision has not worked in practice, but simplifying and consolidating it may still be a better bet his own proposal. More can be said on all this, and indeed, a substantial economic literature has grown around Basu's proposal as well as various critiques (not just mine). Dufwenberg and Spagnolo 2015 is one useful introduction to it, if you are interested.

The Quiet Grip of Caste*

Some time ago I visited a Dalit hamlet in Rewa district. It was hemmed in on all sides by the fields of upper-caste farmers who refused to allow any sort of approach road to reach the hamlet. There were short roads inside the hamlet, but they stopped abruptly at the edge of it. The hamlet had the feel of an island surrounded by hostile territory. I wondered whether any other country in the world still cultivated such absurd and monstrous practices as the caste system.

The next day I read an interesting article on this subject by André Béteille ("India's Destiny not Caste in Stone", *The Hindu*, 21 February 2012). The article began by pointing out, plausibly enough, that the hold of caste in social life is subsiding in many ways. For instance, the association between caste and occupation is not as rigid as it used to be (as Chandra Bhan Prasad puts it more succinctly, "pizza delivery is caste neutral"). Similarly, the rules of purity and pollution tend to be a little more relaxed today than a hundred years ago, at least in public spaces. Following on this, Béteille blames electoral politics, and the coverage of it in the media, for the perpetuation of caste consciousness: "If, in spite of all this, caste is maintaining or even strengthening its hold over the public consciousness, there has to be a reason for it. That reason is to be found in the domain of organised politics." I submit, however, that there are simpler reasons for the survival of caste consciousness.

The real issue, actually, is not so much caste consciousness as the role of caste as an instrument of power. But the two are linked. To

*November 2012.

convey the point, some of us collected information on the share of the upper castes in positions of power and influence (POPIs) in Allahabad – the press club, the university faculty, the bar association, the top police posts, and the commanding positions in trade unions, NGOs, media houses, among other public institutions. The sample covers more than a thousand POPIs of Allahabad, spread over twenty-five public institutions. The share of the upper castes in this sample turns out to be over 75 per cent, compared with a share of around 20 per cent in the population of Uttar Pradesh as a whole. Brahmins and Kayasthas alone have cornered about half of the POPIs – more than four times their share in the population of Uttar Pradesh (they could be said to constitute a sea of POPIs). These are approximate figures, partly based on guessing castes from surnames, but the pattern is clear enough: the upper castes continue their overwhelming control over public institutions. It is not that other castes (or communities) are completely unrepresented, but, with such a large majority, it stands to reason that the upper castes call the shots.

An attempt was also made to identify Dalits in the sample. This required further enquiries, since Dalits (unlike many upper castes) often do not have recognisable surnames. In fact, many of them do not have a surname at all, or, at any rate, are listed in official documents (such as employee registers) under names – or nicknames – such as "Chote" or "Sunita". That itself is quite telling. More importantly, there was no evidence of any significant presence of Dalits in the sample institutions, except a few – such as the university faculty – where mandatory quotas apply.

It is worth noting that the dominance of the upper castes seems to be, if anything, even stronger in institutions of "civil society" than in state institutions. For instance, in Allahabad the share of the upper castes is around 80 per cent among NGO leaders and trade union leaders, close to 90 per cent in the executive committee of the Bar Association, and a full 100 per cent among office bearers of the Press Club (which is, in fact, made up almost entirely of Brahmins and Kayasthas). Even trade unions of workers who belong mainly to disadvantaged castes are often under the control of upper-caste leaders. There is some food for thought here about the grip of the caste hierarchy on social institutions, including some that are otherwise anti-establishment.

There is a little (not much) more balance in state institutions such as the municipality staff or the faculty of Allahabad University. Even there, however, the share of Dalits is minuscule, especially in the more prestigious categories such as "head of department". The reservation norms are evidently being circumvented with abandon.

Perhaps Allahabad is particularly conservative in caste matters. It is, of course, just one city, though it is worth mentioning that Allahabad is a bit of a centre of power in its own right. For instance, at least seven of India's fourteen prime ministers were born, brought up, educated, or elected in Allahabad. And the alumni of Allahabad University are found in large numbers in the civil services and other public institutions across India. Still, there is no intention here of singling out Allahabad, where the numbers happen to come from, for special attention. The point is to illustrate a general pattern that also applies to varying extents in many other parts of India. Indeed, a number of recent studies have brought out, in similar ways, the continued dominance of the upper castes in media houses, corporate boards, judicial institutions, and even cricket teams.

Coming back to the issues raised earlier, it is far from clear why "caste consciousness" has any reason to die down in such circumstances. There is really no need to invoke electoral politics (important as that factor may be) to understand why caste consciousness persists. The dying of caste consciousness, in this situation, would sound like a good deal for the upper castes, since the system of domination would continue, but little notice would be taken of it – and this is indeed happening to some extent. Dalits, however, have absolutely no reason to be "unconscious" of the dominance of the upper castes. A Brahmin who enters the Press Club and finds himself in the company of other Brahmins and upper castes may be unconscious of the situation, and even feel somewhat proud of this lack of caste consciousness. But a

Dalit who enters the same room and finds himself surrounded by upper-caste colleagues, some of them possibly active custodians of the caste hierarchy, is unlikely to feel at home. Similarly, the Dalits who are marooned in isolated hamlets of Rewa district can be forgiven for feeling a little caste conscious.

No-one can be blamed for being born in an upper caste, since it is not a matter of choice. But perhaps this privilege entails a special responsibility to fight the caste system, instead of leaving that to the Dalits – or worse, obstructing their struggle for equality (like the landlords of Rewa). Surely, for instance, there is a role for greater attention to "diversity" in public institutions, of the sort that has significantly reduced ethnic or gender imbalances in other countries. What prevents the bar association, NGOs, or trade unions in Allahabad from ensuring that they do not become upper-caste clubs? Perhaps there is a constructive role here for caste consciousness of a different kind.

The Gujarat Muddle*

As the nation heads for the polling booths in the numbing hot winds of April, objective facts and rational enquiry are taking a holiday and the public relations industry is taking over. Gujarat's image, for one, has been spruced up for the occasion. Many voters are likely to go to the polling booth under the impression that Gujarat resembles Japan, and that letting Narendra Modi take charge is a chance for the whole of India to follow suit.

Three Misconceptions

Some of Modi's admirers in the economics profession have readily supplied an explanation for Gujarat's dazzling development performance: it is due to private enterprise and economic growth. This interpretation is popular in the business media. Indeed, it fits very well with the corporate sector's own view that the primary role of the state is to promote business interests.

However, as more sober scholars (Raghuram Rajan, Ashok Kotwal, Maitreesh Ghatak, among other eminent economists) have shown, Gujarat's development achievements are actually far from dazzling. Yes, the state has grown fast in the last twenty years. And anyone who travels around Gujarat is bound to notice the good roads, mushrooming factories, and regular power supply. But what about people's

*April–May 2014. Note that this essay was written before the findings of the Rapid Survey on Children (RSOC) were released. RSOC data reinforce the point being made in this essay – see "Kerala Tops, Gujarat Flops, Bihar Hops" in section 4.

living conditions? Whether we look at poverty, nutrition, education, health, or related indicators, the dominant pattern is one of indifferent outcomes: Gujarat is doing a little better than the all-India average in many respects, but there is nothing there that justifies it being called a "model". Anyone who doubts this can download the latest National Family Health Survey report, or the Raghuram Rajan Committee report, and verify the facts – no Ph.D. required.

To this, the votaries of the Gujarat model respond that the right thing to look at is not the level of Gujarat's social indicators, but how they have improved over time. Gujarat's progress, they claim, has been faster than that of other states, especially under Modi. Alas, this claim too has been debunked. Indeed, Gujarat was doing quite well in comparison with other states in the 1980s. Since then, its relative position has remained much the same, and even deteriorated in some respects.

An illustration may help. The infant mortality rate in Gujarat is not very different from the all-India average: 38 and 42 deaths per 1000 live births, respectively. Nor is it the case that Gujarat is progressing faster than India in this respect: the gap (in favour of Gujarat) was a little *larger* twenty years ago – in both absolute and proportionate terms. For other indicators, the picture looks a little more or a little less favourable to Gujarat depending on the focus. Overall, no clear pattern of outstanding progress emerges from the available data.

In short, Gujarat's development record is not bad in comparative terms, but it is nothing like that of (say) Tamil Nadu or Himachal Pradesh, let alone Kerala. But there is another issue. Are Gujarat's achievements really based on private enterprise and economic growth? This is only one part of the story. When I visited Gujarat in the 1980s, I was quite impressed with many of the state's social services and public facilities, certainly in comparison with the large North Indian states. For instance, Gujarat already had midday meals in primary schools at that time – decades later than Tamil Nadu, but decades earlier than the rest of India. It had a functional public distribution system – again, not as effective as in Tamil Nadu, but much better than in North India. Gujarat also had the best system of drought relief works in the country, and (with Maharashtra) pioneered many of the provisions that were later included in the National Rural Employment Guarantee Act. Gujarat's achievements today, such as they are, build as much on its ability to put in place functional public services as on private enterprise and growth.

To sum up, the "Gujarat model" story, recently embellished for the elections, is misleading in at least three ways. First, it exaggerates Gujarat's development achievements. Second, it fails to recognise that many of these achievements have little to do with Narendra Modi. Third, it casually attributes these achievements to private enterprise and economic growth. All this is without going into murkier aspects of Gujarat's experience, such as environmental destruction or state repression.

At the end of the day, Gujarat poses an interesting puzzle: why does it have indifferent social indicators, in spite of having enjoyed runaway economic growth for so long, as well as relatively high standards of governance? Perhaps this has something to do with economic and social inequality (including highly unequal gender relations), or with the outdated nature of some of India's social statistics, or with a slackening of Gujarat's earlier commitment to effective public services. Resolving this puzzle would be a far more useful application of mind than cheap propaganda for NaMo.

The Gujarat Middle

As mentioned earlier, the point that Gujarat's development achievements are hardly model has been made by a long list of eminent economists. Yet confusion persists, so I decided to take another look at the data, just in case.

This time I looked at a bunch of summary indexes based on multiple development indicators. One advantage of summary indexes is that they make it harder to cheat by focusing selectively on particular indicators that happen to suit one's purpose. The human development index (HDI) is a good starting point. The latest HDI computations for Indian states, presented by Reetika Khera and myself in *Economic and Political Weekly*, place Gujarat in the ninth position among twenty major states – very close to the middle of the ranking. In the same paper, we also looked at a summary index of child well-being, nicknamed "achievements of babies and children" (ABC) index. This index is based on four indicators, related to child nutrition, survival, education, and immunisation, respectively. In the ABC ranking, too, Gujarat occupies exactly the same spot, ninth among twenty major states.

Another useful summary index is the "multi-dimensional poverty index" (MPI). Briefly, the idea is that poverty manifests itself in different kinds of deprivation – for instance, lack of food, shelter, sanitation, schooling, health care, and so on. Starting with a list of basic deprivations, a household is considered "poor" if it has more than a given proportion (say one-third) of these deprivations. There is some inevitable arbitrariness in the specification of basic deprivations, but nevertheless, the MPI is a useful supplement to other poverty indicators. In the latest MPI ranking of Indian states, due to Sabina Alkire and her colleagues at Oxford University, Gujarat occupies, once more, exactly the same spot.

A new entrant in this family of summary statistics is the "composite development index" devised by the Raghuram Rajan Committee. This index has ten components, related to per capita consumption, household amenities, health, education, urbanisation, connectivity, financial inclusion, and so on. It is based on the latest available data. Looking at the list of component indicators, an unsuspecting reader of the mainstream media might expect Gujarat to emerge pretty close to the top of the state ranking. Alas not. Here again, the result is identical!

There is something almost uncanny about this pattern, since the summary indexes are based on very different indicators. And it's not that I am selectively focusing on particular rankings where Gujarat happens to rank ninth out of twenty. I have reported all the recent summary indexes I know of. If you don't like them, we can always fall back on the Planning Commission's standard poverty estimates based on per capita expenditure. But then Gujarat slips from ninth to tenth position among twenty major states, according to the latest estimates for 2011–12.

The Raghuram Rajan Committee also devised another interesting index: the "performance index", which captures the *progress* that states are making over time in terms of the composite development index. This is an important indicator, bearing in mind that some proponents of the Gujarat model argue that what we should look at is not the level of Gujarat's development indicators, but how they change over time. Which is precisely what the performance index does. Further, it focuses on performance in the decade of the 2000s, when Gujarat was supposed to be at its best. Surely, Gujarat will fare well this time? On the contrary, it slips from ninth to twelfth in the ranking of twenty major states.

In short, whichever way we look at it, Gujarat looks less like a model state than a "middle state" – far from the bottom in inter-state rankings, but far from the top too. If there is a Gujarat model, then there must also be a Haryana model and perhaps a Karnataka model. Incidentally, Maharashtra does better than Gujarat on *all* the summary indexes mentioned earlier. Why, then, is Gujarat held as a model and not Maharashtra? Your guess is as good as mine.

If Gujarat is a model, then the real toppers, like Kerala and Tamil Nadu, must be super-models. Indeed, not only do Kerala and Tamil Nadu routinely come at – or near – the top in rankings of summary development indexes, they also surpass other states in terms of the speed of improvement. For instance, Kerala and Tamil Nadu do better than any other major state in terms of *both* level and change of the composite development index devised by the Raghuram Rajan Committee. Of course, if you believe the touching story whereby Kerala's achievements are actually based on the Gujarat model, then we are back to square one.

An interesting question arises: how did Gujarat acquire an inflated image? No doubt, this optical illusion partly reflects Narendra

Modi's outstanding ability to confuse the public. But perhaps it also has something to do with the fact that our perception of India is over-influenced by the large North Indian states – the former "BIMARU" states. These states have dismal infrastructure, awful public services, and abysmal social indicators. Gujarat certainly shines in comparison – but so do many other states.

Mind you, the "G spot" (ninth out of twenty) may be auspicious. The number nine, according to Wikipedia, "is revered in Hinduism and considered a complete, perfected [sic] and divine number". The Chinese, for their part, associate the number nine with the dragon, "a symbol of magic and power", which also "symbolises the Emperor". If the numerologists got this right, NaMo is well placed.

On the Mythology of
Social Policy*

Few people today remember the letter written on 7 August 2013 by Narendra Modi, then chief minister of Gujarat, to the prime minister, Manmohan Singh. In this letter, available on the Bharatiya Janata Party website, Modi criticised the National Food Security Act (more precisely, the Ordinance) for providing too little. He felt "pained to note that the Food Security Ordinance does not assure an individual of having two meals a day", and pointed out that "[the] proposed entitlement of 5 kg per month per person . . . is hardly 20 per cent of his [sic] daily calorie requirement." Similar sentiments were expressed in parliament on 27 August 2013, during the Lok Sabha debate on food security, when one BJP speaker after another criticised the act for being measly and restrictive – "half-baked" as Sushma Swaraj put it.

One reason why these and related facts tend to be forgotten is that they are at odds with the mythology of social policy cultivated by some sections of the media. This mythology involves a number of fallacies. First, India is in danger of becoming a nanny state, with lavish and unsustainable levels of social spending. Second, social spending is largely a waste – unproductive "handouts" that don't even reach the poor due to corruption and inefficiency. Third, this wasteful extravaganza is the work of a bunch of old-fashioned Nehruvian socialists and assorted jholawalas who took the country down the garden path during the last ten years. Fourth, the electorate has

*July 2014.

rejected this entire approach – people want growth, not entitlements. Fifth, the BJP-led government is all set to reverse these follies and roll back the welfare state.

These five claims have acquired an aura of plausibility by sheer repetition, yet they have no factual basis. Let us examine them one by one.

Facts and Fiction

The idea that social spending in India is too high would be amusing if it were not so harmful. According to the latest *World Development Indicators* (WDI) data, public spending on health and education is just 4.4 per cent of GDP in India, compared with 7 per cent in sub-Saharan Africa, 7.2 per cent in East Asia, 8.5 per cent in Latin America, and 13.3 per cent in OECD countries. Even the corresponding figure for "least developed countries", 6.3 per cent, is much higher than India's. The WDI database does not include social security spending, but the recent Asia Development Bank report on social protection in Asia suggests that India is even more of an outlier in that respect, with only 1.7 per cent of GDP being spent on social support compared with an average of 3.4 per cent for Asia's lower-middle-income countries, 5.4 per cent in China, 10.2 per cent in Asia's high-income countries, and a cool 19.2 per cent in Japan. If anything, India is among the world champions of social under-spending.

The view that social spending is a waste has no factual basis either. The critical importance of mass education for economic development and the quality of life is one of the most robust findings of economic research. From Kerala to Bangladesh, simple public health interventions have brought down mortality and fertility rates. India's midday meal programme has well-documented effects on school attendance, child nutrition, and even pupil achievements. Social security pensions, meagre as they are, bring some relief in the harsh lives of millions of widowed, elderly, or disabled persons. The public distribution system has become an invaluable source of economic security for poor households, not just in showcase states like Tamil Nadu but even in states like Bihar and Jharkhand, where it used to be non-functional. Of course, there is some waste in the social sector, just as there is much waste in (say) universities. In both cases, the lesson is not to dismantle the system but to improve it – there is plenty of evidence that this can be done.

The expansion of public services and social support in India, such as it is, has little to do with any nostalgia of Nehruvian socialism. It is a natural development in a country with a modicum of democracy. A similar expansion, on a much larger scale, happened during the twentieth century in all industrialised democracies (with the partial exception of the United States). It also happened in communist countries, for different reasons. Many developing countries, especially in Latin America and East Asia, have gone through a similar transition in recent decades. So have Indian states where the underprivileged have some sort of political voice, such as Kerala and Tamil Nadu. Many other states, including Gujarat, are now learning from these experiences at varying speed.

Did the UPA lose the recent elections because voters were fed up with "handouts"? This is an odd idea in many ways, starting with the fact that there were few handouts to be fed up with. The UPA did launch the National Rural Employment Guarantee Act (NREGA – not exactly a "handout"), but that was in 2005, and if anything, it helped rather than hindered the UPA in the 2009 elections. After that, there were no major social policy initiatives on the part of the UPA, except for the National Food Security Act which is yet to be implemented. By 2014 the UPA-2 government had little to claim credit for, and plenty to be blamed for – scams, ineptitude, food inflation, the "direct benefit transfer" fiasco, and more. Meanwhile, the BJP had the three things that really matter in an election (money, organisation, and rhetoric) – is it a surprise that three voters out of ten decided to give it a chance?

Coming to the fifth claim, there is little evidence that a rollback of social programmes is part of the BJP's core agenda. As mentioned earlier, many BJP leaders (including Narendra Modi as well the new finance minister, Arun Jaitley) have vociferously demanded a more ambitious National Food Security Act. Some of this is posturing of course, but the BJP's willingness to support food security initiatives is already well demonstrated in Chhattisgarh. Nothing prevents it from doing the same at the national level. Similar remarks apply to the National Rural Employment Guarantee Act: some BJP-led state governments did a relatively good job of implementing it, and the late Gopinath Munde clearly expressed his support for the act as soon as he was appointed minister for rural development.

Possible Backlash

Having said this, there are also ominous signs of a possible backlash against these and other social programmes. Some overenthusiastic advisers of the new government have already put forward explicit proposals to wind up the employment guarantee act and the food security act within ten years, along with accelerated privatis-ation of health and education services. As if on cue, Rajasthan's chief minister Vasundhara Raje recently sent a letter to the prime minister questioning the need for an employment guarantee act. The corporate sector also tends to be hostile to social spending, if only because it means higher taxes, or higher interest rates, or fewer handouts ("incentives" as they are called) for business. Corporate lobbies, already influential under the UPA government (remember the guy who said that the Congress was his dukaan [racket]?) are all the more gung-ho now that their man, Narendra Modi, is at the helm. Even a casual reading of recent editorials in the business media suggests that they have high expectations of devastating "reforms" in the social sector. That is what the mythology of social policy is really about.

This is not to deny the need for constructive reform in health, education, and social security. If one thing has been learnt in the last ten years, it is the possibility of improving public services, whether by expanding the right to information, or introducing eggs in school meals, or computerising the public distribution system, or ensuring a reliable supply of free drugs at primary health centres. But these small steps always begin with an appreciation of the fundamental importance of social support in poor people's lives.

The forthcoming budget is an opportunity for the new government to clarify its stand on these issues. Without enlightened social policies, growth mania is unlikely to deliver more under the new government than it did under the previous one.

The Bullet Train Syndrome*

Anyone who actually travels by train is bound to be a little baffled by recent comments on railway policy in the Indian parliament and the mainstream media. According to the railway minister, for instance, "it is the wish and dream of every Indian that India runs a bullet train as early as possible". Really? To be frank, the average Indian is more likely to dream about a train that runs on time. That may not apply to those who use expensive priority trains like the Rajdhani, because these trains are relatively punctual (at the cost of delaying other trains if need be). But the ordinary traveller is familiar with the debilitating frustration of sitting in trains that routinely reach their destination hours behind schedule.

It is interesting to compare the state of the Indian Railways today with what it was (say) thirty-five years ago, for different classes of travellers. For privileged travellers, there have been major improvements: internet bookings, SMS enquiry services, tatkal quotas, food plazas, and a whole fleet of priority trains (not only the old Rajdhani but also Shatabdis, Durontos, Yuvas, and the oddly named Garib Rath). If you have money, the Indian Railways is great fun, bullet or no bullet. But the lesser mortal who travels without reservation is exactly where she was thirty-five years ago: she has to queue for up to an hour in agonising heat to buy a ticket, there is no functional board to tell her where or when the train is likely to arrive, the enquiry counter is jammed, and more often than not the train is so packed that boarding it is a feat of acrobatics.

*February 2016.

Crowding in unreserved coaches has reached crisis proportions. Thirty-five years ago, it was possible to travel unreserved on most routes and have a reasonably pleasant journey. That is still possible on some routes, especially in south and western India. But in North India, unreserved travel has become a relentless nightmare. Passenger traffic has shot up, but the number of unreserved coaches has barely increased even as numerous priority trains were launched. On the more crowded routes, the boarding of unreserved coaches is now policed by constables with lathis – it is a pathetic sight to see people being herded like cattle into coaches that are already jampacked.

If the focus were on the convenience of ordinary passengers rather than national prestige (at the cost of Rs 60,000 crores per bullet train), big improvements would be possible within a few weeks. Train delays are now tracked to the minute on the net – is anyone using this data to ease the bottlenecks? The queuing system at ticket counters is a disgrace. A single snake queue leading to multiple counters, with railings on each side to prevent leapfrogging, would work wonders. That's how it works in many airports – why not railway stations?

And how about a functional display board? Even in New Delhi railway station, I can testify that the electronic board rarely works. Sometimes it gives wrong or irrelevant information, like the departure time of trains that have already departed. Sometimes it flashes at random like a Christmas tree, or looks plain dead. What does work, in New Delhi and elsewhere, is the good old manual board where a sleepy employee writes down the expected arrival time of each train with a chalk or marker. To read the board, however, you have to carve your way through the crowd of anxious passengers who are trying to get close to it.

Catering is another sad song of the Indian Railways. In the good old days you could get a safe and sound puri-sabzi anywhere for a few rupees, aside from seasonal goodies (cucumber, mangoes, guavas, jamun . . .) from a steady stream of local vendors. Now food contractors have taken over, and often kicked out the barefoot vendors. They sell mainly branded products, from biscuits to bottled water. In textbook fashion, they segment the market and make money by catering to the well-off. Not only is puri-sabzi off the shelf, so are cheap glucose biscuits, because stocking fancy cream biscuits is more profitable. In many stations, there is literally nothing to eat for the ordinary person – whether aam aadmi or aam mahila.

Perhaps all this sounds unkind. All said and done, I love the Indian Railways and have high hopes of it. I doubt that railway services in any other country can match the experience of a long-distance train journey in India – the stunning landscapes, the soothing breezes, the animated discussions, the long hours of peaceful reading punctuated by freelance entertainment from wandering musicians, enigmatic sadhus, and fellow travellers. But I yearn for this great enterprise of public service to flourish even more, for everyone's benefit. The bullet train syndrome perpetuates an elitist approach to the Indian Railways, which consists of creating a pleasant fast track for a privileged minority at the cost of slumdog treatment for the rest. It is, alas, a metaphor for public policy in many other fields as well.

The Mother
of All Disruptions*

Much has been written about the recent move to renew currency notes, known as demonetisation. And yet, confusion persists on basic aspects of this issue. Consider for instance the term "black money". This term has two distinct connotations. In economics, black money refers to illegal earnings. Income earned by evading taxes is black money; so is income earned by selling drugs or accepting a bribe. In the public imagination, however, black money stands for a stock of banknotes, hidden in suitcases or basements, accumulated in the course of these illegal activities. The two concepts are very different, and confusion between the two is a common source of misunderstanding in the debate on demonetisation.

Gambling with People's Lives

Demonetisation, in itself, does not prevent illegal earnings at all. It targets black money in the sense of illegally acquired bank notes. But this stock of tainted banknotes may not be large. Crooks know better than to keep their illegal income in suitcases of cash. Instead, they spend, invest, launder, or convert it in one way or another. They use it to buy property, fund lavish weddings, shop in Dubai, or oblige politicians. Of course, at any point of time some tainted banknotes are likely to be lying in jars or pillowcases. But going after that residual liquidity is like mopping the floor under the shower. Thinking of it as a decisive strike on the black economy is a severe delusion. This

*November–December 2016.

point has already been made by many eminent economists, but the government seems to prefer its own echo chamber.

The main cash hoarders are likely to be political parties. For them, it makes sense to accumulate cash over time, in anticipation of electoral campaigns. Opposition parties may well be the real targets of the demonetisation move. Being in power, the ruling party is less vulnerable. I am all for preventing fraud among political parties, but this is not the best way to go about it.

Aside from exaggerating the benefits of demonetisation, the government has downplayed the costs. Some short-term costs are already evident – the time people waste in long queues, the liquidity crisis in the informal economy, the worker layoffs, and of course many tragic deaths. Wider economic costs are likely to be felt soon. Some reports already suggest that economic activity in rural markets has slowed down. For instance, a study by Nidhi Aggrawal and Sudha Narayanan at the Indira Gandhi Institute of Development Research shows that mandi arrivals of non-perishable agricultural commodities crashed across the board within a week of demonetisation. The declines range from 23 per cent for cotton to 87 per cent for soyabean, and did not occur last year at this time. When farmers are short of cash, agricultural labourers and local artisans are bound to suffer too. NREGA workers are also likely to be badly hit. As it is, they are affected by chronic delays in wage payments. With bank staff out of action for weeks, it is bound to become even harder for them to collect their meagre wages. The same applies to social security pensions, a lifeline for millions of poor widows and elderly persons. For people who live on the margin of subsistence, this is a scary situation.

And then there are other possible costs we know little about, such as creeping corruption in the banking system as bank managers oblige powerful customers who are desperate to change their obsolete banknotes. It would be ironic, but not entirely surprising, if demonetisation ended up breeding a little black economy of its own.

The costs and benefits, of course, are quite speculative. Demonetisation on this scale is a huge gamble with the economy. The full consequences are difficult to predict. The best-case scenario is that the economy will stay the course, after the initial disruption, and that significant sums of black money will be neutralised. The worst-case scenario is a prolonged economic slowdown, with very little result in terms of preventing illegal activity. The initial economic shock, already visible, can easily have ripple effects over the next few months. For instance, delayed sowing of rabi crops today could affect the harvest months from now. With employers short of cash, labourers are likely to lose jobs. It is also important to remember that macroeconomic trends depend a lot on expectations. If the initial shock creates adverse expectations, the economy's growth trajectory could be derailed. In a booming economy, blanket demonetisation is a little bit like shooting at the tyres of a racing car.

The stakes in the gamble include not only macroeconomic indicators but also real lives. An old widow who depends on her meagre pension to survive could easily be pushed to the wall if she is unable to access her bank account for a few weeks. A migrant labourer who is told by his employer that he will be paid after the crisis is over may be forced to return to his village empty-handed. A village carpenter who is out of work because people prefer to keep their cash for more urgent needs may have no other means of survival. It is this lethal aspect of demonetisation, as it is happening today, that makes it unacceptable.

Disruption as an Opportunity

Evidence of the disruptive effects of demonetisation is growing every day. Disruption is actually a mild expression – what is happening is a catastrophe for large sections of the population. The post-demonetisation slump in consumer demand has affected numerous occupation groups, from farmers and artisans to construction workers and street vendors. And of course, many people have died in bank queues or committed suicide after unsuccessful attempts to get cash from the banks.

What is astonishing is how little concern this catastrophe is causing in the corridors of power. Smug reference is made from time to time to the "inconvenience" faced by the public, and people are asked to grin and bear it for the sake of the nation. Little is being done to alleviate their pains.

To understand this inertia, it helps to remember that the word "disruption" has a positive connotation is some circles, particularly that of technological innovation and especially software innovation. For instance, when Nandan Nilekani stated in an interview with *Business Standard* last August that "disruption is waiting to happen" in the banking system, he saw that as a very positive prospect – an opportunity for new financial technologies to step in.

One possible reason why disruption is so popular among software developers is the role of "network effects" in this field. New software typically becomes viable only if a sufficiently large number of people use it. This may require displacing the dominant product, and that, in turn, often involves a disruption of some sort. Displacing Google, for instance, would definitely require some kind of tectonic shift in the world of search engines. Similarly, cashless payment systems like Paytm and Mobikwik work best when large numbers of people adopt these new products at the same time.

Seen in this light, there is something miraculously providential in the demonetisation move as far as the cashless payments industry and its offshoots (including online security services) are concerned. This must have been beyond the wildest dreams of the wizards of cashless payments. Just a year ago, the idea of a cashless economy sounded like utopian waffle. Today, it is the buzzword. Not only are cashless payment systems riding on the wave of demonetisation, the government is also throwing its weight behind the technology, mobilising numerous departments for this purpose and lending its advertisement powers to the industry.

The problem with the "disruption" lingo is that it easily becomes a licence for inflicting hardship on ordinary people and making a virtue of it. Bank premises are overcrowded? Wonderful, that's disruption at its best. ATM queues are getting longer? Nothing like it. People are losing jobs? Well, disruption can afford some short-term collateral damage. In fact, objectively speaking, the more the disruption, the better for those who are trying to use this situation as an opportunity to promote their new products. I am not saying that they are responsible for creating the disruption, or applauding it, but it is a fact that they benefit from it. Considering the tremendous power of the software industry in India, this may help to explain why the disruptive effects of demonetisation are taken lightly.

Among the leading lights of this lobby is the Indian Software Product Industry Roundtable (iSPIRT), an association of black-belt innovators and entrepreneurs. Take a look at their website if you have time – it is an eye-opening exercise. These guys (and they are mainly guys) are smart, they think big, and they have ideas. The question remains – ideas for whom? The website makes no secret of the fact that the ultimate purpose of iSPIRT's work is to create business opportunities for the Indian software industry, not just at home but in the entire world. Under the title "Our Game Plan", for instance, the site explains that "our ambitious goal is to create an adoption wave for software products within the Indian SMB sector". And guess what, the way to do this is to "create a new generation of software product companies" and "disrupt global markets", no less.

The first step, still according to the iSPIRT website, is "smart demand side evangelisation" (sic). Presumably, this involves things like selling Aadhaar to the public as a "voluntary facility", or claiming that the purpose of Aadhaar is to improve welfare programmes. In fact, as Reetika Khera has lucidly explained in a series of articles, it is Aadhaar that has benefited from welfare programmes (by using them to push people to Aadhaar enrolment centres), not the other way around. Quite often, the impact of Aadhaar on welfare programmes has actually been disruptive, in the literal sense of the term. For instance, the recent imposition of Aadhaar-based biometric authentication on the public distribution system has caused havoc in several states, notably Jharkhand and Rajasthan.

What is disturbing is how government policy is now aligned with the interests of these business lobbies. The government's advertisements for cashless payment systems read like a rehash of the private companies' own rhetoric (as a private consultant recently confided, "our marketing costs have gone down", because the government is doing the advertising). The revolving door between government and corporations is getting wider every day. And as mentioned earlier, the entire demonetisation drive is an uncanny miracle for the software industry, as if the industry itself had written the script.

None of this is to deny that cashless payments may have some merits. But there is no reason for state power to promote them single-mindedly, that too by risking economic disaster.

Decoding
Universal Basic Income*

A recent headline in *Quartz*, an otherwise serious media agency, claims that Jammu and Kashmir is the first state in India to "commit to a universal basic income" (UBI). A glance at the original source quickly negates this claim: it is based on nothing more than "seeds of a thought" (*sic*) from the finance minister of J&K about possible cash transfers for a small minority of poor households. This is not a commitment, and it is not UBI anyway.

Premature Articulation

There have been other cases of active promotion of UBI in the business media in recent weeks. For instance, reference is often made to Finland as "the first country with UBI", yet Finland has gone no further than a tiny pilot scheme of unconditional cash transfers for 2000-odd recipients. Clearly, UBI has become a subject of half-truths if not post-truths.

But let's leave propaganda aside for now, and look at UBI proposals on their own merits. Two influential proposals have been made recently. Pranab Bardhan, citing National Institute of Public Finance and Policy (NIPFP) estimates of "non-merit subsidies" to the tune of 9 per cent of GDP, argues for the bulk of this to be spent on UBI instead. With a little top-up from reduced tax exemptions, he proposes a basic income of Rs 10,000 per person per year at a cost of 10 per cent of GDP. On a more modest note, Vijay Joshi proposes spending

*January–February 2017.

3.5 per cent of GDP on a UBI scheme where everyone from aam aadmi to Ambani gets a cash transfer equivalent to one-fifth of the poverty line. Even 3.5 per cent of GDP is ambitious: about three times as much as public expenditure on health care, and more than ten times the cost of the National Rural Employment Guarantee Act (NREGA).

I have liked the idea of UBI for a long time. In countries (like Finland) that can afford a generous UBI and also have first-rate public services, it has two attractive features. First, UBI is a foolproof way of safeguarding the right to dignified living. Second, it gives people the option to live without working (or rather, without doing paid work) if they are willing to settle for a simple life. And why not?

As far as India today is concerned, however, UBI proposals strike me as a case of premature articulation. To start with, the said NIPFP estimates go back to a study published in 2003 and based on 1998–9 data – almost twenty years old. More recent work, also at NIPFP, produces a much lower estimate of non-merit subsidies – about 5 per cent of GDP in 2011–12. That suggests an even lower figure today (perhaps 3.5 per cent or so), bearing in mind that petroleum and fertiliser subsidies have sharply declined in recent years, as a percentage of GDP. Note also that many of these subsidies are implicit (for instance, railway tickets sold below transport costs), and that the bulk of the non-merit subsidies are given by state rather than central governments. Recovering this so-called "fiscal space" is not going to be easy.

Further, why should the bulk of this fiscal space (such as it is) be claimed by UBI alone? There are many other urgent claims on public expenditure – education, health care, environmental protection, essential infrastructure, to name a few. Mobilising 3.5 per cent of GDP for UBI is bound to take many years under any plausible script, not to speak of 10 per cent (if it is advisable at all).

Meanwhile, should the limited resources available for cash transfers be used to kickstart UBI at a very low level of "basic income", or are there better options? I believe there are. Universal maternity entitlements and social security pensions would be a good start. If UBI "is really an extension of the idea of pension", as Bardhan aptly points out, then why not begin with pensions? Maternity entitlements, for their part, are due since 2013 under the National Food Security Act.

Incidentally, India already has one of the closest things that any country has by way of UBI, though it is not quite universal and the transfers are in kind not cash: the public distribution system (PDS). There is no plausible scenario whereby the Indian government would retain the PDS along with a cash-based UBI scheme. Therefore, the main question a low-level UBI proposal would raise is whether, when, and how the PDS should be replaced with cash transfers. The sobering results of recent attempts to do that in Puducherry and Chandigarh suggest that it would be unwise to go beyond these pilot areas for the time being. Earlier experiences of messy transition to bank payments of NREGA wages, and of chaotic imposition of biometric authentication on the PDS, reinforce the need for great caution in these matters.

It is often pointed out that UBI has supporters on both the right and the left. This shared support, however, comes from incompatible perspectives. For the left, UBI is part of a comprehensive social security system that would also include universal health care, free education, good public services, some transfers in kind (e.g. school meals) and other forms of social support. For the right, especially in India, UBI is an adjunct of deep cuts in other social programmes such as the PDS and NREGA. Some UBI advocates have already made an explicit case for dismantling both.

Finally, UBI proposals need to be distinguished from what the Government of India is likely to do with them. It is not difficult to imagine how these proposals might be reduced to a half-baked scheme of targeted cash transfers with no legal safeguards and no indexation to the price level, combined with closing the PDS and possibly NREGA as well. Indeed, highly targeted schemes of the sort envisaged by the finance minister of J&K (or, say, by Surjit Bhalla) are already passing for "UBI".

Seen in this light, there is a real danger of UBI becoming a Trojan horse for the dismantling of hard-won entitlements of the underprivileged. The recent wave of pro-UBI propaganda in the business media (generally hostile to ambitious social programmes) is suspicious in this regard. These issues, in my view, need greater attention in the lively debate on UBI among development economists.

UBI in the Economic Survey

The Economic Survey 2016–17 includes a much-awaited presentation of the finance ministry's thinking on universal basic income. Desisting from specific recommendations, the survey comes to the mild conclusion that UBI "if not ripe for implementation is ripe for serious discussion". But there is certainly a tone of enthusiasm in the chapter on UBI.

The chapter begins with an upbeat discussion of the idea of UBI, and then gets a little entangled in the fiscal maths. In their enthusiasm for UBI, the authors make somewhat simplistic arguments for it. For instance, it is asserted that UBI benefits the poorest by minimising exclusion errors. However, universalisation is bound to come at a cost – either lower per capita benefits, or less spending on other schemes, or higher taxes. Depending on who bears that cost, the argument may or may not be correct. Similarly, UBI is presented as a way of rectifying the current imbalance of social spending across districts: the poorest districts' share of social spending is typically less than their share of poverty. Quite likely, however, UBI would fare worse than many existing schemes in that respect.

Coming to the options, what the survey discusses is not really UBI but what might be called quasi-universal income top-up (QUIT). Let me explain. It is an essential part of the principle of UBI that the transfers involved should cover the basic costs of subsistence – hence the term "basic income". If UBI provides less than that, it is often called "partial basic income". In this case, since the proposed transfers are tiny in per capita terms (less than half of the Tendulkar poverty line), "income top-up" would be more accurate.

Quasi-universal (the term is used in the survey itself) refers to the fact that while universality may be the ideal, in practice, the transfers will be less than universal. The survey first suggests something like 75 per cent of the population, identified by including all those who do not meet simple exclusion criteria. Later, various ways of further reducing the costs are discussed, such as restricting the coverage – initially at least – to women, to specific groups, or to urban areas. It is not difficult to see how further restrictions might reduce QUIT to a targeted income top-up.

In the quasi-universal variant with 75 per cent coverage, UBI (read QUIT) costs as much as 4 to 5 per cent of GDP. Here the survey hits a roadblock, and initiates a worrying shift in thinking about how UBI is to be financed. As mentioned earlier, it seems that the potential savings from non-merit subsidies were overestimated in recent UBI proposals. In the Economic Survey, therefore, fiscal space is sought not so much in reducing subsidies (also because "taking away subsidies to the middle class is politically difficult for any government") as in phasing out a range of welfare schemes that are held to be ineffective. A partial list of possible target schemes is given, including items like midday meals and ICDS, but the survey fails to clarify whether they are really ineffective, if so why, whether they can be improved, and so on. Since the extent of this fiscal space is hard to assess, the authors discuss various UBI options in general terms without backing a specific proposal.

It is in this argument for pruning other welfare schemes that the most simplistic argument for UBI (or rather, for cash transfers) is invoked. Other schemes are construed as "transfers in kind", and cash transfers are held to be superior because they give people "agency", i.e. they allow people to decide what to do with the transfers. However, there are arguments for in-kind transfers too, and further, many welfare schemes are not just transfers in kind. For instance, school meals are both excellent in-kind transfers and also a constructive activity with valuable aims such as nutrition education, employment generation, and social equity. Similarly, the National

Rural Employment Guarantee Act is not a scheme of in-kind transfers (in fact, wages are paid in cash). Aside from income support, it serves other useful purposes such as asset creation, women's empowerment, and environmental protection. Most of the eleven target schemes mentioned in the survey are of that nature.

There is a serious blind spot here. During the last fifteen years or so, India has developed the semblance of a social security framework. Aside from essential health and education services, this framework has five pillars as things stand: employment guarantee in rural areas; the public distribution system; child development programmes (including the ICDS); social security pensions; and maternity entitlements. Far from being wasteful, these programmes play a critical role in protecting people from deprivation and also help to create a better society. This framework (enshrined in legal guarantees) needs to be consolidated, not demolished.

This is not to deny that there are many wasteful schemes and subsidies, or to dismiss the idea of universal basic income. But the fiscal space available from pruning wasteful schemes and subsidies is more restricted than many advocates of UBI claim. And UBI, if and when desirable, must be planned as an extension or modification of the existing framework, not as an alternative to it. UBI is an idea whose time will come, but that time is still quite distant as far as India is concerned.

Development
and Public-Spiritedness*

Word has it that most people are self-interested. At least that is what an unsuspecting reader of mainstream economic theory might conclude. The literature makes constant reference to "rational self-interest" as the prime motivation of economic agents. Of course, there is also a specialised literature on other possible motives, such as sympathy and commitment. And even in the mainstream literature, a discerning economist would point out that the crucial assumption is not really that people are self-interested, but that they have consistent "preferences", whatever these are – not necessarily selfish. But most of the time, these subtleties are ignored, and the assumption of rational self-interest is taken at face value. The assumption is so pervasive that rationality and self-interest are often conflated. As Nobel Laureate Robert Aumann puts it: "The assumption of rationality – that people act in their own best interests, given their information – underlies most of economic theory and indeed of economics as a whole."

This self-interest assumption, read literally, has no theoretical or empirical support of any sort. It is a kind of superstition. Anyone who has bothered to look around, or to read the world's history and literature, or even just to watch a few Bollywood films, would notice that people often act on the basis of other-regarding motives – love, kindness, solidarity, compassion, reciprocity, patriotism, public-spiritedness, and more. Some even make great sacrifices for their friends, family, community, or country.

*February 2017.

Further, it is not always clear where self-interest ends and concern for others begins. Human beings, by nature, are interested in each other's lives. Whether an active schoolteacher, a committed trade unionist, or a passionate artist are acting out of self-interest may be hard to tell – not only for others but even for themselves. It is difficult to imagine what a totally selfish person might look like (perhaps hard-core egoists don't have babies, so they are not around any more).

Even in the animal world, there are many instances of co-operative behaviour or even self-sacrifice, as Peter Kropotkin pointed out long ago in his wonderful book *Mutual Aid*. From ants to elephants, animals have learnt to behave in ways that further not only their own interest but also that of other members of the species. Ants work hard to build common nests, migratory birds fly in formation, elephants help the wounded – examples are aplenty.

These instincts are not based on any sort of ethical reasoning – they are the product of biological evolution. Human beings, however, do not have to wait for long-run evolution to develop habits of co-operation or public-spiritedness. Social norms can also change, more rapidly, through ethical reasoning, public discussion, value education, institutional innovation, and other means.

With this preamble, let me turn to a specific type of non-selfish motive: public-spiritedness, broadly defined as "a reasoned habit of consideration for the public interest". The use of the term "habit" acknowledges the fact that we often act on the basis of habits of thought or behaviour rather than case-by-case optimisation. For instance, many people are used to standing in a queue at the bus stand or railway counter, without getting into a cost–benefit analysis of the choice between joining or jumping the queue (based for instance on the length of the queue, the cost of missing the bus, the risk of being beaten up for jumping the queue, and so on). Of course, we may be able to justify these habits if need be – hence the term "reasoned habit", which also helps to distinguish public-spiritedness from the sort of instinctive co-operative behaviour that can be found among animals.

The term "public interest" may or may not be well defined, depending on the situation. The public interest of British citizens in Brexit is not clear – it is a matter of judgement. But the public interest of Indian and Pakistani citizens in avoiding nuclear war is reasonably clear. So is the public interest of humanity in avoiding self-destruction through global warming. The term "public" need not refer to the society at large – depending on the contexts, it could mean a smaller group such as a family or local community.

The importance of public-spiritedness in social life, and for human development, can be conveyed with two simple examples. The first is punctuality. When we go to (say) a meeting, there is a temptation to go a few minutes – say, five minutes – late, to avoid the inconvenience of waiting for others. But then, others may also reason that way, so ten minutes may be safer. Extending the argument further, we may end up going very late indeed, if we stick to this self-interested reasoning. Formally, the situation has the basic structure of an "escalation game". Game theory tells us two important things about escalation games: first, things can go badly out of hand in such situations, and second, many escalation games are such that there is no rational way to play. Both insights (already discussed in the section on "War and Peace") are consistent with real-life experience. Stories of trivial quarrels that got out of hand by escalation, sometimes ending with a murder, are reported almost every day in the newspapers. Even the First World War, as mentioned earlier, can be interpreted in those terms.

In these circumstances, it may be best (from a collective point of view) not to play the game at all. That is what punctuality is about. In societies with punctual habits, people refrain from embarking in this escalatory reasoning – they simply turn up on time, as a matter of social norm or habit of thought. For whatever reason, some societies have cultivated habits of punctuality, others have not. The contrast struck me a few years ago when I spent some time with a mixed team of Indian and Japanese visitors. The Japanese were obsessively punctual, the Indians blissfully oblivious of time. This is not to say that the Japanese are somehow less selfish than Indians, or that they have more evolved ethics. Punctuality is just a habit of thought they have cultivated.

This may seem like a trivial example. Punctuality may or may not matter much for development. R.K. Narayan, the celebrated writer, argued that it does not: "Personally speaking, I feel, under normal circumstances, most things can survive a little delay . . . In a country like ours, the preoccupation is with eternity, and little measures of time are hardly ever noticed." It is, however, not difficult to cite examples where a modicum of punctuality would make a big difference. For instance, punctuality can greatly facilitate collective action. In some parts of rural India, gram sabhas (village councils) have proved very difficult to convene because people have no sense of time: many turn up hours late, and by the time the laggards arrive, the early birds have lost patience and left the venue.

Turning to a more significant example, it is often forgotten that the entire edifice of electoral democracy rests on a simple act of public-spiritedness: voting. Every voter knows that his or her vote will not make any difference (except in the miraculous situation where there would be a "tie" without it). Yet a large proportion – typically a majority – of people do vote in democratic countries. Many people even vote in difficult circumstances, trekking long distances or queuing for hours in chilly weather. This is a telling example because many of the arguments that are often invoked to explain co-operation within the self-interest paradigm (e.g. repetition of the game, reputation effects, and so on) do not apply in this case – in the framework of game theory, this looks like a one-shot Prisoners' Dilemma. Even social norms explain little: there is, typically, no social norm against abstention from voting. Plausible interpretations of the situation must clearly go beyond self-interest. One of them is that voting is a simple act of public-spiritedness.

As these examples illustrate, public-spiritedness does not always require self-sacrifice or deep ethical thinking. Ethics, of course, can help: someone who considers it unethical to make other people wait for no good reason is more likely to develop a habit of punctuality.

But often we act – or can act – in a public-spirited way as a matter of habit. Punctuality, for one, is a habit that many people imbibe in the course of a healthy upbringing or social life. If called to justify this habit, they may invoke ethical principles, but some may give other reasons, like "I hate being late".

Someone who acts out of habit may sound less than perfectly rational, because he or she misses the opportunity to "optimise" (make the best of a situation) on a case-by-case basis. This argument, however, is deceptive. One of the main insights of game theory is that, in situations where people's decisions are interdependent, optimization may not be well defined (this point has already been illustrated with reference to escalation games). In these situations, it often helps to fall back on some sort of rule of thumb or "bounded rationality". A related escape route (proposed by Robert Aumann) is "rule rationality" – settling for a rule of behaviour that serves us well in general, even if it may not be the best thing to do in every single case. There is, thus, nothing wrong in acting on the basis of habits of thought.

All this may sound like hair-splitting, but I believe that it has an important bearing on the scope for cultivating public-spiritedness in social life. If public-spiritedness required strong ethical commitments, we might be sceptical of the possibility of it spreading beyond a minority of principled individuals. On the other hand, if it takes the form of sensible habits of thought that can be rationalised (if need be) with light-touch ethical reasoning, public-spiritedness may have much more of a future. This is not a small matter – it could help not only to avoid many day-to-day tragedies (from vandalism to violence) but also to build social institutions that reconcile liberty and equality. Dr Ambedkar put it very well in his stirring speech to the Constituent Assembly on 25 November 1949: "Without equality, liberty would produce the supremacy of the few over the many. Equality without liberty would kill individual initiative. *Without fraternity, liberty and equality would not become a natural course of thing.*" Public-spiritedness is not quite fraternity (alias solidarity), but it is a step in that direction at least.

Notes

Rang de Basti

Sanjay Basti, I am glad to say, is still in place. However, slum demolitions have taken place elsewhere in Delhi from time to time in recent years.

Voting in Maoist Land

This essay is based on enquiries conducted on 18 October 2009 in Latehar district, with James Herenj and Mithilesh Kumar. On the Maoist movement in this area (formerly south Bihar), see Bhatia 2005.

The Bribing Game

This essay belongs to a series of rejoinders that appeared soon after Kaushik Basu's (2011) original paper was posted on the website of the finance ministry, Government of India. The paper and rejoinders led to a substantial literature on this issue, both in the mainstream media and in professional economic journals. For a valuable introduction to this literature, see Dufwenberg and Spagnolo 2015.

The Quiet Grip of Caste

The findings of the Allahabad survey mentioned in this essay are presented in more detail in Aggarwal, Drèze, and Gupta 2015, where many other recent studies on the continued dominance of the upper castes in Indian society are also discussed.

The Gujarat Muddle

The sources cited in this paper include: Government of India 2013b, also known as Raghuram Rajan committee report; Drèze and Khera 2012 for the human development index and "achievements of babies and children" index; Government of India 2013c for official poverty estimates; Alkire and Seth 2012 for the multi-dimensional poverty index (also available in Drèze and Sen 2013); and the Sample Registration System for infant mortality figures. The text also refers to earlier work by Maitreesh Ghatak, Ashok Kotwal, and their colleagues, on which see e.g. Ghatak and Roy 2014, and Chaudhuri and Kotwal 2014.

On the Mythology of Social Policy

The figures on social protection expenditure as a proportion of GDP are from Asian Development Bank 2013. Other international data are from the World Bank's *World Development Indicators* (latest edition at the time of writing). On Mukesh Ambani saying, in one of the leaked Niira Radia tapes, "*Congress toh apna dukaan hai*" (the Congress Party is in our pocket), see e.g. Anuradha Raman 2014.

The Bullet Train Syndrome

The statement that a bullet train is "the wish and dream of every Indian" was made by the railway minister D.V. Sadananda Gowda in his budget speech of 8 July 2014 (available on the net).

The Mother of All Disruptions

The statement attributed to Nandan Nilekani was made in an interview published in *Business Standard* on 8 August 2016 (available on the net). The IGIDR study on mandi arrivals is summarised in Aggrawal and Narayanan 2016. On the disruption of the PDS by Aadhaar-based biometric authentication in Jharkhand and Rajasthan, see section 7.

The full economic impact of demonetisation is yet to become clear as this book goes to press. Reddy 2017 presents a useful overview of the evidence so far.

Decoding Universal Basic Income

The "seeds of thought" of the finance minister of Jammu and Kashmir (about a possible cash transfer scheme for BPL families) were shared in passing on the occasion of his budget presentation on 11 January 2017. The UBI proposals by Pranab Bardhan and Vijay Joshi are available on the Ideas for India website (www.ideasforindia.in). The NIPFP subsidy estimates based on 1998–9 data are available in National Institute of Public Finance and Policy 2003.

There is a full chapter on UBI in the Economic Survey 2016–17, prepared by the ministry of finance. The eleven major schemes and subsidies listed there as possible targets for replacement with UBI (figure 1, p. 176) are: midday meal; Swachh Bharat Abhiyan; ICDS; Pradhan Mantri Gram

Sadak Yojana; National Health Mission; Pradhan Mantri Awas Yojana; LPG subsidy; Sarva Shiksha Abhiyan; NREGA; urea subsidy; food subsidy. The passing mention of Surjit Bhalla refers to his article "Financing Basic Income for the Bottom 50 Per Cent", *Indian Express*, 6 January 2017 (the title of that article is a little misleading because the expenditure levels proposed in the text actually suffice for 25 per cent coverage only).

Development and Public-Spiritedness

This is an unpublished paper. On related matters, including the reasons why habits of thought are important in social life, see also Drèze 2016b.

The Narayan quote is from the story "Better Late" in Narayan 1988. I have quoted Aumann 2008 to illustrate the pervasive nature of the self-interest assumption in economics, but similar statements can be found all over the economic literature, starting at least as early as 1881 when F.Y. Edgeworth, one of the founders of modern economics, stated in his *Mathematical Psychics* that "the first principle of Economics is that every agent is actuated only by self-interest". The self-interest assumption, of course, has its critics, notably Amartya Sen (see Sen 1977).

One branch of mainstream economics does depart in a fundamental way from the rational self-interest paradigm – behavioural economics (for a useful introduction, see Camerer, *et al.*, 2014). Much of that literature, however, does not really shed the assumption of self-interest; rather, it explores psychological and other reasons why people are not always able to pursue their self-interest in a rational manner – for instance, for lack of will-power or clear-mindedness. It is mainly in the literature on "social preferences", often considered a field of behavioural economics, that serious consideration is given to non-selfish motives. For an enlightening introduction to that literature, see the work of Sam Bowles (Bowles 2004, 2008). The question remains whether unselfish behaviour is really a matter of "preferences", but that is another story.

REFERENCES

Adhikari, A., and Bhatia, K. (2010), "NREGA Wage Payments: Can We Bank on the Banks?", *Economic and Political Weekly*, 2 January.

Afridi, Farzana (2010), "Child Welfare Programs and Child Nutrition: Evidence from a Mandated School Meal Program in India", *Journal of Development Economics*, 92.

Aggarwal, A., Drèze, J.P., and Gupta, A. (2015), "Caste and the Power Elite in Allahabad", *Economic and Political Weekly*, 7 February.

Aggrawal, N., and Narayanan, S. (2016), "Demonetisation Alone Can't Turn Agricultural Markets Cashless", *The Wire*, 25 November.

Alkire, S., and Seth, S. (2012), "Multidimensional Poverty Index (MPI) Rates in Rural and Urban Indian States", mimeo, Oxford Poverty and Human Development Initiative, University of Oxford; available at http://ophi.qeh.ox.ac.uk.

Ambedkar, B.R. (1957), *The Buddha and His Dhamma* (Bombay: People's Education Society).

Applegate, Elizabeth (2000), "Introduction: Nutritional and Functional Roles of Eggs in the Diet", *Journal of the American College of Nutrition*, 19.

Arrow, K. (1963), "Uncertainty and the Welfare Economics of Medical Care", *American Economic Review*, 53.

Asian Development Bank (2013), *The Social Protection Index* (Bangkok: ADB).

Aumann, Robert J. (2008), "Rule-Rationality versus Act-Rationality", Discussion Paper 497, Center for the Study of Rationality, The Hebrew University of Jerusalem.

Banerjee, A., Deaton, A., and Duflo, E. (2004), "Health Care Delivery in Rural Rajasthan", *Economic and Political Weekly*, 28 February.

Balasubramanyam, V.N. (2001), *Conversations with Indian Economists* (New Delhi: Macmillan).

Basu, Kaushik (2011), "Why, for a Class of Bribes, the Act of *Giving* a Bribe Should be Treated as Legal", Working Paper, Department of Economic Affairs, Ministry of Finance, New Delhi.

Bhaskar, A., Gupta, S., and Yadav, P. (2016), "Well Worth the Effort: Value of MGNREGA Wells in Jharkhand", *Economic and Political Weekly*, 7 May.

Bhatia, Bela (2005), "The Naxalite Movement in Central Bihar", *Economic and Political Weekly,* 9 April.

—— (2012), "Of Human Bondage in Baran, Rajasthan", *Economic and Political Weekly*, 30 June.

Bhatia, B., and Drèze, J.P. (2002), "Still Starving in Jharkhand", *Frontline*, 16 August.

Bloch, Jan de (1899), *The Future of War*, translated by R.C. Long (Boston: Ginn).

Bowles, Samuel (2004), *Microeconomics: Behavior, Institutions, and Evolution* (Princeton: Princeton University Press).

—— (2008), "Policies Designed for Self-interested Citizens May Undermine the 'Moral Sentiments'", *Science*, 320.

Brewer, M., Menzies, N., and Schott, J. (2015), "Identification Systems Don't Always Serve the Bottom 40%", *Just Development*, No. 8, World Bank, Washington, DC.

Camerer, C.F., Loewenstein, G., and Rabin, M. (2004), *Advances in Behavioral Economics* (Princeton: Princeton University Press).

Centre for Equity Studies (2016), *Progress of Children Under Six: Revisiting ICDS in the FOCUS Districts* (New Delhi: Centre for Equity Studies).

Chang, A.C., and Li, P. (2015), "Is Economics Research Replicable? Sixty Research Papers from Thirteen Journals Say 'Usually Not'", Finance and Economics Discussion Series 2015-083, Board of Governors of the Federal Reserve System, Washington, DC.

Chaudhuri, A.R., and Kotwal, A. (2014), "The Perplexing Case of Gujarat", available at www.ideasforindia.in (initially published in the *Indian Express*).

Chaudhury, N., Hammer, J., Kremer, M., Muralidharan, K., and Rogers, F.H. (2006), "Missing in Action: Teacher and Health Worker Absence in Developing Countries", *Journal of Economic Perspectives*, 20.

Chomsky, Noam (1999), *Powers and Prospects* (London: Pluto).

Chopra, S., and Pudussery, J. (2014), "Social Security Pensions in India: An Assessment", *Economic and Political Weekly*, 10 May; reprinted in Drèze 2016a.

Citizens' Initiative for the Rights of Children Under Six (2016), *Focus on Children Under Six* (New Delhi: Secretariat of the Right to Food Campaign).

De, A., Khera, R., Samson, M., and Shiva Kumar, A.K. (2011), *PROBE Revisited: A Report on Elementary Education in India* (New Delhi: Oxford University Press).

De, A., Noronha, C., and Samson, M. (2008), "Towards More Benefits from Delhi's Mid-day Meal Scheme", in Baru, R. (ed.), *School Health Services in India* (New Delhi: Sage).

Deaton, Angus (2013), *The Great Escape: Health, Wealth, and the Origins of Inequality* (Princeton: Princeton University Press).

———, and Cartwright, N. (2016), "Understanding and Misunderstanding Randomized Controlled Trials", NBER Working Paper 22595, National Bureau of Economics Research, Cambridge, MA.

Deaton, Angus, and Drèze, J.P. (2009), "Food and Nutrition in India: Facts and Interpretations", *Economic and Political Weekly*, 14 February.

Desai, S., Vashishtha, P., and Joshi, O. (2015), *Mahatma Gandhi National Rural Employment Guarantee Act: A Catalyst for Rural Transformation* (New Delhi: National Council of Applied Economic Research).

Drèze, Jean (2000), "Militarism, Development and Democracy", *Economic and Political Weekly*, 1 April.

——— (2002), "On Research and Action", *Economic and Political Weekly*, 2 March 2002.

——— (2004a), "Democracy and the Right to Food", *Economic and Political Weekly*, 24 April.

——— (2004b), "Unemployment Guarantee Bill", *The Hindu*, 31 December.

——— (2006), "Universalization with Quality: ICDS in a Rights Perspective", *Economic and Political Weekly*, 26 August.

———, ed. (2016a), *Social Policy: Essays from Economic and Political Weekly* (New Delhi: Orient Blackswan).

——— (2016b), "The Real Insights of Game Theory", *Economic and Political Weekly*, 2 April 2016.

————— (2017a), "Giving Short Shrift to Children's Rights", *The Hindu*, 28 March.

————— (2017b), "In Jharkhand, Compulsory Biometric Authentication for Rations Sends Many Away Empty-handed", *Scroll.in*, 12 February.

Drèze, J.P., and Goyal, A. (2003), "The Future of Midday Meals", *Economic and Political Weekly*, 1 November.

Drèze, J.P., Gupta, P., Khera, R., and Pimenta, I. (2016), "Food Security Act: How are India's Poorest States Faring?", available at www.ideasforindia.in.

Drèze, J.P., and Khera, R. (2009), "Mid-Day Meals in Primary Schools", in Kumar, A., and Singh, A.P., eds (2009), *Elementary Education in India: Issues and Challenges* (New Delhi: Uppal).

————— (2010), "The BPL Census and a Possible Alternative", *Economic and Political Weekly*, 27 February.

————— (2012), "Regional Patterns of Human and Child Deprivation in India", *Economic and Political Weekly*, 29 September.

————— (2013), "Rural Poverty and the Public Distribution System", *Economic and Political Weekly*, 16 November.

—————, with the PEEP team (2014) "A PEEP at Another India", survey report, Indian Institute of Technology, Delhi; partly published in *Outlook*, 24 March.

Drèze, J.P., and Khera, R. (2015a), "Understanding Leakages in the Public Distribution System", *Economic and Political Weekly*, 14 February.

————— (2015b), "Thought for Food", *Outlook*, 31 August.

————— (2017), "Recent Social Security Initiatives in India", *World Development*, 98.

—————, and Pudussery, J. (2015), "Food Security: Bihar on the Move", *Economic and Political Weekly*, 22 August.

Drèze, J.P., and Kingdon, G.G. (2001), "School Participation in Rural India", *Review of Development Economics*, 5.

Drèze, J.P., and Lall, B. (2002), "Hunger Deaths in Manatu", survey report, Gram Swaraj Abhiyan, Jharkhand.

Drèze, J.P., and Sen, A.K. (2002), *India: Development and Participation* (New Delhi: Oxford University Press).

————— (2013), *An Uncertain Glory: India and Its Contradictions* (New Delhi: Penguin).

Dufwenberg, M., and Spagnolo, G. (2015), "Legalizing Bribe Giving", *Economic Inquiry*, 53.

Friedman, Milton (1955), "A Memorandum to the Government of India", New Delhi, 5 November; available at http://www.indiapolicy.org/debate/Notes/friedman.htm.

Garg, Samir (2013), "Twin Strategies for Food Security and Productive Inclusion: PDS Reforms in Chhattisgarh, India", *Poverty in Focus*, No. 25, International Policy Centre for Inclusive Growth, Brasilia.

Ghatak, M., and Roy, S. (2014), "A Look in the Mirror", *Outlook*, 31 March (also available at www.ideasforindia.in).

Ghosh, S., with Guha-Thakurta, P. (2016), *Sue the Messenger* (AuthorsUp Front).

Godse, Nathuram (2015), *Why I Assassinated Gandhi*, revised edition, compiled and edited by Virender Mehra (Delhi: Farsight).

Goel, K., and Khera, R. (2015), "Public Health Facilities in North India: An Exploratory Study in Four States", *Economic and Political Weekly*, 23 May.

Government of India (2004), *Report of the Task Force on Implementation of the Fiscal Responsibility and Budget Management Act, 2003* (New Delhi: Ministry of Finance).

——— (2005), "Performance Evaluation of Targeted Public Distribution System", Programme Evaluation Organisation, Planning Commission, New Delhi.

——— (2009a), *Report of the Expert Group to Review the Methodology for Estimation of Poverty* (New Delhi: Planning Commission).

——— (2009b), *Report of the Expert Group to Advise the Ministry of Rural Development on the Methodology for Conducting the Below Poverty Line (BPL) Census for 11th Five Year Plan* (New Delhi: Ministry of Rural Development).

——— (2013a), *Proposal for Comprehensive National Social Assistance Programme: Report of the Task Force* (New Delhi: Ministry of Rural Development).

——— (2013b), *Report of the Committee for Evolving a Composite Development Index of States* (New Delhi: Ministry of Finance).

——— (2013c), *Press Note on Poverty Estimates 2011–12* (New Delhi: Planning Commission).

——— (2014), *Report of the Expert Group to Review the Methodology for Measurement of Poverty* (New Delhi: Planning Commission).

Gram Swaraj Abhiyan (2002), "Manatu: A Development Catastrophe", survey report, Gram Swaraj Abhiyan, Jharkhand.

Greenwald, Glenn (2014), *No Place to Hide* (New York: Metropolitan Books).

Imbert, C., and Papp, J. (2015), "Estimating Leakages in India's Employment Guarantee: An Update", Working Paper, Research Institute for Compassionate Economics (available at riceinstitute.org).

International Institute for Population Sciences (2000), *National Family Health Survey (NFHS-2), 1998–99: India* (Mumbai: IIPS).

——— (2005), *India: Facility Survey, Phase-II, 2003* (Mumbai: IIPS).

——— (2006), *Reproductive and Child Health: District Level Household Survey 2002–4* (Mumbai: IIPS).

——— (2007), *National Family Health Survey (NFHS-3), 2005–6: India* (Mumbai: IIPS).

Jain, J., and Shah, M. (2005), "Antyodaya Anna Yojana and Mid-day Meals in MP", *Economic and Political Weekly*, 26 November.

Jayachandran, S., and Pande, R. (2013), "Choice not Genes", *Economic and Political Weekly*, 24 August.

Jenkins, R., and Manor, J. (2016), *Politics and the Right to Work: India's National Rural Employment Guarantee Act* (New Delhi: Orient Blackswan).

Jervis, Robert (1989), *The Meaning of the Nuclear Revolution* (Ithaca: Cornell University Press).

Khera, Reetika (2006), "Mid-Day Meals in Primary Schools: Achievements and Challenges", *Economic and Political Weekly*, 18 November.

——— (2008), "Starvation Deaths and 'Primitive Tribal Groups'", *Economic and Political Weekly*, 27 December.

——— (2011a), *The Battle for Employment Guarantee* (New Delhi: Oxford University Press).

——— (2011b), "Revival of the Public Distribution System: Evidence and Explanations", *Economic and Political Weekly*, 5 November.

——— (2013), "Mid-Day Meals: Looking Ahead", *Economic and Political Weekly*, 10 August; reprinted in Drèze 2016a.

——— (2015), "Children's Development: Baby Steps in Odisha", *Economic and Political Weekly*, 3 October.

Kropotkin, Peter (1902), *Mutual Aid: A Factor in Evolution* (London: Heinemann).

Kulkarni, Sudheendra (2016), "A Self-Goal by the RSS", *Indian Express*, 6 January.

Mander, Harsh (2012), "Barefoot: The Other Side of Life", *The Hindu*, 11 February.

———, and Mehrotra, S. (2009), "How to Identify the Poor? A Proposal", *Economic and Political Weekly*, 9 May.

May, E.R., and Zelikow, P.D., eds (1997), *The Kennedy Tapes: Inside the White House during the Cuban Missile Crisis* (Cambridge, MA: Harvard University Press).

McDonald, Hamish (1998), *The Polyester Prince: The Rise of Dhirubhai Ambani* (Australia: Allen and Unwin).

Mohanty, Gopinath (1987), *Paraja: A Novel*, translated from the Oriya by Bikram K. Das (New Delhi: Oxford University Press).

Narayan, R.K. (1988), *A Writer's Nightmare* (New Delhi: Penguin).

Narayan, Swati (2016), "Towards Equality in Healthcare: Trends over Two Decades", *Economic and Political Weekly*, 19 March.

National Institute of Public Finance and Policy (2003), *Budgetary Subsidies in India* (New Delhi: NIPFP).

Oldiges, Christian (2012), "Cereal Consumption and Per-capita Income in India", *Economic and Political Weekly*, 11 February.

PROBE Team (1999), *Public Report on Basic Education* (New Delhi: Oxford University Press).

Puri, Raghav (2012), "Reforming the Public Distribution System: Lessons from Chhattisgarh", *Economic and Political Weekly*, 4 February.

Rajan, Raghuram (2014), "Saving Credit", Third Dr Verghese Kurien Memorial Lecture, delivered at the Institute of Rural Management, Anand, 25 November (available at www.rbi.org.in).

Raman, Anuradha (2014), "Big ED in the Chair", *Outlook*, 14 July.

Ranaware, K., Das, U., Kulkarni, A., and Narayanan, S. (2015), "MGNREGA Works and Their Impacts", *Economic and Political Weekly*, 28 March; reprinted in Drèze 2016a.

Rangarajan, C., and Mahendra Dev, S. (2015), "Counting the Poor: Measurement and Other Issues", *Economic and Political Weekly*, 10 January.

Rapoport, Anatol (1960), *Fights, Games and Debates* (Ann Arbor: University of Michigan Press).

————— (1992), *Peace: An Idea Whose Time Has Come* (Ann Arbor: University of Michigan Press).

————— (1997), *The Origins of Violence: Approaches to the Study of Conflict* (London: Transaction Publishers).

Reddy, Rammanohar (2017), *Demonetisation and Black Money* (New Delhi: Orient Blackswan).

Sainath, P. (1996), *Everybody Loves a Good Drought* (New Delhi: Penguin).

Sarmah, Sasanka (2001), "Agricultural Wages in India: A Study of States and Regions", *Indian Journal of Agricultural Economics*, 45.

Schelling, Thomas (1960), *The Strategy of Conflict* (Cambridge, MA: Harvard University Press).

————— (1961), *Arms and Influence* (New Haven: Yale University Press).

————— (1962), "Nuclear Strategy in Europe", *World Politics*, 14.

Sen, Amartya (1977), "Rational Fools: A Critique of the Behavioral Foundations of Economic Theory", *Philosophy and Public Affairs*, 6.

————— (1993), "Positional Objectivity", *Philosophy and Public Affairs*, 22.

Sengupta, A., Kannan, K.P., and Raveendran, G. (2008), "India's Common People", *Economic and Political Weekly*, 15 March.

Shubik, Martin (1971), "The Dollar Auction Game: A Paradox in Non-cooperative Behaviour and Escalation", *Journal of Conflict Resolution*, 15.

Siddhartha and Vanaik, A. (2008), "CAG Report on NREGA: Fact and Fiction", *Economic and Political Weekly*, 21 June.

Sinha, Dipa (2015), "Maternal and Child Health: Inching Ahead, Miles to Go", *Economic and Political Weekly*, 5 December.

Tellis, Ashley (2005), *India as a New Global Power: An Action Agenda for the United States* (New Delhi: Carnegie Endowment for International Peace).

Viswanath, Apurva (2017), "What are the Lessons Learnt from the Right to Food Case?", *Livemint*, 20 March.

Visaria, Leela (2000a), "From Contraceptive Targets to Reproductive Health: Evolution of India's Policies and Programmes", mimeo, New Delhi.

————— (2000b), 'Innovations in Tamil Nadu', *Seminar*, 489.

Vivek S. (2015), *Delivering Public Services Effectively: Tamil Nadu and Beyond* (New Delhi: Oxford University Press).

World Bank (2004), "State Fiscal Reforms in India: Progress and Prospects", Report No. 28849-IN, Poverty Reduction and Economic Management Sector Unit, World Bank, Washington, DC.

Wright Mills, C. (1958), *The Causes of World War Three* (London: Secker and Warburg).

Young, Alwyn (2016), "Channelling Fisher: Randomization Tests and the Statistical Insignificance of Seemingly Significant Experimental Results", draft paper, London School of Economics.

SOURCE
ACKNOWLEDGEMENTS

In cases where the original essay title (often chosen by an editor rather than the author) is different from the one used in this book, the original title appears after the date of publication. Essays that draw on two different articles are marked with an asterisk.

Drought and Hunger

"Starving the Poor": *The Hindu*, 26 February 2001.

"Fragile Lifelines, Robust Oppression": *Times of India*, 17 September 2001 ("No More Lifelines: Political Economy of Hunger in Orissa").

"The Right to Food and Public Accountability": *The Hindu*, 5 December 2001.

"Memories of Kusumatand" (with Bela Bhatia): *Frontline*, 16 August 2002 ("Still Starving in Jharkhand").

"The Dark Well of Hunger": *Hindustan Times*, 21 May 2003 ("On the Hunger Trail").

Poverty

"The Poverty Trap*": *Hindustan Times*, 22 September 2011 ("The Poverty Trap") and also *The Hindu*, 3 October 2011 ("The BPL Club").

"On the Poverty Line": Unpublished article, partly included in Drèze and Sen (2013), chapter 7.

"Beyond Small Mercies": *The Hindu*, 25 December 2013.

"Squaring the Poverty Circle" (with Angus Deaton): *The Hindu*, 25 July 2014.

School Meals

"Hunger in the Classroom" (with Vivek S.): *Food and Nutrition World*, sample issue (2002); also published in abridged form in *Hindustan Times*, 15 October 2002.

323

"Food for Equality*": *Hindustan Times*, July 2003 ("Digesting Inequality") and also *Hindustan Times*, 29 August 2003 ("Beyond Ghoogri"); with minor update of survey findings using Drèze and Goyal 2003.

"Mid-day Meals and the Joy of Learning": *Learning Curve*, 2006.

"Caste, Class and Eggs": *Times of India*, 9 June 2015.

Health Care

"Health Checkup": *The Hindu*, 12 March 2004.

"India Leapfrogged": *The Hindu*, 17 September 2004 ("Bangladesh Shows the Way").

"Health at Sixty-Six": *Hindustan Times*, 15 August 2013 ("Still a Sick Man of South Asia").

"Small Leap Forward in Child Health": *The Hindu*, 16 September 2015.

"Kerala Tops, Gujarat Flops, Bihar Hops" (with Reetika Khera): www.ndtv. com, 18 November 2015.

Child Development and Elementary Education

"Class Struggle" (with the PROBE Team): Adapted from The PROBE Team (1999), also using "Class Struggle", *India Today*, 13 October 1997.

"The Welfare State in Tamil Nadu": *Times of India*, 21 May 2003 ("Children First: The Welfare State in Tamil Nadu").

"Children Under Six: Out of Focus", *The Hindu*, 20 October 2006 ("Children Under Six: Out of the Spotlight").

"Struggling to Learn" (with A. De, M. Samson, and A.K. Shiva Kumar), *The Hindu*, 20 February 2009 ("School Education: Struggling to Learn"); also draws on "Education: Report Card" (with A. De, M. Samson, A.K. Shiva Kumar, and S. Dasgupta), *Frontline*, 14 March 2009.

"Progress of Children Under Six": Adapted from the foreword of the Progress of Children Under Six report, September 2016 (Centre for Equity Studies, 2016).

Employment Guarantee

"Employment as a Social Responsibility": *The Hindu*, 21 November 2004.

"Employment Guarantee and Its Discontents*": *Times of India*, 12 August 2005 ("Totally Off Target") and 13 August 2005 ("Time to Clean Up").

"Corruption in NREGA: Myths and Reality" (with Reetika Khera and Siddhartha): *The Hindu*, 22 January 2008.

"Employment Guarantee or Slave Labour?": *The Hindu*, 18 September 2009.

"Guaranteeing Productive Work*": *The Hindu*, 23 August 2014 ("Learning from NREGA") and also *Indian Express*, 1 July 2015 ("The Digging-holes Myth").

Food Security and the Public Distribution System

"Food Security Act: Indecent Proposal?": *The Hindu*, 8 July 2010 ("The Task of Making the PDS Work").

"The PDS Turnaround in Chhattisgarh" (with Reetika Khera): *The Hindu*, 13 November 2010 ("Chhattisgarh Shows the Way").

"Rural Poverty and the Public Distribution System" (with Reetika Khera): *The Hindu*, 5 September 2012 ("A Bill that Asks too Much of the Poor").

"The Food Security Debate in India": *India Ink* (New York Times blog), 9 July 2013.

"The Poor States Catch Up": *The Hindu*, 13 January 2016 ("Leaving No Poor Person Behind").

Corporate Power and Technocracy

"Glucose for the Lok Sabha?" (with Reetika Khera): *Hindustan Times*, 14 April 2008.

"Nehruvian Budget in the Corporate Age": *The Hindu*, 5 March 2015.

"Unique Identity Dilemma": *Indian Express*, 19 March 2015.

"The Aadhaar Coup": *The Hindu*, 15 March 2016.

"Dark Clouds over the PDS", *The Hindu*, 10 September 2016.

War and Peace

"Nuclear Deterrence: From MAD to Worse": *The Hindu*, 6 August 1999.

"The Future of War in Retrospect": *Hindustan Times*, 15 January 2000 ("Day of the Bayonet").

"Kashmir: Manufacturing Ethnic Conflict": *The Hindu*, 29 March 2000.

"The Warped Logic of Nuclear Gambles": *The Hindu*, 27 May 2002.

"India and the Deal: Partner or Pawn?": *The Hindu*, 7 September 2007.

"Kashmir's Hidden Uprising*": *The Hindu*, 25 November 2016 ("The New Abnormal in Kashmir") and also *Indian Express*, 5 December 2016 ("Kashmir's Hidden Uprising").

Top-up

"Rang de Basti" (with Bela Bhatia): *Hindustan Times*, 7 May 2007.

"Voting in Maoist Land": *The Hindu*, 10 January 2010.

"The Bribing Game": *Indian Express*, 23 April 2011.

"The Quiet Grip of Caste": *Hindustan Times*, 29 November 2012.

"The Gujarat Muddle*": *The Hindu*, 11 April 2014 ("The Gujarat Muddle") and 12 May 2014 ("The Gujarat Middle").

"On the Mythology of Social Policy": *The Hindu*, 8 July 2014.

"The Bullet Train Syndrome": *Scroll.in*, 23 February 2016 ("The Bullet Train Syndrome Perpetuates an Elitist Approach to the Indian Railways").

"The Mother of All Disruptions*": www.bbc.com/hindi ("*Notebandi Logon ke Jeevan ke Oopar Khela Gaya Jua Hai*") and also *The Hindu*, 27 December 2016 ("The Mother of All Disruptions").

"Decoding Universal Basic Income*": www.ndtv.com, 16 January 2017 ("Decoding Universal Basic Income") and 2 February 2017 ("The Tale and Maths of Universal Basic Income").

"Development and Public-Spiritedness": Unpublished.

NAME INDEX

SUBJECT INDEX